Apache Wicket Cookbook

Master Wicket by example by implementing real-life solutions to everyday tasks

Igor Vaynberg

PUBLISHING

BIRMINGHAM - MUMBAI

Apache Wicket Cookbook

First published: March 2011

Production Reference: 1180311

Published by Packt Publishing Ltd.
32 Lincoln Road
Olton
Birmingham, B27 6PA, UK.

ISBN 978-1-849511-60-5

www.packtpub.com

Cover Image by Asher Wishkerman (a.wishkerman@mpic.de)

Credits

Author
Igor Vaynberg

Reviewers
Brandon Fuller
Martin Grigorov
Sven Meier
Erik van Oosten
Jeremy Thomerson

Acquisition Editor
Chaitanya Apte

Development Editor
Neha Mallik

Technical Editor
Gauri Iyer

Indexer
Hemangini Bari

Editorial Team Leader
Mithun Sehgal

Project Team Leader
Ashwin Shetty

Project Coordinator
Michelle Quadros

Proofreader
Aaron Nash

Graphics
Nilesh Mohite

Production Coordinator
Adline Swetha Jesuthas

Cover Work
Adline Swetha Jesuthas

About the Author

Igor Vaynberg is a software architect, residing in Sacramento, California. His liking for computers was sparked when he received a Sinclair Z80 for his birthday at the age of 10. Since then, he has worked in companies both large and small building scalable web applications. Igor's main interest is finding ways to simplify development and maintenance of complex user interfaces for the web tier. Igor is a core committer for the Apache Wicket framework, the aim of which is to simplify the programming model as well as reintroduce OOP to the web UI tier. When he is not head deep in code, he enjoys spending time with his beautiful wife and children, as well as snowboarding and playing video games.

I would like to thank my father for getting me my first computer, and my mother for supporting my obsession. But, most of all, I would like to thank my wife and children for giving me the time, space, love, and support needed to work on this project. I could have never done it without them.

About the Reviewers

Brandon Fuller is a Technical Leader with Cisco Systems. Since 2007, he has been responsible for building web applications to support various Cisco TelePresence services. Those efforts have exclusively used Apache Wicket as the web development framework. When not working, he can often be found running on trails throughout Colorado.

He can be reached at `http://brandon.fuller.name/`.

Martin Grigorov is a committer at Apache Wicket project and software developer and consultant at jWeekend. Since his early days with computers and programming, he has been involved with open source projects.

While away from the keyboard he enjoys spending his time with his wife and friends, and doing different kinds of sports.

Martin loves to travel around the world but his favorite place to live is his natal Bulgaria.

> I would like to thank my wife Nina for being next to me and encouraging me in my adventures.

Sven Meier has more than 13 years of experience in designing and implementing Java Enterprise applications.

He develops applications on a wide range of open source libraries. His toolbox includes a number of application frameworks, including Hibernate, JPA and Spring; user interface libraries like Swing and SWT, and the DB2 and Oracle database engines. Sven has been using Wicket since 2005 and has never looked back since.

Erik van Oosten, writes about software at `http://www.day-to-day-stuff.blogspot.com`, teaches about software, occasionally reviews a book about software, and dreams (too much) about software. He has been working and learning in the ICT industry since he graduated in 1996. His work ranges from embedded C++ protocol stacks to financial Swing applications. For web applications, Wicket is his preferred web framework as this is "the only framework that makes sense". Erik teaches jWeekend's Wicket course and also reviewed early drafts of 'Wicket in Action'.

Jeremy Thomerson is a technology enthusiast who loves exploring, learning, and creating new technologies. One of his earliest programming feats was at the age of eight modifying the game "Nibbles", written in Basic, to be multi-player so he and his neighbor could play together. Since that time, he has continually experimented with any new technology that interested him, and never backed down from a challenge.

He played an instrumental role in building CARad, a software listing tool that was purchased by eBay in 2003. After the acquisition, he worked as a key member in the team that converted an old, tired architecture into a scalable and sustainable architecture written in Java. After leaving eBay, he has helped numerous companies upgrade their architectures to multi-tier architectures primarily based on the leading Java open source technologies, including Wicket, Spring, Lucene, Hibernate and more. For the past several years, he has owned and operated the leading U.S. company providing Wicket training and consulting services.

www.PacktPub.com

Support files, eBooks, discount offers and more

You might want to visit www.PacktPub.com for support files and downloads related to your book.

Did you know that Packt offers eBook versions of every book published, with PDF and ePub files available? You can upgrade to the eBook version at www.PacktPub.com and as a print book customer, you are entitled to a discount on the eBook copy. Get in touch with us at service@packtpub.com for more details.

At www.PacktPub.com, you can also read a collection of free technical articles, sign up for a range of free newsletters and receive exclusive discounts and offers on Packt books and eBooks.

http://PacktLib.PacktPub.com

Do you need instant solutions to your IT questions? PacktLib is Packt's online digital book library. Here, you can access, read and search across Packt's entire library of books.

Why Subscribe?

- ► Fully searchable across every book published by Packt
- ► Copy and paste, print and bookmark content
- ► On demand and accessible via web browser

Free Access for Packt account holders

If you have an account with Packt at www.PacktPub.com, you can use this to access PacktLib today and view nine entirely free books. Simply use your login credentials for immediate access.

Table of Contents

Preface   **1**

Chapter 1: Validating and Converting User Input   **7**

Introduction   **7**

Performing form-level custom validation   **7**

Creating a custom validator   **12**

Composing multiple validators into a single reusable validator   **18**

Converting string inputs to objects   **23**

Chapter 2: Getting Down and Dirty with Forms and Form Components   **33**

Introduction   **33**

Creating linked selectboxes   **34**

Composing multiple form components into a single reusable component   **39**

Preventing multiple form submits   **45**

Protecting against spam with a CAPTCHA   **55**

Chapter 3: Making Forms Presentable   **61**

Introduction   **61**

Changing form component CSS class on validation errors   **62**

Using FeedbackPanel to output form component specific messages   **65**

Streamlining form component presentation using behaviors   **67**

Chapter 4: Taking your Application Abroad   **75**

Introduction   **75**

Storing module resource strings in package properties   **76**

Retrieving a localized string   **80**

Feeding dynamic localized strings to components using StringResourceModel   **84**

Using wicket:message to output localized markup   **86**

Overriding localized resources on a case by case basis   **89**

Chapter 5: Displaying Data Using DataTable — 95

Introduction — 95
Sorting — 96
Filtering — 100
Making cells clickable — 106
Making rows selectable with checkboxes — 110
Exporting data to CSV — 120

Chapter 6: Enhancing your UI with Tabs and Borders — 129

Introduction — 129
Creating tabs with dynamic titles — 130
Making a tabbed panel play nice with forms — 136
Creating a client-side JavaScript tabbed panel — 140
Using borders to decorate components — 143
Creating a collapsible border — 148

Chapter 7: Deeper into Ajax — 157

Introduction — 157
Adding Ajax validation to individual form components — 158
Blocking until an Ajax request is complete — 162
Providing Ajax feedback automatically — 168

Chapter 8: Visualizing Data with Charts — 177

Introduction — 177
Charting with Open Flash Chart — 178
Feeding chart data using a SharedResource — 191
Responding to clicks — 199

Chapter 9: Building Dynamic and Rich UI — 207

Introduction — 207
Swapping components using a select box — 208
Creating dynamic forms — 214
Creating a dynamic portal layout — 222

Chapter 10: Securing your Application — 235

Introduction — 235
Creating a login page and forcing the user to log in — 236
Authenticating with OpenID — 243
Securing components using — 251
IAuthorizationStrategy — 251
Securing URLs and protecting against cross-site request forgery — 258
Switching from HTTP to HTTPS and back again — 260

Chapter 11: Integrating Wicket with Middleware   263

Introduction   263
Integrating with Spring   264
Integrating with CDI   268
Populating repeaters from a JPA query   272
Creating a model for a JPA entity   282

Chapter 12

This chapter is not present in the book but is available as a free download from:
http://www.packtpub.com/sites/default/files/downloads/
1605_Chapter12.pdf

Index   291

Preface

Apache Wicket is one of the most famous Java web application frameworks. Wicket simplifies web development and makes it fun. Are you bored of going through countless pages of theory to find out how to get your web development done? With this book in hand, you don't need to go through hundreds of pages to figure out how you will actually build a web application. You will get practical solutions to your common everyday development tasks to pace up your development activities.

Apache Wicket Cookbook provides you with information that gets your problems solved quickly without beating around the bush. This book is perfect for you if you are ready to take the next step from tutorials and step into the practical world. It will take you beyond the basics of using Apache Wicket and show you how to leverage Wicket's advanced features to create simpler and more maintainable solutions to what at first may seem complex problems.

You will learn how to integrate with client-side technologies such as JavaScript libraries or Flash components, which will help you to build your application faster. You will discover how to use Wicket paradigms to factor out commonly used code into custom Components, which will reduce the maintenance cost of your application, and how to leverage the existing Wicket Components to make your own code simpler.

A straightforward Cookbook with over 70 highly focused practical recipes to make your web application development easier with the Wicket web framework.

What this book covers

Chapter 1, Validating and Converting User Input: This chapter is all about form validation and input conversion. Learn how to enforce constraints on the inputs and how to convert string inputs into other types so the rest of your code can be type-safe.

Chapter 2, Getting Down and Dirty with Forms and Form Components: In this chapter, we will examine some of the in-depth form patterns such as preventing double submits and refactoring form components to make them more reusable.

Chapter 3, Making Forms Presentable: This chapter is all about making your forms look good. Here we will see how to change presentation of form components and labels to give the user better feedback and how to package that code in a reusable manner.

Chapter 4, Taking your Application Abroad: This chapter is about internationalization. Here you will learn how to take advantage of the many features Wicket offers to make your application a good international citizen.

Chapter 5, Displaying Data Using DataTable: No web application is complete without a page that has a table of data. In this chapter we will learn how to make great use of Wicket's `DataTable` components to make displaying awesome tables a snap.

Chapter 6, Enhancing your UI with Tabs and Borders: In this chapter we will take a look at some of the more advanced use cases of using `TabbedPanel` and `Border` components.

Chapter 7, Deeper into Ajax: Are you ready to take your Ajax knowledge past the basics? This chapter will show you how.

Chapter 8, Visualizing Data with Charts: Build an awesome Wicket component that can display charts using OpenFlashCharts; and as a bonus, learn how to integrate Wicket with client-side components built with Flash or JavaScript.

Chapter 9, Building Dynamic and Rich UI: In this chapter, we will learn how to take advantage of Wicket's dynamic component hierarchy to easily manipulate the user interface of our applications.

Chapter 10, Securing your Application: Ever wish you had a read recipe to follow for how to integrate services such as OpenID into your application? Have you spent nights thinking of ways to assign roles and permissions to individual Wicket components easily? This chapter covers all that and more.

Chapter 11, Integrating Wicket with Middleware: Wicket tries to do one thing, but do it very well – allow you to build awesome user interfaces. But, web applications are made up of more than just interfaces. In this chapter, we will learn how to integrate Wicket with middleware such as Spring, CDI, and JPA.

Chapter 12, General Wicket Patterns: This chapter is like a small encyclopedia of recipes for common but non-trivial use cases that make you scratch your head.

Chapter 12, General Wicket Patterns is not present in the book but is available as a free download from the following link: `http://www.packtpub.com/sites/default/files/downloads/1605_Chapter12.pdf`

What you need for this book

The following software are required for this book:

- ▶ Java 1.5+
- ▶ Apache Wicket 1.4.15+
- ▶ To build and run the examples you will need Apache Maven 2.2.1+

Who this book is for

This book is for current users of the Apache Wicket framework; it is not an introduction to Wicket that will bore you with tons of theory. You are expected to have built or maintained a simple Wicket application in the past and to be looking to learn new and better ways of using Wicket. If you are ready to take your Wicket skills to the next level this book is for you.

Conventions

In this book, you will find a number of styles of text that distinguish between different kinds of information. Here are some examples of these styles, and an explanation of their meaning.

Code words in text are shown as follows: "Refer to `HomePage.html` and `HomePage.java` in the code bundle."

A block of code is set as follows:

```
if (value.equalsIgnoreCase("johndoe")) {
    ValidationError error = new ValidationError();
    error.setMessage("Username "+value+" is already taken");
    validatable.error(error);
```

When we wish to draw your attention to a particular part of a code block, the relevant lines or items are set in bold:

```
try {
    Thread.sleep(2000);
} catch (InterruptedException e) {}
```

New terms and **important words** are shown in bold. Words that you see on the screen, in menus or dialog boxes for example, appear in the text like this: "As we can see, just like before, the user withdraws **$100** from a new account **888** with a starting balance of **$1000**".

 Warnings or important notes appear in a box like this.

Tips and tricks appear like this.

Reader feedback

Feedback from our readers is always welcome. Let us know what you think about this book—what you liked or may have disliked. Reader feedback is important for us to develop titles that you really get the most out of.

To send us general feedback, simply send an e-mail to feedback@packtpub.com, and mention the book title via the subject of your message.

If there is a book that you need and would like to see us publish, please send us a note in the **SUGGEST A TITLE** form on www.packtpub.com or e-mail suggest@packtpub.com.

If there is a topic that you have expertise in and you are interested in either writing or contributing to a book, see our author guide on www.packtpub.com/authors.

Customer support

Now that you are the proud owner of a Packt book, we have a number of things to help you to get the most from your purchase.

Downloading the example code

You can download the example code files for all Packt books you have purchased from your account at http://www.PacktPub.com. If you purchased this book elsewhere, you can visit http://www.PacktPub.com/support and register to have the files e-mailed directly to you.

Errata

Although we have taken every care to ensure the accuracy of our content, mistakes do happen. If you find a mistake in one of our books—maybe a mistake in the text or the code—we would be grateful if you would report this to us. By doing so, you can save other readers from frustration and help us improve subsequent versions of this book. If you find any errata, please report them by visiting http://www.packtpub.com/support, selecting your book, clicking on the **errata submission form** link, and entering the details of your errata. Once your errata are verified, your submission will be accepted and the errata will be uploaded on our website, or added to any list of existing errata, under the Errata section of that title. Any existing errata can be viewed by selecting your title from http://www.packtpub.com/support.

Piracy

Piracy of copyright material on the Internet is an ongoing problem across all media. At Packt, we take the protection of our copyright and licenses very seriously. If you come across any illegal copies of our works, in any form, on the Internet, please provide us with the location address or website name immediately so that we can pursue a remedy.

Please contact us at `copyright@packtpub.com` with a link to the suspected pirated material.

We appreciate your help in protecting our authors, and our ability to bring you valuable content.

Questions

You can contact us at `questions@packtpub.com` if you are having a problem with any aspect of the book, and we will do our best to address it.

1
Validating and Converting User Input

In this chapter, we will cover:

- ▶ Performing form-level custom validation
- ▶ Creating a custom validator
- ▶ Validating unique values like a username or an e-mail address
- ▶ Composing multiple validators into a single reusable validator
- ▶ Converting string inputs to objects

Introduction

In this chapter, you will learn how to validate user input inside forms. You will learn how to handle validation constraints that involve more than one field as well as how to create custom validators for individual fields. You will also learn how to convert users' input from strings into Java objects.

Performing form-level custom validation

Frequently, complex forms contain dependencies between various fields that need to be validated in a dynamic manner. For example, the value of one field needs to be validated based on rules that vary with the value of another field.

Let's take a look at a search form where the **keywords** textfield needs to be validated with rules dictated by the selection in the `search type` drop-down box:

We would like the `keywords` field to be validated as a zip code or a phone number based on what is selected in the dropdown list.

Getting ready

We will get started by creating the **Search Customers** form without validation.

Create the page:

`HomePage.html`

```html
<html>
  <body>
      <h1>Search Customers</h1>
      <div wicket:id="feedback"></div>
        <form wicket:id="form">
          <select wicket:id="type"></select>
          <input wicket:id="keywords" type="text" size="20"/>
          <input type="submit" value="Search"/>
        </form>
    </body>
</html>
```

`HomePage.java`

```java
public class HomePage extends WebPage {
  private static final String ZIPCODE = "ZIPCODE";
  private static final String PHONE = "PHONE";
  private static final List<String> TYPES = Arrays.asList(new String[]
{
      ZIPCODE, PHONE });
  public HomePage(final PageParameters parameters) {
    add(new FeedbackPanel("feedback"));
```

```
final DropDownChoice<String> type = new
  DropDownChoice<String>("type",
    new Model<String>(ZIPCODE), TYPES);
type.setRequired(true);

final TextField<String> keywords = new
  TextField<String>("keywords",
    new Model<String>());
keywords.setRequired(true);

Form< ? > form = new Form<Void>("form") {
   @Override
  protected void onSubmit() {
     info("Form successfully submitted");
   }
}
add(form);
form.add(type);
form.add(keywords);
    }
}
```

Downloading the example code

You can download the example code files for all Packt books you have purchased from your account at http://www.PacktPub.com. If you purchased this book elsewhere, you can visit http://www. PacktPub.com/ support and register to have the files e-mailed directly to you.

How to do it...

We are going to implement our validation by overriding `Form#onValidate()` method and putting our validation logic there.

1. Implement validation logic:

```
Form< ? > form = new Form<Void>("form") {
   @Override
  protected void onSubmit() {
     info("Form successfully submitted");
   }
  @Override
  protected void onValidate() {
     super.onValidate();

     if (hasError()) {
```

```
        return;
      }
      final String selectedType = type.getConvertedInput();
      final String query = keywords.getConvertedInput();
      if (ZIPCODE.equals(selectedType)) {
        if (!Pattern.matches("[0-9]{5}", query)) {
          keywords.error((IValidationError)new ValidationError()
            .addMessageKey("invalidZipcode"));
        }
      }
      else if (PHONE.equals(selectedType)) {
        if (!Pattern.matches("[0-9]{10}", query)) {
          keywords.error((IValidationError)new ValidationError()
            .addMessageKey("invalidPhone"));
        }
      }
    }
  };
  add(form);
  form.add(type);
  form.add(keywords);
  }
}
```

2. Provide definitions for the error message resources used to construct error messages:

```
HomePage.properties
invalidZipcode=Invalid Zipcode
invalidPhone=Invalid Phone Number
```

How it works...

Wicket provides ample opportunity for developers to interact with its form processing work-flow. In this particular instance, we use the `Form#onValidate()` callback to insert our own validation logic. This callback will be invoked after the form has validated all fields and form validators.

The first thing we do is check if the form contains any errors so far, and if it does, skip our validation. We do this by checking the return value of the form's `Form#hasError()` method:

```
protected void onValidate() {
  if (hasError()) {
  return;
}
```

Next, we retrieve the submitted values of the *search type* and *keywords* fields:

```
final String selectedType = type.getConvertedInput();
final String query = keywords.getConvertedInput();
```

 Notice that we use `FormComponent#getConvertedInput()` method instead of accessing the field's value via its model. We do this because we are still in the validation stage of the form's work-flow and so the models of form components have not yet been updated.

Finally, we check the values and report any errors using the `FormComponent#error(IValidationError) FormComponent#error(IValidataionError)` method:

```
if (ZIPCODE.equals(selectedType)) {
  if (!Pattern.matches("[0-9]{5}", query)) {
    keywords.error((IValidationError)new ValidationError()
      .addMessageKey("invalidZipcode"));
  }
}
```

There's more...

Wicket offers developers more than one place to plug-into form validation workflow. Here we take a look at an alternative.

Making validation logic reusable

If the inter-field constraints being validated will be used on multiple fields across multiple pages and forms, the validation logic can be externalized into Wicket's `org.apache.wicket.markup.html.form.validation.IFormValidator`.

See also

- See the *Creating a custom validator* recipe in this chapter for how to validate individual fields.
- See the *Composing multiple form components into a single reusable component* recipe for how to combine form components

Creating a custom validator

While Wicket provides a lot of built-in validators to help us with various common constraints, more often than not, we find ourselves needing to perform validation based on some business rules. For this reason, Wicket makes it very easy to implement a custom validation by creating a validator that can be added to form fields.

One example of a custom validation that most web applications will have is a password policy. Outside of the password length itself, which can be validated using Wicket's `StringValidator`, most applications also require the password to meet other security requirements that would make it more secure.

Let's build a user registration form which enforces the following password requirements:

- ▸ Password must be at least eight characters long
- ▸ Password must contain at least one lower case letter
- ▸ Password must contain at least one upper case letter
- ▸ Password must contain at least one digit

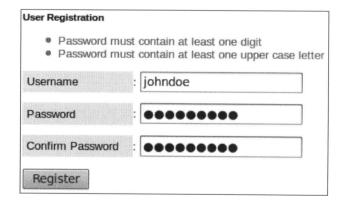

Getting ready

Let's get started by creating the form without password validation:

1. Create the web page:

```
HomePage.html
<html>
  <body>
  <h1>User Registration</h1>
  <div wicket:id="feedback"></div>
    <form wicket:id="form">
```

```html
    <p><label>Username</label>: <input wicket:id="username"
      type="text" size="20"/></p>
    <p><label>Password</label>: <input wicket:id="password1"
      type="password" size="20"/></p>
    <p><label>Confirm Password</label>: <input
      wicket:id="password2" type="password" size="20"/></p>
    <input type="submit" value="Register"/>
    </form>
  </body>
</html>
```

HomePage.java
```java
public class HomePage extends WebPage {
  public HomePage(final PageParameters parameters) {
    add(new FeedbackPanel("feedback"));

    TextField< ? > username = new TextField<String>("username",
      Model.of(""));Model.of(""));
    username.setRequired(true);

    FormComponent<String> password1 = new
      PasswordTextField("password1", Model.of(""));
```

 You might be wondering what the Model.of("") does. The method simply returns a new instance of Model constructed with the empty string parameter we passed in. Model comes with a few variations of the of() convenience factory methods which help the compiler infer the generic type rather than forcing us to specify it manually: new Model<String>(""), allowing us to write shorter code in the process.

```java
    password1.setLabel(Model.of("Password"));
    FormComponent< ? > password2 = new
      PasswordTextField("password2", Model
        .of(""));

    Form< ? > form = new Form<Void>("form") {
      @Override
      protected void onSubmit() {
        info("Form successfully submitted");
      }
    };
    form.add(new EqualPasswordInputValidator(password1,
      password2));
    add(form);
    form.add(username);
```

```
        form.add(password1);
        form.add(password2);
    }
}
```

How to do it...

1. Create a Wicket field validator:

    PasswordPolicyValidator.java

    ```
    public class PasswordPolicyValidator implements IValidator<String>
    {
        private static final Pattern UPPER = Pattern.compile("[A-Z]");
        private static final Pattern LOWER = Pattern.compile("[a-z]");
        private static final Pattern NUMBER = Pattern.compile("[0-9]");

        public void validate(IValidatable<String> validatable) {
            final String password = validatable.getValue();

        if (!NUMBER.matcher(password).find()) {
            error(validatable, "no-digit");
                }
        if (!LOWER.matcher(password).find()) {
            error(validatable, "no-lower");
                }
         if (!UPPER.matcher(password).find()) {
            error(validatable, "no-upper");
            }
        }

        private void error(IValidatable<String> validatable, String
            errorKey) {
            ValidationError error = new ValidationError();
            error.addMessageKey(getClass().getSimpleName() + "." +
                errorKey);
            validatable.error(error);
        }
    }
    ```

2. PasswordPolicyValidator.properties

    ```
    PasswordPolicyValidator.no-digit=${label} must contain at least
    one digit
    PasswordPolicyValidator.no-lower=${label} must contain at least
    one lower case letter
    PasswordPolicyValidator.no-upper=${label} must contain at least
    one upper case letter
    ```

3. Add validation to the form:

```
FormComponent<String> password1 = new
PasswordTextField("password1", Model.of(""));
    password1.setLabel(Model.of("Password"));
    password1.add(StringValidator.minimumLength(8));
    password1.add(new PasswordPolicyValidator());
```

Notice that we are able to implement the minimum length requirement using Wicket's `StringValidator`.

How it works...

A field validator in Wicket is any class that implements the `org.apache.wicket.validation.IValidator` interface and is added to the form component that represents a form field. When the form is submitted Wicket will call all the validators added to each form component and give them a chance to inspect the input and report any errors.

We begin by creating a `PasswordPolicyValidator` class that implements the `IValidator` interface:

```
public class PasswordPolicyValidator implements IValidator<String>
{
    public void validate(IValidatable<String> validatable)
    {
    }
}
```

When it is time to validate the field, Wicket will call the `validate(IValidatable<String> validatable)` method on our validator. The passed in `validatable` parameter is our validator's view into the field that is being validated. It provides a method to retrieve the current value of the field as well as a method to report errors.

The first thing we must do is retrieve the current value of the field. We do this by calling `validatable`'s `IValidatable#getValue()` method:

```
final String password = validatable.getValue();
```

Notice that we do not check if `validatable.getValue()` returns `null`; Wicket will check the value prior to calling validators and if it is null, validators will be skipped.

If a validator does want to be called even if the value is `null` it can implement a tagging interface: `org.apache.wicket.validation.INullAcceptingValidator`.

Once we have the value, we can perform our validation. In this case, we use a simple regular expression matcher to implement the password policy checks. Whenever we find a policy violation, we call our `error(IValidatable,String)` helper method and pass in an `errorKey` parameter to represent the violation:

```
error(validatable, "no-digit");
```

The `errorKey` parameter, in the above example: "no-digit", is used to construct the error message resource key unique to the violation. This is how a single validator can display multiple error messages.

The `error(IValidatable,String)` method constructs a `ValidationError` object with the correct error message resource key and passes it to `validatable's IValidatable#error(IValidationError)` method to report the error:

```
private void error(IValidatable<String> validatable, String errorKey)
{
    ValidationError error = new ValidationError();
    error.addMessageKey(getClass().getSimpleName() + "." + errorKey);
    validatable.error(error);
}
```

Using the validator's simple class name concatenated with a more specific error key is Wicket's convention for creating resource keys for validation error messages. It is advised that the users follow the same convention when creating custom validators.

If we take a close look at the code for the validator, we will see that we can construct three distinct error key strings, each representing a single password policy violation:

- ► `PasswordPolicyValidator.no-digit`
- ► `PasswordPolicyValidator.no-lower`
- ► `PasswordPolicyValidator.no-upper`

We use these strings as error message resource keys for the message instead of the message itself, so that we can internationalize them if needed. Therefore, we need to put the resource values somewhere where Wicket can find them. By default, one of the places Wicket will check is a property file named with the same name as the validator class that reported the error. This is why in our example we named the property file `PasswordPolicyValidator.properties` and put it next to `PasswordPolicyValidator.java` in your package structure.

There's more...

Validators are only as good as the errors they produce. Wicket offers a lot of ways to build the validation message; here we explore ways of customizing error messages to the specifics of the error.

Using Wicket's built-in error variables

In our example we have defined error messages containing: `"${label}"`. The `"${label}"` string tells wicket to substitute the entire snippet with the value of a variable named `"label"`. Wicket defines the following standard variables:

- `label`: The label of the `FormComponent`, usually set by calling `FormComponent#setLabel(IModel)`
- `input`: The value being validated
- `name`: The Wicket id of the `FormComponent`

Using custom error variables

Users can provide custom variables to be used when error messages are interpolated; new variables can be added using `ValidationError#setVariable(String,Object)` method. For example, let's create a `MaximumStringLengthValidator`:

```java
public class MaximumStringLengthValidator implements
IValidator<String>
  {
    private final int max;
    public MaximumStringLengthValidator(int max)
      {
        this.max = max;
      }
  public void validate(IValidatable<String> validatable)
    {
    if (validatable.getValue().length() > max)
      {
        ValidationError error = new ValidationError();
        error.addMessageKey(getClass().getSimpleName());
        error.setVariable("max", max);
```

```
        validatable.error(error);
      }
    }
  }
```

As our validator specifies the maximum length by adding the "max" variable, we can construct error messages that reference it, for example:

```
MaximumStringLengthValidator=${label} must contain a string no longer
than ${max} characters.
```

See also

▶ See the *Composing multiple validators into a single reusable validator* recipe in this chapter on how to compose multiple validators into a single one.

▶ See the *Storing module resource strings in package properties* recipe for an alternative place to store validation messages.

Composing multiple validators into a single reusable validator

It is rare that we come across a field constraint as simple as "the length of entered string must be at least two characters" or "the entered number must be between five and ten". More often, we find ourselves in a situation where a validation constraint consists of two or more simpler ones. Often, we already have the validators for the simpler constraints written and all we need is a simple and reusable way to compose them together.

Let's build a user registration form where the username needs to comply with the following constraints:

▶ Username must be between 5 and 20 characters long

▶ Username must only contain lower-case letters

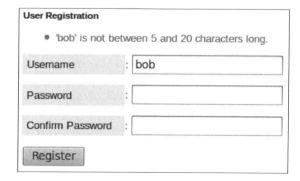

Getting ready

Let's get started by creating the form above without the validation.

1. Create the web page:

```
HomePage.html
<html>
  <body>
  <h1>User Registration</h1>
  <div wicket:id="feedback"></div>
    <form wicket:id="form">
      <p><label>Username</label>: <input wicket:id="username"
        type="text" size="20"/></p>
      <p><label>Password</label>: <input wicket:id="password1"
        type="password" size="20"/></p>
      <p><label>Confirm Password</label>: <input
        wicket:id="password2" type="password" size="20"/></p>
      <input type="submit" value="Register"/>
    </form>
  </body>
</html>
```

```
HomePage.java
public class HomePage extends WebPage {
  public HomePage(final PageParameters parameters) {
    add(new FeedbackPanel("feedback"));

    TextField< ? > username = new TextField<String>("username",
      Model.of(""));
    username.setRequired(true);

    FormComponent<String> password1 = new
      PasswordTextField("password1", Model.of(""));
    password1.setLabel(Model.of("Password"));

    FormComponent< ? > password2 = new
      PasswordTextField("password2", Model
        .of(""));

    Form< ? > form = new Form<Void>("form") {
      @Override
      protected void onSubmit() {
        info("Form successfully submitted");
      }
    };

    form.add(new EqualPasswordInputValidator(password1,
      password2));

    add(form);
```

```
        form.add(username);
        form.add(password1);
        form.add(password2);
    }
}
```

How to do it...

1. Create the validator for the username field:

    ```
    UsernameValidator.java
    public class UsernameValidator extends CompoundValidator<String> {
      public UsernameValidator() {
        add(StringValidator.lengthBetween(5, 20));
        add(new PatternValidator("[a-z]+"));
      }
    }
    ```

2. Install the validator into the username field:

    ```
    HomePage.java
        TextField< ? > username = new TextField<String>("username",
          Model.of(""));
        username.setRequired(true);
        username.add(new UsernameValidator());
    ```

How it works...

To implement the username field validator we extend the org.apache.wicket. validation.CompoundValidator class and inside the constructor use its CompoundV alidator#add(IValidator) method to add all the individual validators which together define our overall constraint:

```
public class UsernameValidator extends CompoundValidator<String>
  {
  public UsernameValidator()
    {
      add(StringValidator.lengthBetween(5, 20));
      add(new PatternValidator("[a-z]+"));
    }
  }
```

The little bit of magic that happens is inside the `CompoundValidator#validate(IValidatable)` method:

```
public class CompoundValidator<T> implements IValidator<T>
  {
    public final void validate(IValidatable<T> validatable)
      {
        Iterator<IValidator<T>> it = validators.iterator();
        while (it.hasNext() && validatable.isValid())
          {
            it.next().validate(validatable);
          }
      }
  }
```

The method loops over all validators that have been added and delegates validation to each one sequentially by invoking their `IValidator#validate(IValidatable)` method. If a validation error is detected, by checking the `IValidatable#isValid()` method, the loop is aborted and the validator returns.

Using this trick it is trivial to compose low-level validators into higher-level validators that are reusable across forms and fields.

There's more...

While validators are very flexible it is important not to abuse them. In this section, we will take a look at some pitfalls.

Pitfalls of not encapsulating validation constraints

It seems easier to accomplish this by invoking `FormComponent#add(IValidator)` multiple times on the username field itself as follows:

```
TextField<String> username = new TextField<String>("username", Model.
of(""));
username.setRequired(true);
username.add(StringValidator.lengthBetween(5, 20));
username.add(new PatternValidator("[a-z]+"));
```

But, it is important to consider the implications:

  ▶ It is easy to forget to add one of the constraints; sometimes fields will have five or six constraints that make up their overall validation. In these cases it is very easy to leave off a constraint or two which will cause a headache down the road.

► What happens if the business logic governing the validation constraint changes? We would need to find all the places in our code where the *username* field is used so we can update it to use the new constraint. It is better to stick to the DRY (don't repeat yourself) principle and have only one place in code that governs this constraint.

Pitfalls of not externalizing validation constraints

Some developers prefer to achieve the same usecase by creating a subclass of the `FormComponent` instead of the `CompoundValidator`. For example, following this methodology, the `username` field can be built as follows:

```
private class UsernameField extends TextField<String>
    {
      public UsernameField(String id, IModel<String> model)
        {
          super(id, model);
          setLabel(new ResourceModel("field.username.label"));
          add(StringValidator.lengthBetween(5, 20));
        }
    }
```

While this does not violate the DRY principle for our particular usecase, it does somewhat limit the further composability and reusability of the validation code. For example, suppose we needed to have a `Referer` field that had the same validation logic as the `Username` field with the additional constraint that it cannot contain the username of the currently logged in user.

Had we chosen to implement our validation exclusively inside the `UsernameField` form component, we would be forced to extend it and use a `TextField` instead of perhaps an `AutocompleteTextField`. But, had we chosen to implement the validation inside the `UsernameValidator`, we could simply wrap it inside another compound validator:

```
public class RefererUsernameValidator extends
CompoundValidator<String>
    {
      public UsernameValidator()
        {
          add(new UsernameValidator());
          add(new NotCurrentlyLoggedInUsernameValidator());
        }
    }
```

See also

▶ See the *Creating a custom validator* recipe in this chapter on how to create field validators.

▶ See the the *Composing multiple form components into a single reusable component* recipe for how to combine form components.

Converting string inputs to objects

The web is built around strings: the html documents are strings, the cookies are strings, and the urls are strings as well. The browser, which is how users interact with our web applications, only understands strings. However, it is rare that Java code which drives all these artifacts is also built around strings. Proper Java code is built around objects, and so when we build web applications with Java we often have to convert between objects and strings. The problem is most apparent when working with web forms where fields that represent things other than strings in the Java code (dates, numbers, and currency) have to be converted. Web application frameworks try to ease the pain as much as possible, but in the end the developer always has to write the logic that does the conversion.

Let's build a **Search Schedule** form where the user has to enter a time value in the h:mma format. The value of the **Time** field will be represented by a cookbook.Time Java object we will create, and we will use Wicket's conversion infrastructure to allow the **Time** textfield to seamlessly convert between the cookbook.Time object and its h:mma string representation.

The user enters a correct time value and it is converted to the **Time** object as shown in the following screenshot:

Search Schedule

- You entered: [Time hour=5 minute=15 am=false]

Time : 5:15pm (h:mma)

Search Schedule

The user enters an incorrect **Time** value and a conversion error is reported as shown in the following screenshot:

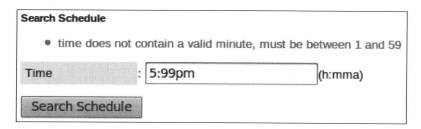

Getting ready

Let's get started by creating a form with a regular `TextField` for time.

Create the web page:

`HomePage.html`

```
<html>
    <body>
            <h1>Search Schedule</h1>
            <div wicket:id="feedback"></div>
          <form wicket:id="form">
            <p><label>Time</label>: <input wicket:id="time" type="text"
              size="20"/>(h:mma)</p>
            <input type="submit" value="Search Schedule"/>
          </form>
    </body>
</html>
```

`HomePage.java`

```
public class HomePage extends WebPage
  {
    public HomePage(final PageParameters parameters)
      {
        add(new FeedbackPanel("feedback"));
        TextField<String> time = new TextField<String>("time", Model.
          of(""));
        Form< ? > form = new Form<Void>("form")
          {
            @Override
            protected void onSubmit()
              {
```

```
            info("You entered: " + HomePage.this.time);
        }
    };
    add(form);
    form.add(time);
    }
}
```

How to do it...

1. Create the object to represent the time:

```
Time.java
public class Time implements Serializable
    {
    private int hour;
    private int minute;
    private boolean am = true;

// getters and setters omitted for brevity

    @Override
    public String toString()
        {
        return String.format("[Time hour=%d minute=%d am=%b]", hour,
            minute, am);
        }
    }
```

2. Create the converter that will convert the object to a string and back:

```
TimeConverter.java
public class TimeConverter implements IConverter
    {
        public Object convertToObject(String val, Locale locale)
            {
            if (Strings.isEmpty(val))
                {
                return null;
                }
        String value = val.toLowerCase();
        if (!Pattern.matches("[0-9]{1,2}:[0-9]{2}(am|pm)", value))
            {
            error(value, "format");
            }
```

```
int colon = value.indexOf(':');
int hour = Integer.parseInt(value.substring(0, colon));
int minute = Integer.parseInt(value.substring(colon + 1, colon
    + 3));
String meridian = value.substring(colon + 3, colon + 5);

if (hour < 1 || hour > 12)
  {
    error(value, "hour");
  }
if (minute < 0 || minute > 59)
  {
    error(value, "minute");
  }

Time time = new Time();
time.setHour(hour);
time.setMinute(minute);
time.setAm("am".equals(meridian));

return time;
}

private void error(String value, String errorKey)
{
  ConversionException e = new ConversionException("Error
    converting value: "
  + value +
      " to an instance of: " + Time.class.getName());
  e.setSourceValue(value);
  e.setResourceKey(getClass().getSimpleName() + "." + errorKey);
  throw e;
}

public String convertToString(Object value, Locale locale)
  {
    if (value == null)
      {
        return null;
      }
    Time time = (Time)value;

    return String.format("%d:%02d%s", time.getHour(), time.
      getMinute(),
      ((time.isAm())
        ? "am"
```

```
        : "pm"));
    }
  }
```

3. Register the converter in the application subclass:

```
WicketApplication.java
public class WicketApplication extends WebApplication {
 public Class<HomePage> getHomePage() {
    return HomePage.class;
 }

  @Override
  protected IConverterLocator newConverterLocator() {
    ConverterLocator locator = (ConverterLocator)super.
      newConverterLocator();
    locator.set(Time.class, new TimeConverter());
    return locator;
  }
}
```

6. Change the time `TextField` to use our `Time` object:

```
HomePage.java
public class HomePage extends WebPage
    {
    private Time time;

    public HomePage(final PageParameters parameters)
      {
        TextField<Time> time = new TextField<Time>("time", new
          PropertyMo
        del<Time>(this, "time"));

      }
    }
```

7. Create message strings for conversion errors:

```
HomePage.html
TimeConverter.format=${label} does not contain a properly
formatted date
TimeConverter.hour=${label} does not contain a valid hour, must be
between 1 and 12
TimeConverter.minute=${label} does not contain a valid minute,
must be between 0 and 59
```

How it works...

All Wicket components that work with models are aware of Wicket's conversion infrastructure. When a component needs to present its model object as a part of html markup, it first runs it through the conversion infrastructure to convert it to a string. When a component needs to convert a user's input, which is typically a string, back to a model object it once again runs it through the conversion infrastructure, this time to convert the string value back to the object.

Wicket's conversion infrastructure is built around converters, represented by objects that implement org.apache.wicket.util.convert.IConverter the interface, and a converter locator responsible for finding converters that can convert from an object of the given class to a string and back.

Let's start creating our converter by letting it implement the IConverter interface:

```
public class TimeConverter implements IConverter
{
  public Object convertToObject(String value, Locale locale)
  {
    return null;
  }
  public String convertToString(Object value, Locale locale)
  {
    return null;
  }
}
```

We can see that each converter consists of two methods:

▶ convertToObject(): It converts a string representation to the object

▶ convertToString(): It converts an object to its string representation

We begin by implementing the easier of the two methods – convertToString() – inside which we simply convert the passed in Time instance to its h:mma string representation:

```
public String convertToString(Object value, Locale locale)
  {
  if (value == null)
    {
      return null;
    }
  Time time = (Time)value;
  return String.format("%d:%02d%s", time.getHour(), time.
    getMinute(),
  ((time.isAm())
```

```
    ? "am"
    : "pm"));
}
```

 Notice that we must correctly handle null values. Wicket does not automatically handle nulls because there are cases where a null object is not represented by a null string.

With the easy part out of the way, let's implement the `convertToObject()` method. The first thing we do is check for null:

```
if (value == null)
  {
    return null;
  }
```

As a null string represents a `null cookbook.Time` instance, we simply return null.

Next we check the overall format of the string, and if it does not match the `h:mma` format we report an error using the helper `error(String,String)` method which we will see later:

```
String value = val.toLowerCase();
if (!Pattern.matches("[0-9]{1,2}:[0-9]{2}(am|pm)", value))
  {
    error(value, "format");
  }
```

Now that we know the string is in the correct format we can tokenize it and do some further checking:

```
int colon = value.indexOf(':');
int hour = Integer.parseInt(value.substring(0, colon));
int minute = Integer.parseInt(value.substring(colon + 1, colon +
    3));
String meridian = value.substring(colon + 3, colon + 5);
if (hour < 1 || hour > 12)
{
  error(value, "hour");
}
if (minute < 0 || minute > 59)
  {
    error(value, "minute");
  }
```

At this point we know that the user has entered a valid h:mma representation of the string and we can construct and return an instance of cookbook.Time object:

```
Time time = new Time();
time.setHour(hour);
time.setMinute(minute);
time.setAm("am".equals(meridian));
return time;
```

The only part we have not looked at is the error(String,String) helper method which reports conversion errors. Converters report conversion errors by throwing a org.apache.wicket.util.convert.ConversionException. ConversionException carries with it such information as the value that failed conversion, as well as a message resource key that will be used to display the error. The helper method does just this: construct and throw an instance of ConversionException that contains the proper message resource key:

```
private void error(String value, String errorKey)
{
  ConversionException e = new ConversionException("Error converting
    value: "
  + value +
  " to an instance of: " + Time.class.getName());
  e.setSourceValue(value);
  e.setResourceKey(getClass().getSimpleName() + "." + errorKey);
  throw e;
}
```

Our converter has three possible errors that it can report to the user as seen in the message resource file we created earlier:

```
TimeConverter.format=${label} does not contain a properly formatted
date
TimeConverter.hour=${label} does not contain a valid hour, must be
between 1 and 12
TimeConverter.minute=${label} does not contain a valid minute, must be
between 0 and 59
```

The error helper method creates these keys by concatenating the simple name of the converter with a dot followed by the error key.

Using the converter's simple class name concatenated with a more specific error key is Wicket's convention for creating resource keys for conversion error messages; it is advised that the users follow the same convention when creating custom converters.

With our converter complete, the only remaining task is to register it with Wicket so it can look it up whenever a conversion to or from `cookbook.Time` is needed. We do this in our application subclass by the overriding application's `newConverterLocator()` factory method:

```
public class WicketApplication extends WebApplication
  {
    @Override
    protected IConverterLocator newConverterLocator()
      {
        ConverterLocator locator = (ConverterLoca
        tor)super.newConverterLocator();
        locator.set(Time.class, new TimeConverter());
        return locator;
      }
  }
```

Once this is done, any `Component` with a model object of type `cookbook.Time` will use our converter to perform the conversion to a string and back.

There's more...

The recipe has covered the core usecase of converters in Wicket. In this section, we will learn how to use them better.

How automatic type conversion works

You may have noticed that we did nothing special when creating the `TextField` component in the form:

```
TextField<Time> time = new TextField<Time>("time", new
PropertyModel<Time>(this, "time"));
```

So how did it know that its model object is of type `cookbook.Time`? Some models are capable of letting components know the type of the object they contain. `PropertyModel` is one such model because it implements `org.apache.wicket.model.IObjectClassAwareModel`. If we did not use such a model we would have to manually set the type on `TextField` via the `FormComponent#setType(Class<?>)` method:

```
TextField<Time> time = new TextField<Time>("time", new
Model<Time>(null));
time.setType(Time.class);
```

Global converters

By registering our converter with the application's ConverterLocator we have made our converter available globally and it will transparently be used any time a conversion to or from cookbook.Time will be needed. However, there are times when we may wish to override the converter on a case by case basis. We can accomplish this by overriding Component#getConverter(Class<?>) method. For example, had we not registered our converter globally we could still use it.

```
TextField<Time> time = new TextField<Time>("time", new
Model<Time>(null)
  {
    public IConverter getConverter(Class<?> type)
      {
        if (Time.class.equals(type)
          {
            return new TimeConverter();
          }
        return super.getConverter(type);
      });
time.setType(Time.class);
```

More on resource strings

In our example, we have put the message resources into HomePage.properties which only made them available in that particular page. In most cases, however, it may make more sense to put them into Application's global property bundle so they are available everywhere.

See also

> ► See the *Creating a custom validator* recipe in this chapter on how to create field validators.

2

Getting Down and Dirty with Forms and Form Components

In this chapter, we will cover:

- ▶ Creating linked selectboxes
- ▶ Composing multiple form components into a single reusable component
- ▶ Preventing multiple form submits
- ▶ Protecting against spam with a CAPTCHA

Introduction

In this chapter, we will cover a wide cross-section of use cases related to working with Wicket forms. We will see how to create form components that depend on each other, how to put form components into chunks that can be reused across forms, and even how to link components to JavaScript.

Creating linked selectboxes

Many of the web applications are interfaces to vast data stores; helping the user sift through these vast amounts of data is often the most important service these applications provide. A common method of filtering data is to allow the user to progressively narrow results by progressively filtering it; this is commonly accomplished by presenting two or more selectboxes linked in a manner where a selection in one helps to narrow the available choices in others.

Let's build a form that allows a user to select their favorite city. We will help the user make the selection quickly by allowing them to first pick the country the city is in, which will reduce the number of cities they can pick from, making sifting through the cities selectbox easier.

The form will look as shown in the following screenshot:

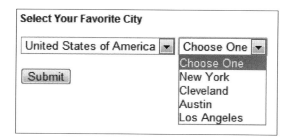

Getting ready

To begin, let's implement value objects that will represent countries and cities, as well as a webpage to hold the form.

Create the country and city objects. Refer to the `City.java` and `Country.java` files in the code bundle.

Create a mock database of countries and cities:

```
public class Database
{
    public static List<Country> getCountries()
    {
        // return a list of countries
        // sample code does it from memory
    }
    public static List<City> getCities(String countryCode)
    {
        // return a list of cities based on country code
        // sample code does it from memory
    }
}
```

Create the page:

HomePage.java

```java
// refer to the code bundle for markup
public class HomePage extends WebPage
{
    private Country country;

    private City city;

    public HomePage(final PageParameters parameters)
    {
        country = Database.getCountries().get(0);
        // add a feedback panel and a form
        // see sample code
    }
}
```

How to do it...

We now have everything necessary to implement the selectboxes.

1. Lets begin by implementing a model that will feed the country selectbox a list of countries. We will implement it as an inner class of our page:

    HomePage.java

    ```java
    private static class CountriesModel extends
    LoadableDetachableModel<List<? extends Country>>
    {
        protected List<? extends Country> load()
        {
            return Database.getCountries();
        }
    }
    ```

2. We will also need a model to feed the city selectbox a list of available cities. We implement it as an inner class as well:

    HomePage.java

    ```java
    private class CitiesModel extends LoadableDetachableModel<List<?
    extends City>>
    {
        protected List<? extends City> load()
        {
            return Database.getCities(country.getCode());
        }
    }
    ```

3. With all the necessary model classes in place we implement the two selectboxes and add them to the form:

HomePage.html

```
<body>
    <h1>Select Your Favorite City</h1>
    <div wicket:id="feedback"></div>
    <form wicket:id="form">
        <select wicket:id="countries"></select>
        <select wicket:id="cities"></select>
        <input type="submit" value="Submit"/>
    </form>
</body>
```

HomePage.java

```
DropDownChoice<Country> countries =
    new DropDownChoice<Country>("countries",
        new PropertyModel<Country>(this, "country"),
        new CountriesModel(),
        new ChoiceRenderer<Country>("name", "code"))
{
    protected boolean
    wantOnSelectionChangedNotifications() {return true;}

    protected void
    onSelectionChanged(Country newSelection) {city = null;}
};
countries.setRequired(true);
form.add(countries);

DropDownChoice<City> cities =
    new DropDownChoice<City>("cities",
        new PropertyModel<City>(this, "city"),
        new CitiesModel(),
        new ChoiceRenderer<City>("name", "code"));
cities.setRequired(true);
form.add(cities);
```

How it works...

The trick to making the selectboxes work together is in how we tied the CitiesModel, which feeds the list of available cities, to the selection made in the Country selectbox. This, coupled with the fact that the Country selectbox automatically submits the form when the selection is changed, allows the two selectboxes to work together seamlessly.

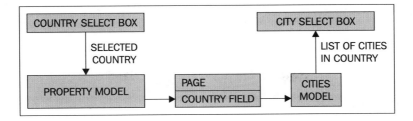

Let's examine the whole recipe in its entirety.

We begin by creating the Country and City objects in step 1. In an actual application, these would most likely be ORM entities retrieved from a database, but to keep things concise in the example they are simple value objects.

In the next step we create a simple in-memory database which contains two methods: one to retrieve all countries and one to retrieve cities based on a country code.

In step 3, we create a page with an empty form that will contain our two selectboxes. The two selectboxes will need to store their selected values somewhere, so we create two fields to hold the currently selected values:

```
// class HomePage
private Country country;
private City city;
```

In step 4 we create the model that will feed the Country selectbox its list of available countries. We retrieve the list by querying the `Database` object:

```
return Database.getCountries();
```

Step 5 is where things get a little more interesting; here we create a model that will feed the City selectbox the list of available cities. But, the list of cities has to be restricted by the country selected in the Country selectbox; we accomplish this by selecting the currently selected country from the `country` field we created earlier, and using it to filter the result:

```
return Database.getCities(country.getCode());
```

At this point all we are missing is a way to force the Country selectbox to push its current selection into its model whenever the value is changed so that the City selectbox can be properly updated. Wicket's `DropDownChoice` has the ability to do this, and we enable it by overriding `wantOnSelectionChangedNotification` method and returning `true`:

```
DropDownChoice<Country> countries =
    new DropDownChoice<Country>("countries",
        new PropertyModel<Country>(this, "country"),
        new CountriesModel(),
```

```
new ChoiceRenderer<Country>("name", "code"))
{
    protected boolean
    wantOnSelectionChangedNotifications()
    {
        return true;
    }
};
```

One last thing we do is wipe out the currently selected city because if the country is changed the previously selected city is no longer valid. We implement this in `DropDownChoice'sonS electionChanged()` callback:

```
DropDownChoice<Country> countries =
    new DropDownChoice<Country>("countries",
        new PropertyModel<Country>(this, "country"),
        new CountriesModel(),
        new ChoiceRenderer<Country>("name", "code"))
    {
            protected void
            onSelectionChanged(Country newSelection)
            {
                city = null;
            }
    };
```

At this point the two selectboxes are properly linked.

There's more...

In the next section, we will see how to trigger the change notification over AJAX rather than a regular request.

How to trigger a change notification over AJAX

We could easily AJAXify the two dropdown lists by adding an `AjaxFormComponentUpdatingBehavior` behavior to the countries selectbox rather than using `DropDownChoice#wantOnSelectionChangedNotifications()`. AJAXifying the two dropdown lists will allow us to avoid a full-page refresh and make the interface feel quicker and more fluid. It would look like this:

```
cities.setOutputMarkupId(true);
countries.add(new AjaxFormComponentUpdatingBehavior("onchange")
{
    protected void onUpdate(AjaxRequestTarget target)
```

```
    {
        city = null;
                target.addComponent(cities);
        }
    });
```

Composing multiple form components into a single reusable component

As applications grow and forms get more and more complex, we often find opportunities to break out a part of a form and use it in others. This recipe will show you how to do it.

In this recipe, we will create a form that allows a user to sign up for a newsletter. The user will enter their e-mail address and their name. However, the name will consist of two fields: first and last. We will create a form component which will encapsulate the two textfields necessary to collect the user's name in such a way that it will be possible to use it in multiple forms or even multiple times in the same form.

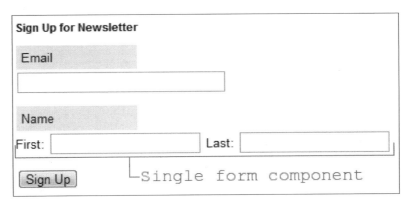

Getting ready

We will get started by creating the above form without the form component that represents the name.

Create the `Name` bean. Refer to the `Name.java` file in the code bundle.

Next, implement the page with a form shown in the screenshot previously. Refer to the `HomePage.java` and `HomePage.html` files in the code bundle.

How to do it...

1. Implement the editor for the name field:

NameEditor.html

```
<wicket:panel>
  First: <input wicket:id="first" type="text" size="20"/>
  Last: <input wicket:id="last" type="text" size="20"/>
</wicket:panel>
```

NameEditor.java

```java
public class NameEditor extends FormComponentPanel<Name>
{
    private final FormComponent<String> first;
    private final FormComponent<String> last;
    public NameEditor(String id, IModel<Name> model)
    {
        super(id, model);
        first = new TextField<String>("first", new Model<String>());
        add(first);

        last = new TextField<String>("last", new Model<String>());
        add(last);

        onModelChanged();

        add(new BothNamesFilledInValidator());
    }
    protected void onModelChanged()
    {
        super.onModelChanged();
        Name name = getModelObject();
        if (name != null)
        {
            first.setModelObject(name.getFirst());
            last.setModelObject(name.getLast());
        } else {
            first.setModelObject(null);
            last.setModelObject(null);
        }
    }

    protected void convertInput()
    {
        Name name = new Name();
        name.setFirst(first.getConvertedInput());
        name.setLast(last.getConvertedInput());
```

```java
        if (Strings.isEmpty(name.getFirst()) && Strings.
isEmpty(name.getLast()))
        {
            name = null;
        }
        setConvertedInput(name);
    }

    private static class BothNamesFilledInValidator implements
IValidator<Name>
    {
        public void validate(IValidatable<Name> validatable)
        {
            Name name = validatable.getValue();
            if (Strings.isEmpty(name.getFirst()) || Strings.
isEmpty(name.getLast()))
            {
                ValidationError error = new ValidationError();
                error.addMessageKey(getClass().getSimpleName());
                validatable.error(error);
            }
        }
    }
}
```

`NameEditor.properties`

`BothNamesFilledInValidator=Both first name and last name must be filled in`

2. Add the editor to the form:

`HomePage.html`

```html
<form wicket:id="form">
<p>
<label>Email</label>
<input wicket:id="email" type="text" size="30"/>
</p>
<p>
<label>Name</label>
<wicket:container wicket:id="name"/>
</p>
<input type="submit" value="Sign Up"/>
</form>
```
`HomePage.java`
```java
FormComponent<Name> name = new NameEditor("name",
    new PropertyModel<Name>(this, "name"));
```

```
name.setRequired(true);
form.add(name);
```

 The `wicket:container` tag we use to add the editor into the markup is a placeholder which leaves no trace once rendered. It is equivalent to adding a component to any tag and also calling `Component#setRenderBodyOnly (true)`.

How it works...

Our `name` editor needs to work as both a panel and a form component so we can reuse it easily by simply dropping it in wherever we need it. This means we would have to extend both Panel and FormComponent. Unfortunately, Java does not support multiple inheritance; for these cases Wicket provides a `FormComponentPanel` class which acts as both a `Panel` and a `FormComponent`.

We begin constructing our editor by extending `FormComponentPanel` and adding the two `TextField` components we need:

```
public class NameEditor extends FormComponentPanel<Name>
{
    private final FormComponent<String> first;
    private final FormComponent<String> last;
    public NameEditor(String id, IModel<Name> model)
    {
        super(id, model);
        first = new TextField<String>("first", new Model<String>());
        add(first);

        last = new TextField<String>("last", new Model<String>());
        add(last);
    }
}
```

Our editor is passed in a model containing a `Name` object. Once we create our editor we have to initialize the textfields with the values passed in the `Name` model object. We would also need to do this any time a new model object is set via a call to `setModelObject()` method. The best place to perform the initialization code would thus be in the `onModelChanged()` method which is called every time `setModelObject()` or `modelChanged()` methods are called:

```
protected void onModelChanged()
{
    super.onModelChanged();
```

```
    Name name = getModelObject();
    if (name != null)
    {
        first.setModelObject(name.getFirst());
        last.setModelObject(name.getLast());
    } else {
        first.setModelObject(null);
        last.setModelObject(null);
    }
}
```

We have to call this method manually from our editor's constructor to initially bootstrap the textfield values.

 Notice that we handle the case where `name` is `null`. It is feasible that an empty model is passed into our editor, in which case the editor should create a new instance of `name` and push it into the model.

The next thing we do is create and add a validator that will make sure both the first and last names are filled in if at least one of them is not empty. We create the validator as an inner class and add an instance in the constructor:

```
private static class BothNamesFilledInValidator
    implements IValidator<Name>
{
    public void validate(IValidatable<Name> validatable)
    {
        Name name = validatable.getValue();
        if (Strings.isEmpty(name.getFirst())
            || Strings.isEmpty(name.getLast()))
        {
            ValidationError error = new ValidationError();
            error.addMessageKey(getClass().getSimpleName());
            validatable.error(error);
        }
    }
}
```

You may have noticed that the validator expects a validatable of type `Name`, and the editor itself is given a model of type `Name`, setting the expectation that the editor will somehow convert the first and last name now stored in strings into a `Name` object and push that object into the model after validating it. Indeed, we accomplish this by overriding `FormComponent#convertInput()` and performing the conversion inside:

```
protected void convertInput()
{
    Name name = new Name();
    name.setFirst(first.getConvertedInput());
    name.setLast(last.getConvertedInput());

    if (Strings.isEmpty(name.getFirst())
        && Strings.isEmpty(name.getLast()))
    {
        name = null;
    }

    setConvertedInput(name);
}
```

Notice we properly handle the null case, converting two empty textfields into a null `Name` instance.

Also notice we access the values of first and last name text fields via `FormComponent#getConvertedInput()`—this is because during this stage of form processing workflow the models of the text fields have not yet been updated.

As the `NameEditor` provides its own markup and resource strings we create them in `NameEditor.html` and `NameEditor.properties` respectively. The resource strings are used for the error message raised by `BothNamesFilledInValidator`.

The `NameEditor` is now complete; all that remains is to add it to our form. We do this in step 4 by simply dropping it into the form and markup.

There's more...

The preceding recipe is based on an immutable model object, but this is often not the case. Let's explore ways of building editors that work with mutable objects, which are more common in everyday code.

Changing the editor to work with a mutable model object

In the preceding example our `NameEditor` always pushes a new instance of `Name` into its model. This works correctly most of the time, but what if `Name` had other fields that we wanted to preserve? In this case, the editor would have to apply the values of first and last names to the instance of `Name` currently in its model instead of pushing a new instance. This could easily be accomplished by overriding how form components update their models. For our particular example we can do this as follows:

```java
public class NameEditor extends FormComponentPanel<Name>
{
    @Override
    public void updateModel()
    {
        Name edited=getConvertedInput();
        Name current=getModelObject();
        if (current!=null) {
            current.setFirst(edited.getFirst());
            current.setLast(edited.getLast());
            getModel().setObject(current);
        } else {
            getModel().setObject(edited);
        }
        super.updateModel();
    }
}
```

 Notice that we still call `getModel().setObject(current)` in the case that a `Name` already exists in the model. While doing so may seem like a loop as we are essentially executing `getModel().setObject(getModel().getObject())`, it is still a good practice in case the model containing the `Name` instance expects to know when the name has been updated.

Preventing multiple form submits

A common problem for web applications is unwanted form resubmits, either via clicking the **Submit** button again before the page finished processing, or by navigating back and submitting the form again. While submitting a search form twice may not be a problem, submitting an order form may lead to two identical orders, or worse, erroneously submitting a bank-related form more than once may lead to serious consequences.

In this example, we will examine how to prevent multiple submits of the same form, and we will do so by constructing a mock ATM. Our ATM will start off all accounts with a $1000 balance and allow users to withdraw money from the accounts.

Here is what a normal withdrawal from a new account might look like:

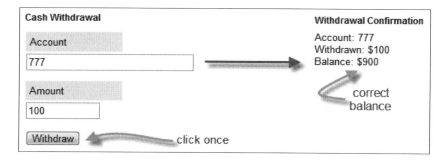

The user selects a new account **777** with a starting balance of $1000 and withdraws $100 dollars ending up with a balance of $900.

Here is what a withdrawal from a new account of a user in a hurry might look like:

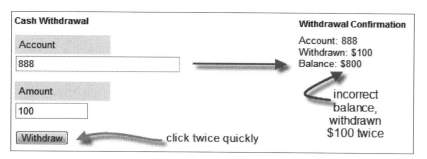

As we can see, just like before, the user withdraws **$100** from a new account **888** with a starting balance of **$1000**. But, this time the user clicks the **Withdraw** button twice before the form has a chance to finish processing, which leads to the withdrawal, being processed twice as can be seen from the finishing balance of $800.

In this recipe, we will build a solution that will detect this situation and correctly ignore duplicate submits, leaving the user with a good user experience:

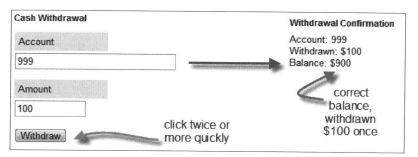

Getting ready

Let's begin by constructing our ATM in its default, vulnerable state.

Create a mock bank:

```
public class Bank
{
    static synchronized int withdraw(String account,int amount)
    {
        // sample code decreases balance of account in memory
    }
    public static synchronized int getBalance(String account)
    {
        // sample code retrieves balance from memory
    }
}
```

Create the **Withdrawal Confirmation** page shown previously and refer to the HomePage. java and ConfirmationPage.java and ConfirmationPage.html files in the code bundle.

Implement the **Cash Withdrawal** page:

HomePage.java

```
// refer to the code bundle for markup
public class HomePage extends WebPage
{
    private String account;
    private Integer amount;
    public HomePage(final PageParameters parameters)
    {
        add(new FeedbackPanel("feedback"));
        Form<?> form = new Form<Void>("form")
        {
            protected void onSubmit()
            {
                Bank.withdraw(account, amount);
                Duration.seconds(5).sleep();
                setResponsePage(
                    new ConfirmationPage(account, amount));
            }
        };
        add(form);
```

```
      // add two text fields to the form to collect the account and
         amount to withdraw linked to the two fields
   }
}
```

How to do it...

We have now implemented the cash withdrawal workflow, but this workflow is vulnerable to double submits. In the next step, we are going to build a subclass of Form which will block resubmits, and install it in our **Funds Transfer** page.

1. Implement a FormToken object. This object will identify a submitted form so we can track them:

    FormToken.java

    ```
    public class FormToken implements Serializable
    {
       private final PageReference reference;
       private final String pathToForm;

       public FormToken(PageReference reference, String pathToForm)
       {
          this.reference = reference;
          this.pathToForm = pathToForm;
       }

       @Override
       public int hashCode()
       {
          return 31 * reference.hashCode() *
             pathToForm.hashCode();
       }

       @Override
       public boolean equals(Object obj)
       {
          if (obj == this)
          {
             return true;
          }
          else if (obj == null)
          {
             return false;
          }
          else if (obj instanceof FormToken)
    ```

```
        {
            FormToken other = (FormToken)obj;
            return other.reference.equals(reference) && other.
pathToForm.equals(pathToForm);
        }
        return false;
    }
}
```

2. Implement the `Form` subclass that blocks resubmits:

`SubmitOnceForm.java`

```java
public class SubmitOnceForm<T> extends Form<T>
{
    private static MetaDataKey<ArrayList<FormToken>> PROCESSED =
        new MetaDataKey<ArrayList<FormToken>>()
    {
    };
    public SubmitOnceForm(String id)
    {
        super(id);
    }
    protected void onRepeatSubmit()
    {
        error(getString("alreadySubmitted"));
    }
    @Override
    public void process(IFormSubmittingComponent
        submittingComponent)
    {
        if (isAlreadyProcessed())
        {
            onRepeatSubmit();
            return;
        }
        super.process(submittingComponent);
        updateProcessedForms();
    }
    private FormToken getToken()
    {
        return new FormToken(getPage().getPageReference(),
            getPageRelativePath());
    }
```

```
    private synchronized boolean isAlreadyProcessed()
    {
        ArrayList<FormToken> tokens = getSession().
getMetaData(PROCESSED);

        if (tokens != null)
        {
            FormToken token = getToken();
            if (tokens.contains(token))
            {
                return true;
            }
        }
        return false;
    }

    private synchronized void updateProcessedForms()
    {
        if (hasError())
        {
            return;
        }

        ArrayList<FormToken> tokens = getSession().
getMetaData(PROCESSED);
        if (tokens == null)
        {
            tokens = new ArrayList<FormToken>();
        }

        FormToken token = getToken();

        if (!tokens.contains(token))
        {
            tokens.add(token);
            while (tokens.size() > 20)
            {
                tokens.remove(0);
            }
            getSession().setMetaData(PROCESSED, tokens);
        }
    }
}

SubmitOnceForm.properties

alreadySubmitted=This form has already been processed
```

3. Replace the use of normal `Form` with our `SubmitOnceForm` in the
   Cash Withdrawal page:

   ```
   HomePage.java
   Form<?> form = new SubmitOnceForm<Void>("form")
   {
       @Override
       protected void onSubmit()
       {
           Bank.withdraw(account, amount);
           Duration.seconds(5).sleep();
           setResponsePage(new ConfirmationPage(account, amount));
       }
       @Override
       protected void onRepeatSubmit()
       {
           setResponsePage(new ConfirmationPage(account, amount));
       }
   };
   add(form);
   ```

How it works...

There are many ways to implement resubmit protection. In this example, we implement it by tracking submitted forms in the user's HTTP session.

The first step is to be able to identify each form uniquely. In Wicket, any component can be uniquely identified by combining:

- The page it is on
- The path from the page to the component

In order to store this information we create the `FormToken` object in step 5:

```
public class FormToken implements Serializable
{
    private final PageReference reference;
    private String pathToForm;
    // getters and setters omitted for brevity
    // hashcode and equals are omitted for brevity
}
```

Not that we use `PageReference` to reference the `Page` and not the page instance itself. There are two reasons for doing this: we do not want the page instance serialized into session if the session is ever replicated, and `PageReference` references a specific version of the page whereas a `Page` instance's version can still change.

The remaining tasks are:

- Store the token in a list kept in the session
- Intercept the submit and make sure the form is not already in the list

We are going to encapsulate this behavior in a `SubmitOnceForm` class which is a subclass of `Form`.

We are going to use Wicket's metadata facility to store the list in session; this way, we will not need to force the application to use a special subclass of `Session`. Wicket's metadata is a key-value store, so first we must create a key. Keys are created by subclassing `MetaDataKey`:

```
private static MetaDataKey<ArrayList<FormToken>> PROCESSED = new MetaD
ataKey<ArrayList<FormToken>>() {};
```

Notice that keys specify which type of object they store, so the metadata facility is typesafe.

Now that we have a metadata key, let's start by implementing the storage of submitted forms. First we must intercept the post-submit event; we do this by overriding `Form#process(IForm mSubmittingComponent)`:

```
public class SubmitOnceForm<T> extends Form<T>
{

    public void process(IFormSubmittingComponent submittingComponent)
    {
        super.process(submittingComponent);
        updateProcessedForms();
    }
}
```

Next, we implement the `updateProcessedForms()` function:

```
    private synchronized void updateProcessedForms()
    {
        if (hasError())
        {
            return;
        }
        ArrayList<FormToken> tokens = getSession().
    getMetaData(PROCESSED);
```

```
        if (tokens == null)
        {
            tokens = new ArrayList<FormToken>();
        }
        FormToken token = getToken();
        if (!tokens.contains(token))
        {
            tokens.add(token);
            while (tokens.size() > 20)
            {
                tokens.remove(0);
            }
            getSession().setMetaData(PROCESSED, tokens);
        }
    }
}
```

When implementing `updateProcessedForms()` we first check if there were errors processing the current form, and if there were, we do not record the form as processed. Next we create a token to represent the form and store it in a list and then store the list in session.

Now that we can record submitted forms we can check if the form has already been submitted. We do it once again using `Form#Process(IFormSubmittingComponent)`:

```
public class SubmitOnceForm<T> extends Form<T>
{
    @Override
    public void process(IFormSubmittingComponent submittingComponent)
    {
        if (isAlreadyProcessed())
        {
            onRepeatSubmit();
            return;
        }
        super.process(submittingComponent);
        updateProcessedForms();
    }
```

Now we implement `ifAlreadyProcessed()`; this is a simple function that checks if a `FormToken` for the current form is already in the list we keep in session:

```
private synchronized boolean isAlreadyProcessed()
{
    ArrayList<FormToken> tokens = getSession().getMetaData(PROCESSED);
    if (tokens != null)
```

```
    {
        FormToken token = getToken();
        if (tokens.contains(token))
        {
            return true;
        }
    }
    return false;
}
```

We complete our recipe with step 6 where we replace the use of a normal `Form` with our `SubmitOnceForm`.

There's more...

Preventing double submits may appear easy, but in practice can be tricky. Let's take a look at some traps that are easy to fall into.

Understanding page versioning

At first glance it may seem like we are overcomplicating things. A more obvious solution may be to simply keep a `submitted` boolean and use it as a flag to see if the form has already been submitted:

```java
public class SubmitOnceFormBad<T> extends Form<T>
{
    private boolean submitted = false;

    @Override
    public void process(IFormSubmittingComponent submittingComponent)
    {
        if (submitted)
        {
            error(getString("alreadySubmitted"));
        }
        super.process(submittingComponent);
        if (!hasError())
        {
            submitted = true;
        }
    }
}
```

While this will work for our preceding example, it will fail in a variety of other situations. Namely, it will fail if the page version is incremented after the form is submitted. What will happen is that the `true` value of the `submitted` boolean will be stored in the new page version, and so when the user clicks the back button to submit the form again Wicket will roll the state of the page back to the old version in which the `submitted boolean` is still `false`.

The reason we do not increment the page version in the preceding example is because we simply navigate to another page and do not modify the state of the current page. A lot of applications, however, navigate by using panel-swapping instead of pages. A panel swap increments the page version and the `SubmitOnceFormBad` would fail to protect against a repeat submit.

Protecting against spam with a CAPTCHA

Spam is becoming more and more of a problem, especially for web applications that do not require users to have accounts, such as blogs or wikis. In this recipe, we are going to construct a reusable CAPTCHA form component that will help us protect our forms from spammers.

To test our component, we will construct a trivial **Leave a Comment** form as follows and add a CAPTCHA to protect it:

Getting ready

Create the page with the form shown precedingly, without the CAPTCHA component for now. Refer to the `HomePage.java` and `HomePage.html` files in the code bundle.

How to do it...

1. Create a model to supply CAPTCHA challenges:

   `ChallengeModel.java`

   ```java
   public class ChallengeModel extends AbstractReadOnlyModel<String>
   {
       private String challenge;

       @Override
       public String getObject() {
           if (challenge == null) {
               challenge = String.format("%04d",
                  (int)(Math.random() * 10000));
           }
           return challenge;
       }
       public void reset() {
           challenge = null;
       }
   }
   ```

2. Create a validator to check user's responses to challenges:

   `ChallengeValidator.java`

   ```java
   public class ChallengeValidator implements IValidator<String> {
       private final IModel<String> challenge;

       public ChallengeValidator(IModel<String> challenge) {
           this.challenge = challenge;
       }

       public void validate(IValidatable<String> validatable) {
           if (!challenge.getObject()
              .equals(validatable.getValue())) {
              ValidationError error = new ValidationError();
              error.addMessageKey(getClass().getSimpleName());
              validatable.error(error);
           }
       }
   }
   ```

```
ChallengeValidator.properties

ChallengeValidator=You did not correctly answer the CAPTCHA
```

3. Create the CAPTCHA component:

```
Captcha.html
<wicket:panel>
<img wicket:id="challenge"/><br/>
<input wicket:id="result" type="text" size="20"
autocomplete="off"/>
</wicket:panel>
```

```java
Captcha.java
public class Captcha extends Panel {
    private ChallengeModel challenge = new ChallengeModel();
    private TextField<String> result;

    public Captcha(String id) {
        super(id);
        setDefaultModel(challenge);

        add(new Image("challenge", new CaptchaImageResource(challen
          ge)));
        result = new TextField<String>("result", new
        Model<String>(null));
        result.setRequired(true);
        result.add(new ChallengeValidator(challenge));
        add(result);
    }

    @Override
    protected void onBeforeRender() {
        result.clearInput();
        result.setModelObject(null);
        challenge.reset();
        super.onBeforeRender();
    }
}
```

4. Install the component in the form:

```java
HomePage.java

form.add(new Captcha("captcha"));
```

```
HomePage.html
<p>
<label>Captcha</label>
<wicket:container wicket:id="captcha"/>
</p>
```

How it works...

In order to create a CAPTCHA component, we need to accomplish the following tasks:

- ▶ Generate challenges and store them in session
- ▶ Validate that the user's response is correct
- ▶ Create an image to present challenges
- ▶ Create a text field where the user can respond to challenges
- ▶ Regenerate the challenge on every render

We begin by creating a `Model` that will supply challenges in step 1. It is a simple model that generates a challenge string consisting of some numbers and stores it until we call the `reset()` method:

```
public String getObject()
  {
    if (challenge == null)
      {
        //generate challenge
      }
    return challenge;
  }
public void reset()
  {
    challenge = null;
  }
```

As we do not clear the challenge string in the `IModel#detach()` method it will be stored in session along with the model.

In step 2, we create a validator that compares the user's input to the challenge string and raises an error if they do not match. We give our validator access to the challenge string by passing in the challenge model; this is also how we are going to give it to the component that will draw the CAPTCHA as an image:

```
public class ChallengeValidator implements IValidator<String>
  {
    private final IModel<String> challenge;
    public ChallengeValidator(IModel<String> challenge)
      {
        this.challenge = challenge;
      }
```

In our case the model we pass in will be an instance of `ChallengeModel`, but this does not matter to a validator – it just needs a model of type `String` that it can call `getObject()` on. The validator compares the string it pulls out of the challenge model to the user's input, and if they do not match it raises an error:

```
public void validate(IValidatable<String> validatable)
    {
        if (!challenge.getObject()
            .equals(validatable.getValue())) {
            // raise error
        }
    }
```

Now that we have a way to generate challenges and validate them we can move on to creating the `Captcha` component itself. The component will take care of the last three tasks in our to-do list:

► Create an image to present challenges

► Create a textfield where the user can response to challenges

► Regenerate the challenge on every render

Wicket ships with a `wicket-extensions` module which serves as a repository for non-critical components. One of these components is: `org.apache.wicket.extensions.markup.html.captcha.CaptchaImageResource`, which given a challenge string can render a CAPTCHA image for it. We will use this component to generate the image part of our CAPTCHA:

```
add(new Image("challenge",
    new CaptchaImageResource(challenge)));
```

With the image out of the way, we move on to creating the textfield our users will use to respond to the challenge:

```
result = new TextField<String>("result",
    new Model<String>(""));
result.setRequired(true);
result.add(new ChallengeValidator(challenge));
```

We give the textfield a blank model because we do not need to reference the value users will enter, the only piece of code that needs access to this value is the `ChallengeValidator`, and it will have it via Wicket's validation mechanism.

The last task is to regenerate the challenge string on every render. We accomplish this by overriding `Captcha`'s `Component#onBeforeRender()` method:

```
protected void onBeforeRender()
    {
        result.clearInput();
```

```
        result.setModelObject(null);
        challenge.reset();
        super.onBeforeRender();
    }
```

The first two lines take care of clearing any previous response the user may have given to the challenge. The next line calls `ChallengeModel#reset()` which forces the `ChallengeModel` to create a new response whenever `getObject()` is called next.

The `Captcha` component is now complete. We add it to our form in step 4.

 As we have built `Captcha` as a `Panel` which encapsulates both code and markup we are now free to drop it into any form and it will just work. This is one of the most powerful things about Wicket.

3
Making Forms Presentable

In this chapter, we will cover:

- ► Changing form component CSS class on validation errors
- ► Using `FeedbackPanel` to output form component specific messages
- ► Streamlining form component presentation using behaviors

Introduction

Forms are probably the most important parts of any web application because they are what the users interact with the most. In this chapter, we will see how to make forms friendlier and more efficient to use by providing visual feedback to our users.

Changing form component CSS class on validation errors

Making incorrectly filled-in form fields visually stand out is an important aspect of usability design because it allows the user to quickly find and correct their mistakes. A common technique for accomplishing this is to append a CSS class that will change how the fields are displayed. In this recipe, we will learn how to do that in a simple and reusable manner and apply it to a simple Newsletter Sign Up form as shown in the following screenshot:

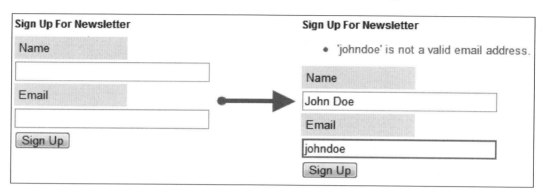

Getting ready

Create the form shown in the preceding screenshot. Refer to `HomePage.html` and `HomePage.java` in the code bundle.

How to do it...

1. Create the behavior that will output the `error` CSS class:

```
ErrorClassAppender.java
public class ErrorClassAppender extends AbstractBehavior
{
    @Override
    public void onComponentTag(Component component, ComponentTag
      tag) {
        if (((FormComponent<?>) component).isValid() == false) {
            String cl = tag.getAttribute("class");
            if (cl == null) {
                tag.put("class", "error");
            } else {
                tag.put("class", "error " + cl);
            }
```

```
        }
    }
}
```

2. Add the behavior to the desired form components:

```
HomePage.java
TextField<String> name = new TextField<String>("name",Model.
of(""));
name.add(new ErrorClassAppender());

TextField<String> email = new TextField<String>("email",Model.
of(""));
email.add(new ErrorClassAppender());
```

How it works...

To make fields with errors stand out in our form we will append a CSS class `error` to the input tag. We have defined this CSS class in Step 1:

```
<style>
    input.error { border: 2px solid red; }
</style>
```

We have also defined the form in Step 1, so what is left is to make sure the `class="error"` CSS attribute is added to the `name` and `email` input tags in our form whenever they are in an invalid state.

We accomplish this by creating a Wicket behavior in Step 2. Wicket behaviors have an `onCo mponentTag(Component, ComponentTag)` method that is called when the markup tag of the component the behavior is attached to is being rendered. We will override this method and add our logic there. As we only want to output the CSS class when the form component is in an invalid state we use `FormComponent#isValid()` to check the current state of the form component:

```
if (((FormComponent<?>) component).isValid() == false) {
    // output the class="error" attribute
}
```

Once we know the component is in an invalid state we use the passed in `ComponentTag` object to add the attribute:

```
String cl = tag.getAttribute("class");
if (cl == null) {
    tag.put("class", "error");
} else {
    tag.put("class", "error " + cl);
}
```

Notice that we take care to append the `error` class instead of simply setting it; this is so we do not wipe out any other CSS class the component may have specified in the markup.

The remaining step is to add the behavior to the desired form components; we do this in Step 3 by adding it to the `name` and `email` components:

```
name.add(new ErrorClassAppender());
email.add(new ErrorClassAppender());
```

Now, whenever `name` or `email` components have invalid values their rendered markup will look like this:

```
<input wicket:id="email" type="text"
 size="30" value="johndoe" name="email"
class="error"/>
```

And will appear with the red border we have defined previously.

There's more...

In this section, we will examine some opportunities which we will make using our `ErrorClassAppender` simpler.

Automating component decoration

In our example the form has two fields, so it required only two calls to add `ErrorClassAppender` to all the fields. But, what if our form had twenty fields; would we have to call `field.add(new ErrorClassAppender())` twenty times? This would be very error-prone; instead we can automate the process by using visitors. By adding the following code at the end of our page's constructor we can automate the process of adding the behavior to each field:

```
form.visitChildren(FormComponent.class,
    new IVisitor<FormComponent<?>>() {
       public Object component(FormComponent<?> component) {
          component.add(new ErrorClassAppender());
          return CONTINUE_TRAVERSAL;
       }
    });
```

Using FeedbackPanel to output form component specific messages

As web applications get more complex the forms they use get larger. At some point of time, having a long list of errors at the top of the form becomes inefficient. A better way to display errors is to display them next to the fields that caused them. In this example, we are going to modify a **Sign Up For Newsletter** form to display errors next to the fields instead of at the top:

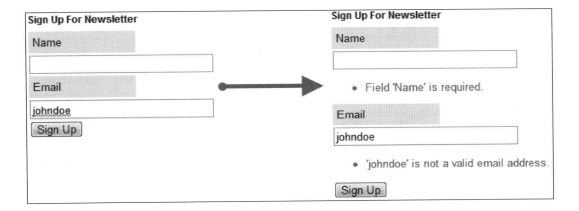

Getting ready

Create the form shown in the preceding screenshot. Refer to HomePage.html and HomePage.java in the code bundle.

How to do it...

1. Add two separate FeedbackPanels that will display field-related errors:

```
HomePage.html
<label>Name</label>
<input wicket:id="name" type="text" size="30"/><br/>
<div wicket:id="nameFeedback"></div>
<label>Email</label>
<input wicket:id="email" type="text" size="30"/><br/>
<div wicket:id="emailFeedback"></div>

HomePage.java
TextField<String> name = new TextField<String>("name", Model.
of(""));
form.add(name);
form.add(new FeedbackPanel("nameFeedback",
```

```
        new ComponentFeedbackMessageFilter(name)));

    TextField<String> email = new TextField<String>("email", Model.
    of(""));
    form.add(email);
    form.add(new FeedbackPanel("emailFeedback",
            new ComponentFeedbackMessageFilter(email)));
```

How it works...

By default, each `FeedbackPanel` added to the page will display all feedback messages reported by any component in that page. What we want is to restrict the `FeedbackPanel` to only show messages related to a specific `FormComponent` in our form. This way we can add a `FeedbackPanel` for every field in our form and have it display only errors produced by that field.

`FeedbackPanels` have built in support for filtering messages that display in the form of `IFeedbackMessageFilter` which looks like this:

```
public interface IFeedbackMessageFilter extends IClusterable
{
    boolean accept(FeedbackMessage message);
}
```

What we need is to implement a filter that only accepts messages from a specific form field; luckily Wicket ships with a filter we can use to do just that, the `ComponentFeedbackMessageFilter`.

Armed with this knowledge we can easily create a `FeedbackPanel` that will display errors for a specific form field. We create two such panels in Step 2 – one for each field. We do this by passing in the filter to `FeedbackPanel`'s constructor:

```
    TextField<String> name = new TextField<String>("name", Model.
    of(""));
    form.add(name);
    form.add(new FeedbackPanel("nameFeedback",
            new ComponentFeedbackMessageFilter(name)));
```

The `FeedbackPanel` will only display errors produced by the name field because that is the component we give to the `ComponentFeedbackMessageFilter`. All that is left is to position the `nameFeedback` component next to its form field and the errors will show up where we want:

```
    <input wicket:id="name" type="text" size="30"/><br/>
    <div wicket:id="nameFeedback"></div>
```

Streamlining form component presentation using behaviors

Setting up fields in forms involves a lot of repetitive steps for each field: adding a field label, adding a `FeedbackPanel` to display errors, adding some sort of field indicator that indicates whether the field is required or not, and so on. Lucky, all of the above can be accomplished by creating and adding a single behavior to each field; in this recipe we are going to create such a behavior and add it to fields in a Newsletter Sign Up form:

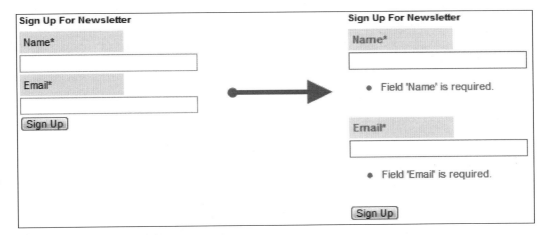

Getting ready

Create the form shown in the figure above. Refer to `HomePage.html` and `HomePage.java` in the code bundle.

How to do it...

1. Create the behavior we will use to decorate each form field:

```
FieldDecorator.java
public class FieldDecorator extends AbstractBehavior {
    public void bind(Component component) {
        component.setOutputMarkupId(true);
    }

    public void beforeRender(Component component) {
        FormComponent<?> fc = (FormComponent<?>) component;
        Response r = component.getResponse();
        String label =
```

```
            (fc.getLabel() != null) ? fc.getLabel().getObject(): null;
            if (label != null) {
                r.write("<label for=\"");
                r.write(fc.getMarkupId());
                r.write("\"");
                if (fc.isValid() == false) {
                    r.write(" class=\"error\"");
                }
                r.write(">");
                r.write(Strings.escapeMarkup(label));
                if (fc.isRequired()) {
                    r.write("<span class=\"required\">*</span>");
                }
                r.write("</label>");
            }

            super.beforeRender(component);
        }

        @Override
        public void onRendered(Component component) {
            FormComponent<?> fc = (FormComponent<?>) component;
            Response r = component.getResponse();
            FeedbackMessages messages = fc.getSession().
              getFeedbackMessages();

            if (messages.hasMessageFor(component)) {
                r.write("<ul class=\"feedbackPanel\">");
                IFeedbackMessageFilter filter = new
                  ComponentFeedbackMessageFilter(
                      component);

                for (FeedbackMessage message : messages.messages(filter))
{
                    r.write("<li class=\"feedbackPanel");
                    r.write(message.getLevelAsString().toUpperCase());
                    r.write("\">");
                    r.write(Strings.escapeMarkup(message.getMessage().
                      toString()));
                    r.write("</li>");
                }
                r.write("</ul>");
            }
        }

        @Override
        public void onComponentTag(Component component, ComponentTag
          tag) {
```

```
        FormComponent<?> fc = (FormComponent<?>) component;
        if (fc.isValid() == false) {
            String cl = tag.getAttribute("class");
            if (cl == null) {
                tag.put("class", "error");
            } else {
                tag.put("class", "error " + cl);
            }
        }
    }
}
```

2. Add it to each form field:

    HomePage.java

    ```
    TextField<String> name = new TextField<String>("name", Model.
    of(""));
    name.add(new FieldDecorator());
    TextField<String> email=new TextField<String>("email", Model.
    of(""));
    email.add(new FieldDecorator());
    ```

How it works...

As we want to skip the hassle of adding label components, feedback components, and so on, we are going to accomplish our task by writing directly into the markup. While, at first, this may seem to be going against the component-oriented methodology, it is a perfectly normal way of doing things when circumstances require it. In this particular case, we can justify using this technique by explaining that the markup we are writing out is small, well-defined, and not particularly dynamic; it will also not need to be tweaked by the designer nor changed for a different use case by a developer.

Our `FieldDecorator` behavior accomplishes the following:

  ► Write out the `<label>` tag
  ► Add 'error' css class to the label if the field is invalid
  ► Write out a * indicator if the field is required
  ► Write out any errors the field produces
  ► Add 'error' css class to the field tag if the field is in valid

Let's begin by writing out the `<label>` tag. A proper label tag looks like this:

```
<label for="name">Name</label>
```

The first thing we must do is ensure that the field outputs its markup id so the label can use it in the `for` attribute. We accomplish it by overriding `IBehavior:bind(Component)` which is called every time a behavior is added to a component. In the method, we simply call `Compon ent#setOutputMarkupId(boolean)` on the component that is passed in (the component to which the behavior was added):

```
@Override
public void bind(Component component) {
    component.setOutputMarkupId(true);
}
```

Next we write out the `<label>` tag itself. We do this in `IBehavior:beforeRender(Compo nent)` because we want the label tag to appear in the markup before the form field:

```
@Override
public void beforeRender(Component component) {
    FormComponent<?> fc = (FormComponent<?>) component;
    Response r = component.getResponse();
    String label = (fc.getLabel() != null) ?
        fc.getLabel().getObject()    : null;
    if (label != null) {
        r.write("<label for=\"");
        r.write(fc.getMarkupId());
        r.write("\"");
        r.write(">");
        r.write(Strings.escapeMarkup(label));
        r.write("</label>");
    }
}
```

We get a hold of the `Response` object by calling the `Component#getResponse()` method, once we have the `Response` we can write anything we want into the markup by using `Response#write(String)`.

Notice that when writing out the label itself we first run it through `Strings#escapeMarkup(String)`. As we are not using a component to output the label for us we cannot rely on it to escape possible markup, so we have to do it ourselves. Not doing so may open our application to XSS attacks.

Next, we move on to appending the 'error' css class to the label if the field is invalid. We can test whether the field is valid or not by using `FormComponent#isValid()`, and the rest is easy:

```
if (label != null) {
    r.write("<label for=\"");
    r.write(fc.getMarkupId());
```

```
r.write("\"");
if (fc.isValid() == false) {
    r.write(" class=\"error\"");
}
```

With the label tag taken care of, we move on to writing out the required field indicator; in our case we will simply output a star next to fields that are required. We are going to accomplish this in much the same way as above, but instead of testing with `FormComponent#isValid()` we are going to use `FormComponent#isRequired()`:

```
if (label != null) {
    if (fc.isRequired()) {
        r.write("<span class=\"required\">*</span>");
    }
    r.write("</label>");
}
```

Let's take care of writing out the field errors. We will implement this in the `IBehavior#componentRendered(Component)` because we want the errors rendered after the field's tag. We will output the errors using exact markup used by the `FeedbackPanel` so any CSS styling could be easily reused. First, we check if the field has any errors associated with it by obtaining the `FeedbackMessages` component that stores all messages reported by all components:

```
@Override
public void onRendered(Component component) {
    FeedbackMessages messages = fc.getSession().
      getFeedbackMessages();

    if (messages.hasMessageFor(component)) {
```

Next, we will loop over each error and write out the necessary markup:

```
if (messages.hasMessageFor(component)) {
    r.write("<ul class=\"feedbackPanel\">");
    IFeedbackMessageFilter filter = new ComponentFeedbackMessageFilter
      (component);
    for (FeedbackMessage message : messages.messages(filter)) {
        r.write("<li class=\"feedbackPanel");
        r.write(message.getLevelAsString().toUpperCase());
        r.write("\">");
        r.write(Strings.escapeMarkup(
            message.getMessage().toString()));
        r.write("</li>");
    }
```

Notice that we once again use `Strings#escapeMarkup(String)` when writing out values we do not have direct control over.

The last remaining task of our `FieldDecorator` is to append an 'error' CSS class to the field it is attached to; in our example this is used to add a red border to the field. We do this by overriding `IBehavior#onComponentTag(Component)` which is called when the component's markup tag is being rendered:

```
@Override
public void onComponentTag(Component component, ComponentTag tag) {
    FormComponent<?> fc = (FormComponent<?>) component;
    if (fc.isValid() == false) {
        String cl = tag.getAttribute("class");
        if (cl == null) {
            tag.put("class", "error");
        } else {
            tag.put("class", "error " + cl);
        }
    }
}
```

 Notice we take care to append the 'error' class to the CSS class attribute so that we can preserve any other classes set by the user or other behaviors such as `AttributeModifiers`.

Our `FieldDecorator`, once added to a form component can now transform markup like this:

```
<input wicket:id="email" type="text" size="30"/><br/>
```

Into the following:

```
<label for="email3" class="error">
    Email
    <span class="required">*</span>
</label>
<input wicket:id="email" type="text" size="30" value="" name="email"
id="email3" class="error"/>
<ul class="feedbackPanel">
    <li class="feedbackPanelERROR">
        Field Email is required.
    </li>
</ul>
```

Not bad for a single line of code:

```
email.add(new FieldDecorator());
```

There's more...

As I have mentioned previously, writing directly into markup is not the Wicket way in most situations. As such, it comes with a few caveats of its own; here we will examine how to smooth out the rough edges.

Making the decorator work with AJAX

If we repainted a field that has a `FieldDecorator` via AJAX, like when using `AjaxFormComponentUpdatingBehavior`, we would notice a strange behavior:

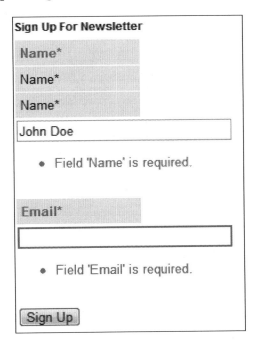

This is happening because we are replacing the `input` tag of our field with the entire markup produced by `FieldDecorator` every time we update the field with Ajax.

Starting with version 1.4.10, Wicket provides a simple solution: `IAjaxRegionMarkupIdProvider` – a mixing interface that allows us to override what markup region should be updated via Ajax. Let's modify `FieldDecorator` to take advantage of this and properly render when updated via AJAX.

1. Implement the interface and provide a markup id of the region we want updated:

```
    public class FieldDecorator extends AbstractBehavior
implements IAjaxRegionMarkupIdProvider {
    public String getAjaxRegionMarkupId(Component component) {
        return component.getMarkupId() + "_fd";
    }
}
```

2. Create the region around the output so the entire region can be repainted:

```
public void beforeRender(Component component) {
    Response r = component.getResponse();

    r.write("<div id=\"");
    r.write(getAjaxRegionMarkupId(component));
    r.write("\">");

    // rest of code
}

public void onRendered(Component component) {
    Response r = component.getResponse();

    // rest of code

    r.write("</div>");
}
```

Now when we try to update the field with AJAX it will work properly.

4

Taking your Application Abroad

In this chapter, we will cover:

- ▶ Storing module resource strings in package properties
- ▶ Retrieving a localized string
- ▶ Feeding dynamic localized strings to components using `StringResourceModel`
- ▶ Using `wicket:message` to output localized markup
- ▶ Overriding localized resources on a case by case basis

Introduction

In today's international world web applications need to support multiple locales. Wicket comes with first-class support for localizing and internationalizing web applications built with it. In this chapter, we will examine how to effectively use Wicket's localization support.

Storing module resource strings in package properties

Wicket is all about breaking down user interfaces into components and reusing those components over and over to speed up the development process. After a while, every Wicket application evolves a library of reusable components. Some are reusable across applications, while others only make sense with the application they were built for. In this recipe, we will see how to package resource properties along with component libraries without polluting the global `Application.properties` resource.

Wicket has many places where resource properties can be kept, but for reusable component libraries it is best to store the resource files in the same package. Wicket will attempt to load resources from a file called `package.properties` in the Java package that contains the component requesting the resource as well as all parent packages.

To demonstrate this we are going to create two components: a `NameLabel`, used to display a `Name` object, and a `NameEditor`, used to edit a `Name` object. These two components are going to share resource strings which we will store in `package.properties` so they are accessible by both components.

Here is what `NameLabel` and `NameEditor` look like:

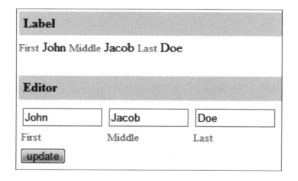

And here is what they look like when viewed with a browser set to `es` locale:

Label
Nombre de pila **John** Segundo nombre **Jacob** Apellido **Doe**

Editor
John   Jacob   Doe
Nombre de pila   Segundo nombre Apellido
[update]

Getting ready

Create the `Name` object:

`Name.java`

```
public class Name implements Serializable {
    private String first;
    private String middle;
    private String last;
    // constructors, getters and setters
}
```

Create the `NameLabel` component:

`NameLabel.java`

```
// for markup see NameLabel.html in the code bundle
public class NameLabel extends Panel {
    public NameLabel(String id, IModel<Name> model) {
        super(id, model);
        add(new Label("firstLabel", new ResourceModel("name.first")));
        add(new Label("first", new PropertyModel<String>(model,
            "first")));
        add(new Label("middleLabel", new ResourceModel("name.middle")));
        add(new Label("middle", new PropertyModel<String>(model,
            "middle")));
        add(new Label("lastLabel", new ResourceModel("name.last")));
        add(new Label("last", new PropertyModel<String>(model,
            "last")));
    }
}
```

Create `NameEditor` component:

`NameEditor.java`

```java
// for markup see NameEditor.html in the code bundle
public class NameEditor extends Panel {
    public NameEditor(String id, IModel<Name> model) {
        super(id, model);
        add("first").add("middle").add("last");
    }
    private NameEditor add(String id) {
        IModel<String> model = new PropertyModel<String>(getDefaultMod
el(), id);
        TextField<String>tf = new TextField<String>(id, model);
        tf.setLabel(new ResourceModel("name." + id));
        add(tf).add(new SimpleFormComponentLabel(id + "Label", tf));
        return this;
    }
}
```

`HomePage.java`

```java
// for markup see HomePage.html in the code bundle
public class HomePage extends WebPage {
    private Name name;
    public HomePage(final PageParameters parameters) {
        name = new Name("John", "Jacob", "Doe");

        add(new NameLabel("label", new PropertyModel<Name>(this,
"name")));

        Form<?> form = new Form<Void>("form");
        add(form);
        form.add(new NameEditor("editor", new PropertyModel<Name>(this,
"name")));
    }
}
```

How to do it...

1. Create `package.properties`next to `NameLabel.java` and `NameEditor.java`:

   `package.properties`

   `name.first=First`

   `name.middle=Middle`

   `name.last=Last`

2. Create `package_es.properties` next to `package.properties` which will contain the Spanish translation:

 As this is a standard property file it should be encoded using `ISO-8859-1` character encoding. If you need to use characters that are not supported by this encoding then use an `xml` property file instead. See JavaDoc of `java.util.Properties` for details.

```
package_es.properties
name.first=Nombre de pila
name.middle=Segundo nombre
name.last=Apellido
```

How it works...

In steps 2 and 3 we create components which require the `name.first`, `name.middle`, and `name.last` resource keys:

`NameLabel.java`

```
add(new Label("firstLabel", new  ResourceModel("name.first")));
```

`NameEditor.java`

```
TextField<String>tf = new TextField<String>(id, model);
tf.setLabel(new ResourceModel("name." + id));
```

In order to provide these resources we can create `NameLabel.properties` and `NameEditor.properties` and define the needed resources twice in each file, or we can create a package-scoped resource file which both components can access. In step 5 we create such a file:

`package.properties`

```
name.first=First
name.middle=Middle
name.last=Last
```

Now when either `NameLabel` or `NameEditor` requests these resources they will come from the same place, allowing us not to have to maintain two duplicate definitions.

There's more...

Wicket's resource loading mechanism is pluggable, and makes it easy to add new places where resources can be loaded from. In the next section we will see how easy it is to add a custom resource loader.

Extending Wicket's resource loading

All resource loading is handled by implementations of `org.apache.wicket.resource.loader.IStringResourceLoader` interface, which looks like this:

```
public interface IStringResourceLoader
{
    String loadStringResource(Class<?>clazz, String key, Locale locale,
        String style);
    String loadStringResource(Component component, String key);
}
```

The methods of the interface are explained in detail in the JavaDoc of the interface. New implementations of resource loaders can be registered like this:

```
public class MyApplication extends WebApplication {
    protected void init() {
        supert.init();
        getResourceSettings().addStringResourceLoader(newMyLoader());
    }
}
```

If you want your resource loader to override Wicket's behavior (have the priority) you can insert it in the beginning of the resource loaders chain:

```
getResourceSettings().addStringResourceLoader(0, newMyLoader());
```

Notice the 0 parameter above which will register `MyLoader` in the beginning of the chain.

Retrieving a localized string

Wicket makes it easy to retrieve and manipulate localized strings. Conventionally users rely on Wicket's `ResourceModel` to retrieve the localized strings and pass them to a component for display; however, sometimes we need to retrieve localized strings programmatically, without a model. One common use case where this is needed is to show feedback in a `FeedbackPanel` when an action occurs.

To demonstrate how to access and build localized strings programmatically let's build a Newsletter Sign Up form where the confirmation message will come from a localized string:

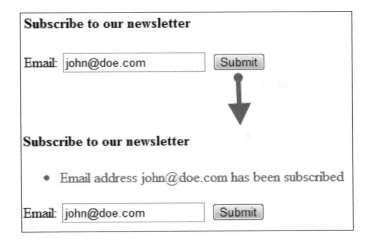

And here is what the user who subscribed with a browser set to es locale will see:

Suscribirse a nuestro boletín

- Dirección de correo electrónico john@doe.com ha sido suscrito

Correo electrónico: john@doe.com   Submit Query

Getting ready

Create the form without the confirmation message:

HomePage.properties

```
email=Email
subscribe=Subscribe to our newsletter
subscribed=Email address ${email} has been subscribed
```

HomePage_es.properties

```
email=Correoelectrónico
subscribe=Suscribirse a nuestroboletín
subscribed=Dirección de correoelectrónico${email} ha sidosuscrito
```

HomePage.java

```
// for markup refer to HomePage.html in the code bundle
public class HomePage extends WebPage {
    publicHomePage()
    {
```

```
        // sample code adds a form and calls the subscribe() method from
        form's onSubmit() handler.
    }
    private void subscribe() {
        // TODO display confirmation message
    }
}
```

How to do it...

1. Build and display the confirmation message:

    ```
    HomePage.java
    private void subscribe() {
        String addr = email.getModelObject();
        Map vars = new MicroMap("email", addr);
        String value=getString("subscribed", Model.ofMap(vars));
        info(value);
    }
    ```

How it works...

In step 1 HomePage.properties, we have defined our confirmation message which looks like this:

```
subscribed=Email address ${email} has been subscribed
```

In step 2, we retrieve the value of the subscribed string and display it.

The message has a variable named email which we want to replace with the email address the user has entered in the form. Wicket has the ability to interpolate variables in the resource strings; all we need to do is to define the values. Wicket can read values from either a Java Bean or a map; in our case we will define the value of the email variable in a map:

```
String addr = email.getModelObject();
Map vars = new MicroMap("email", addr);
```

We put the value into a MicroMap which is a Wicket utility implementation of Java's Map that only holds a single key/value pair. We could have used any implementation of Map such as the HashMap, but MicroMap provides us with a convenient constructor.

Wicket has two utility `Map` implementations called a `MicroMap` and a `MiniMap`. Both of these are primarily designed to be serialized more efficiently than more standard implementations such as the `HashMap`. If a component needs to store a `Map` as its property, consider using one of these implementations in order to optimize the component's footprint in session.

Now we are ready to retrieve the localized string; we do this using the `Component#getString(String key, IModel<Map>variables)` method, and display it using the `Component#info(String message)` method:

```
String value=getString("subscribed", Model.ofMap(vars));
info(value);
```

There's more...

In this section we explore further utilities provided by Wicket to help you in localizing your application.

The Localizer

All localization in Wicket happens through the `org.apache.wicket.Localizer` instance (every application has a single instance), all other methods and objects such as `ResourceModel` and`Component#getString()` simply delegate retrieval of localized strings to the `Localizer` instance. If you are writing your own `ResourceModel`-like models or need to access localized resources in an unconventional manner you will need to use the `Localizer`.

The Localizer instance can be accessed through the Application instance:

```
Application.get().getResourceSettings().getLocalizer();
```

Or, via the helper `Component#getLocalizer()` if you have access to a `Component` instance.

Feeding dynamic localized strings to components using StringResourceModel

Wicket comes with the well-known `ResourceModel` that is used to feed localized strings to components. However, what if we need more advanced features such as variable interpolation and default values? For these use cases, we can use `ResourceModel`'s older but less known `StringResourceModel` cousin.

To demonstrate the use of `StringResourceModel`, we will build a simple click counter page where the counter value and its last increment time stamp is displayed via a localized string:

> **Click Counter Example**
>
> The link has been clicked: 2 times, last click was at: Sat Jul 24 12:28:10 PDT 2010
> increment

And here is what it would look like in `es` locale:

> **Click Counter Example**
>
> este vínculo se ha hecho clic: 3 veces, último clic fue a las: Mon Jul 26 16:24:32 PDT 2010
> increment

Getting ready

Create the page with a placeholder for the message:

`HomePage.properties`

```
count=The link has been clicked: ${count} times, last click was at:
${timestamp}
```

`HomePage_es.properties`

```
count=estevínculo se ha hechoclic: ${count} veces, últimoclicfue a
las: ${timestamp}
```

`HomePage.java`

```java
// for markup refer to HomePage.html in the code bundle
public class HomePage extends WebPage {
    private int counter;
    private Date lastClick;

    public HomePage(final PageParameters parameters) {
```

```
      add(new Label("count", Model.of("placeholder")));
    add(new Link<Void>("increment") {
       public void onClick() {
          counter++;
          lastClick = new Date();
       }
    });
  }
}
```

How to do it...

1. Replace the placeholder label from step 1 with the proper click counter label:

    HomePage.java

    ```
    add(new Label("count", new StringResourceModel("count",
       newLoadableDetachableModel(){
             protected Object load() {
             HashMap map = new HashMap();
             map.put("count", counter);
             map.put("timestamp", (lastClick == null) ? "?"
                : lastClick);
             return map;
          }
    }))));
    ```

How it works...

In step 1 we have defined the click counter message:

HomePage.properties

```
count=The link has been clicked: ${count} times, last click was at:
${timestamp}
```

In step 2 we create a Label that will display the click count message.

The message contains two variables: the count and the timestamp.
StringResourceModel supports variable interpolation in localized strings, but in order for it to work we need to provide the values for the variables. The values can either come in a Java Bean or in a Map. We are going to use a Map to define the variable values:

```
HashMap map = new HashMap();
map.put("count", counter);
```

```
map.put("timestamp", (lastClick == null) ? "?"
    : lastClick);
```

Instead of expected a `Map` instance directly, `StringResourceModel` expects a `Imodel<?>`, so we wrap our map in a model:

```
new LoadableDetachableModel() {
    protected Object load() {
        HashMap map = new HashMap();
        // map definition above
        return map;
    }
```

We used a `LoadableDetachableModel` because there is no need to store the map between requests since we can recreate it every time it is needed.

The last step is to create the label itself with the `StringResourceModel` that uses our resource key: `count` and our map to interpolate the variables:

```
add(new Label("count", new StringResourceModel("count",
    new LoadableDetachableModel() {
        // model definition above
        }
    }))));
```

Using wicket:message to output localized markup

Fully localized pages usually have a lot of places where localized text needs to be inserted. Adding a `Label` component to the page every time we need to insert a bit of localized text adds a lot of noise to the code. Wicket provides a special markup tag that can be used to insert localized text into a page or a panel without requiring a `Component`.

Let's build a simple newsletter sign up form and localize it without adding any Wicket components to the page. The values we will want to localize are:

- ▶ The header of the form
- ▶ The policy message on the bottom
- ▶ The value of the submit button

The form will look like this:

Subscribe to our Newsletter:

[ ] [Subscribe]

Your email address will not be shared with anyone outside this company.

And with a browser set to es locale:

Suscribirse a nuestro boletín:

[ ] [Subscribir]

Su dirección de correo electrónico no será compartida con nadie fuera de esta empresa

Create the form in the previous screenshot. Refer to `HomePage.html` and `HomePage.java` in the code bundle.

How to do it...

1. Add the property files with localized values:

   `HomePage.properties`

   ```
   header=Subscribe to our Newsletter
   subscribe=Subscribe
   policy=Your email address will not be shared with anyone outside
   this company.
   ```

   `HomePage_es.properties`
   ```
   header=Suscribirse a nuestroboletín
   subscribe=Subscribir
   policy=Su dirección de correoelectrónico no serácompartida con
   nadiefuera de estaempresa
   ```

2. Modify the markup to use localized strings:

   `HomePage.html`

   ```html
   <html>
   <body>
      <strong>
         <wicket:message key="header"/>
      </strong>:<br/>
      <form>
          <input type="text"/>
          <input type="submit"
          wicket:message="value:subscribe"/>
          <br/>
   ```

```
        <small><em>
            <wicket:message key="policy"/>
        </em></small>
    </form>
  </body>
</html>
```

How it works...

The first thing we had to do was to define the resource bundles for our page. The following is the resource bundle for the default locale:

```
HomePage.properties

    header=Subscribe to our Newsletter
    subscribe=Subscribe
    policy=Your email address will not be shared with anyone outside this
    company.
```

With our localized strings defined we can begin to insert them into the page. In order to do so we will use the `<wicket:message>` tag. This tag is processed by Wicket and is replaced by the localized strings whose key is defined in the `key` attribute. In order to output the header of our form defined via the `header` resource key we add the following where we want the localized string to appear:

```
<strong>
    <wicket:message key="header"/>
</strong>:<br/>
```

We do the same for the policy string defined with the `policy` key:

```
<small><em>
    <wicket:message key="policy"/>
</em></small>
```

Lastly we need to localize the value of the submit button. Wicket also supports using `wicket:message` as an attribute of a tag; when used in such a way, various attributes of the tag can be localized. The value of the attribute consists of the following pattern:

```
attr:key,attr:key,...,attr:key
```

Here, each `attr` is the name of the attribute we want to localize and each `key` represents the key of the localized string. So, in order to localize the `value` attribute of our submit button we do the following:

```
<input type="submit" wicket:message="value:subscribe"/>
```

The `value:subscribe` string means we want to localize the `value` attribute of the tag with a string whose key is `subscribe`.

Overriding localized resources on a case by case basis

As Wicket components encapsulate all of their internal details, which include localized strings, Wicket provides an easy way for parent components to override resources used by individual child components. One particular use case where this is useful is when we need to use more than one instance of a component on the page.

Suppose that we have created a `NameEditor` panel that is used to edit our `Name` domain object. Now, suppose that we want to create a promotion form where we want the user to enter their name and their spouse's name. We want our form to look like this:

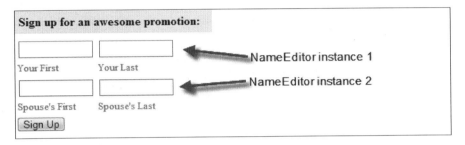

However, unless we can somehow override the resources used by the `NameEditor` to output the field labels our form will look like this:

Notice, that the field labels are the same, which makes the form confusing.

Getting ready

Let's get started by implementing the form without overriding the labels.

Implement the Name domain object:

Name.java

```java
public class Name implements Serializable {
    private String first;
    private String last;
    // constructors, getters and setters
}
```

NameEditor.properties

```
name.first=First
name.last=Last
```

NameEditor.java

```java
// for markup refer to NameEditor.html in the code bundle
public class NameEditor extends Panel {
    public NameEditor(String id, IModel<Name> model) {
        super(id, model);
        add("first").add("last");
    }
    private NameEditor add(String id) {
        IModel<String> model = new PropertyModel<String>(getDefaultMod
          el(), id);
        TextField<String>tf = new TextField<String>(id, model);
        tf.setLabel(new ResourceModel("name." + id));
        add(tf).add(
          newSimpleFormComponentLabel(id + "Label", tf));
        return this;
    }
}
```

HomePage.java

```java
// for markup Refer to HomePage.html in the code bundle
public class HomePage extends WebPage {
    public HomePage(final PageParameters parameters) {
        Form<?> form = new Form<Void>("form");
        add(form);
        form.add(new NameEditor("your", Model.of(new Name())));
        form.add(new NameEditor("spouse",
          Model.of(new Name())));
    }
}
```

How to do it...

1. Override localized strings of the two `NameEditor` instances:

   HomePage.properties

   ```
   form.your.firstLabel.name.first=Your First
   form.your.lastLabel.name.last=Your Last
   form.spouse.firstLabel.name.first=Spouse's First
   form.spouse.lastLabel.name.last=Spouse's Last
   ```

How it works...

When a `Wicket` component requests a value of a localized string, Wicket allows any parent component to provide the value. Wicket does this by asking each parent (from Page to component's parent) to provide the value for a key of the form:

▶ `<relative-path-from-parent-to-requesting-component>.<original-key>`

▶ `<original-key>`

In our example, the component hierarchy is this:

```
HomePage
 +-- form (Form)
       +-- your (NameEditor)
       |     +-- firstLabel (SimpleFormComponentLabel)
       |     +-- lastLabel  SimpleFormComponentLabel)
       +-- spouse (NameEditor)
             +-- firstLabel (SimpleFormComponentLabel)
             +-- lastLabel (SimpleFormComponentLabel)
```

So when the `firstLabel` component in the `spouseNameEditor` asks Wicket for the value of the localized string with key `name.first`, Wicket will ask the following components:

▶ key: `form.your.firstLabel.name.first`; class: `HomePage`

▶ key: `name.first`; class: `HomePage`

▶ key: `your.firstLabel.name.first`; class: `org.apache.wicket.markup.html.form.Form`

▶ key: `name.first`; class: `org.apache.wicket.markup.html.form.Form`

▶ key: `firstLabel.name.first`; class: `NameEditor`

▶ key: `name.first`; class: `NameEditor`

We override the resources of the `yourNameEditor` by providing the following localized strings:

`HomePage.properties`

```
form.your.firstLabel.name.first=Your First
form.your.lastLabel.name.last=Your Last
```

And the strings of spouse `NameEditor` by providing the following:

`HomePage.properties`

```
form.spouse.firstLabel.name.first=Spouse's First
form.spouse.lastLabel.name.last=Spouse's Last
```

Which will be the first key tried by Wicket, and so they will be used instead of strings defined in `NameEditor.properties`.

There's more...

The actual algorithm used by Wicket when looking for resource strings is more complex than what is described previously, especially when we throw in resource bundles for various locales. In the next section, we will see how to debug missing or incorrect resource keys in Wicket.

Debugging loading of resources

Coupled together with complex pages that contain deep component hierarchies, looking for the right resource key to override can cause quite a headache. To solve this problem, Wicket is nice enough to log all resource keys it tries when looking for a particular resource string. This logging is turned on by enabling the `org.apache.wicket.resource` logger. For example, if you are using `log4j` the logger can be enabled like this:

`log4j.properties`

```
log4j.logger.org.apache.wicket.resource=DEBUG
```

In the previous example the logging output for the `firstLabel` in the `yoursNameEditor` had we not overridden it in `Homepage.properties` would look like this:

```
DEBUG - ponentStringResourceLoader-
component: '[MarkupContainer [Component id = firstLabel]]';
key: 'name.first'
DEBUG - ponentStringResourceLoader-
key: 'form.your.firstLabel.name.first';
class: 'cookbook.HomePage';
locale: 'en_US'; Style: 'null'
```

```
INFO  -PropertiesFactory            -
Loading properties files from
file:recipe0405/target/classes/cookbook/HomePage.properties
DEBUG - ponentStringResourceLoader-
Found properties file: 'cookbook/HomePage.'
but it doesn't contain the property
DEBUG - ponentStringResourceLoader-
key: 'name.first';
class: 'cookbook.HomePage';
locale: 'en_US'; Style: 'null'
DEBUG - ponentStringResourceLoader-
Found properties file: 'cookbook/HomePage.'
but it doesn't contain the property
DEBUG - ponentStringResourceLoader -
key: 'your.firstLabel.name.first';
class: 'org.apache.wicket.markup.html.form.Form';
locale: 'en_US'; Style: 'null'
DEBUG - ponentStringResourceLoader-
key: 'name.first';
class: 'org.apache.wicket.markup.html.form.Form';
locale: 'en_US'; Style: 'null'
DEBUG - ponentStringResourceLoader-
key: 'firstLabel.name.first';
class: 'cookbook.NameEditor';
locale: 'en_US'; Style: 'null'
INFO  -PropertiesFactory            -
Loading properties files from
file:recipe0405/target/classes/cookbook/NameEditor.properties
DEBUG - ponentStringResourceLoader-
Found properties file: 'cookbook/NameEditor.'
but it doesn't contain the property
DEBUG - ponentStringResourceLoader-
key: 'name.first';
class: 'cookbook.NameEditor';
locale: 'en_US'; Style: 'null'
DEBUG - ponentStringResourceLoader-
```

```
Found property 'name.first'
in: 'cookbook/NameEditor.'; value: 'First'
```

How it works...

Wicket stores the current locale in the `Session` object. Whenever a component needs to access the locale it can do so by using `Session#getLocale()`. Likewise, when a component wants to change the locale it can do so by using `Session#setLocale(Locale)` method.

In our example the `LocaleSwitcher` requests that it is updated every time the user selects a new locale by implementing the `DropDownChoice#wantOnSelectionChangedNotifications()` method:

```
protected boolean wantOnSelectionChangedNotifications() {
    return true;
}
```

And when it gets the notification it forces the newly-selected locale:

```
protected void onSelectionChanged(Locale newSelection) {
    getSession().setLocale(newSelection);
}
```

After the new locale is selected all components will use it on subsequent renders when looking up values of localized strings.

5
Displaying Data Using DataTable

In this chapter, we will cover:

- ▶ Sorting
- ▶ Filtering
- ▶ Making cells clickable
- ▶ Making rows selectable with checkboxes
- ▶ Exporting data to CSV

Introduction

It is hard to find a web application that does not have a single table that presents the user with some data. Building these DataTables, although not very difficult, can be a daunting task because each of these tables must often support paging, sorting, filtering, and so on. Wicket ships with a very powerful component called the DataTable that makes implementing all these features simple and elegant. Because Wicket is component-oriented, once implemented, these features can be easily reused across multiple DataTable deployments. In this chapter, we will see how to implement the features mentioned previously using the DataTable and the infrastructure it provides.

Sorting

A common requirement, when displaying tabular data, is to allow users to sort it by clicking the table headers. Click a header once and the data is sorted on that column in ascending order; click it again, and the data is sorted in the descending order.

In this recipe, we will see how to implement such a behavior when displaying data using a DataTable component. We will build a simple table that will look much like a phone book and will allow the sorting of data on the name and e-mail columns:

Name	Email	Phone
Charles Montgomery Burns	cmb@fox.com	555-5322
Homer Simpson	homer@fox.com	555-1211
Ned Flanders	green@fox.com	555-9732

click

Name	Email	Phone
Charles Montgomery Burns	cmb@fox.com	555-5322
Ned Flanders	green@fox.com	555-9732
Homer Simpson	homer@fox.com	555-1211

click

Name	Email	Phone
Homer Simpson	homer@fox.com	555-1211
Ned Flanders	green@fox.com	555-9732
Charles Montgomery Burns	cmb@fox.com	555-5322

Getting ready

Begin by creating a page that will list contacts using the DataTable, but without sorting:

1. Create `Contact` bean:

   `Contact.java`

   ```
   public class Contact implements Serializable {
       public String name, email, phone;
       // getters, setters, constructors2.
   ```

2. Create the page that will list the contacts:

`HomePage.html`

```
<html>
    <body>
        <table wicket:id="contacts" class="contacts"></table>
    </body>
</html>
```

`HomePage.java`

```
public class HomePage extends WebPage {

    private static List<Contact> contacts = Arrays.asList(
      new Contact("Homer Simpson", "homer@fox.com", "555-1211"),
      new Contact("Charles Burns", "cmb@fox.com", "555-5322"),
      new Contact("Ned Flanders", "green@fox.com", "555-9732"));

    public HomePage(final PageParameters parameters) {
        // sample code adds a DataTable and a data providert hat
          uses the contacts list created above
    }

}
```

How to do it...

1. Enable sorting by letting DataTable columns know they can be sorted by using a constructor that takes the sort data parameter:

`HomePage.java`

```
List<IColumn<Contact>> columns = new
ArrayList<IColumn<Contact>>();
columns.add(new PropertyColumn<Contact>(Model.of("Name"),
"name","name"));
columns.add(new PropertyColumn<Contact>(Model.of("Email"),
"email", "email"));
columns.add(new PropertyColumn<Contact>(Model.of("Phone"),
"phone"));
```

2. Implement sorting by modifying the data provider:

```
private static class ContactsProvider
        extends SortableDataProvider<Contact> {
    public ContactsProvider() {
        setSort("name", true);
    }

    public Iterator<? extends Contact>
    iterator(int first, int count) {
        List<Contact> data = new ArrayList<Contact>(contacts);
```

```
        Collections.sort(data, new Comparator<Contact>() {
            public int compare(Contact o1, Contact o2) {
                int dir = getSort().isAscending() ? 1 : -1;
                if ("name".equals(getSort().getProperty())) {
                    return dir * (o1.name.compareTo(o2.name));
                } else {
                    return dir * (o1.email.compareTo(o2.email));
                }
            }
        });
        return data.subList(first,
            Math.min(first + count, data.size())).iterator();
    }

    public int size() {
        return contacts.size();
    }
    public IModel<Contact> model(Contact object) {
        return Model.of(object);
    }
}
```

How it works...

DataTable supports sorting out of the box. Any column with the
IColumn#getSortProperty() method that returns a non-null value is treated as a
sortable column and Wicket makes its header clickable. When a header of a sortable column
is clicked Wicket will pass the value of IColumn#getSortProperty to the data provider
which should use this value to sort the data. In order to know about the sorting information
the data provider must implement the ISortableDataProvider interface; Wicket provides
the default SortableDataProvider implementation which is commonly used to implement
sort-capable data providers. DataTable will take care of details such as multiple clicks to the
same column resulting in change of sorting direction, so on.

Let's examine how to implement sorting in practice. In step 1 and 2, we have implemented
a basic DataTable that cannot yet sort data. Even though the data provider we have
implemented already extends a SortableDataProvider, it does not yet take advantage of
any sort information that may be passed to it.

We start building support for sorting by enabling it on the columns, in our case the name and
the email columns:

```
List<IColumn<Contact>> columns = new ArrayList<IColumn<Contact>>();
columns.add(new PropertyColumn<Contact>(Model.of("Name"), "name",
"name"));
```

```
columns.add(new PropertyColumn<Contact>(Model.of("Email"), "email",
    "email"));
columns.add(new PropertyColumn<Contact>(Model.of("Phone"), "phone"));
```

We enable sorting on the columns by using the three-argument constructor of the `PropertyColumn`, with the second argument being the "sort data". Whenever a DataTable column with sorting enabled is clicked, the data provider will be given the value of the "sort data". In the example, only the name and e-mail columns have sorting enabled with the sort data defined as a string with values "name" and "e-mail" respectively.

Now, let's implement sorting by making our data provider implementation sort-aware. Since our data provider already extends a provider that implements `ISortableDataProvider` we only need to take advantage of the sort information:

```
public Iterator<? extends Contact> iterator(int first, int count) {
    List<Contact> data = new ArrayList<Contact>(contacts);
    Collections.sort(data, new Comparator<Contact>() {
        public int compare(Contact o1, Contact o2) {
            int dir = getSort().isAscending() ? 1 : -1;
            if ("name".equals(getSort().getProperty())) {
                return dir * (o1.name.compareTo(o2.name));
            } else {
                return dir * (o1.email.compareTo(o2.email));
            }
        }
    });
    return data.subList(first,
        Math.min(first + count, data.size())).iterator();
}
```

First we copy the data into a new list which we can sort as needed and then we sort based on the sort data and direction provided. The value returned by `getSort().getProperty()` is the same sort data values we have defined previously when creating columns.

The only remaining task is to define a default sort which will be used when the table is rendered before the user clicks any header of a sortable column. We do this in the constructor of our data provider:

```
public ContactsProvider() {
    setSort("name", true);
}
```

There's more...

DataTable gives us a lot out of the box; in this section we see how to add some usability enhancements.

Adding sort direction indicators via CSS

DataTable is nice enough to decorate sortable `<th>` elements with sort-related CSS classes out of the box. This makes it trivial to implement sort direction indicators as shown in the following screenshot:

Showing 1 to 8 of 50					<< < 1 2 3 4 5 6 7 > >>
Actions	**ID**	First Name	Last Name	Home Phone	**Cell Phone**
select	26	Abby	**Bailey**	341-555-7681	314-555-3366
select	7	Abner	**Jones**	213-555-2034	477-555-1671
select	9	Abner	**Smiith**	221-555-1572	815-555-3843
select	40	Abner	**Rose**	803-555-3061	270-555-6787
select	33	Brianna	**Moore**	272-555-1606	834-555-4313
select	6	Christopher	**Jones**	767-555-7134	604-555-1211
select	13	Christopher	**Clark**	635-555-5715	320-555-1767
select	46	Christopher	**Black**	712-555-5805	823-555-8836

A possible CSS style definition can look like this:

```
table tr th { background-position: right; background-repeat:no-repeat;
}
table tr th.wicket_orderDown {
   background-image: url(images/arrow_down.png); }
table tr th.wicket_orderUp {
   background-image: url(images/arrow_up.png); }
table tr th.wicket_orderNone {
   background-image: url(images/arrow_off.png);
```

Filtering

One of the more common use cases for using the DataTable component is to display a large data set which often needs to be paged. But, navigating large data sets can be cumbersome even with the best of paging interfaces. Most users prefer to search rather than page to find the information. In this recipe, we will see how to make a DataTable searchable. We will implement a simple quick-search type form which will filter records in the DataTable, shown as follows:

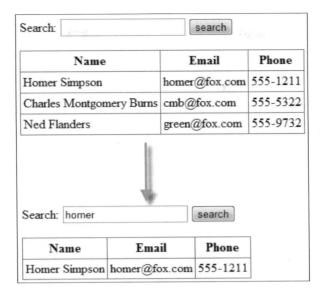

Getting ready

We begin by creating the page without filtering.

Create the contact bean. Refer to `Contact.java` in the code bundle.

Create the page to list contacts:

```
HomePage.java
// for markup refer to HomePage.html in the code bundle
public class HomePage extends WebPage {

    private String filter;

    public HomePage(final PageParameters parameters) {

        // sample code adds DataTable just like the first recipe
        Form<?> form = new Form<Void>("form");
        add(form);
        form.add(new TextField<String>("filter", new
          PropertyModel<String>(
            this, "filter")));

    }

}
```

How to do it...

Modify the data provider to filter data:

```java
HomePage.java
private class ContactsProvider
        extends SortableDataProvider<Contact> {
    private transient List<Contact> filtered;

    private List<Contact> getFiltered() {
        if (filtered == null) {
            filtered = filter();
        }
        return filtered;
    }

    private List<Contact> filter() {
        List<Contact> filtered=new ArrayList<Contact>(contacts);
        if (filter != null) {
            String upper = filter.toUpperCase();

            Iterator<Contact> it = filtered.iterator();

            while (it.hasNext()) {
                Contact contact = it.next();
                if (contact.name.toUpperCase().indexOf(upper) < 0
                        && contact.email.toUpperCase().indexOf(upper) < 0) {
                    it.remove();
                }
            }
        }
        return filtered;
    }
    @Override
    public void detach() {
        filtered = null;
        super.detach();
    }

    public Iterator<? extends Contact> iterator(int first, int count) {
        return getFiltered()
        .subList(
         first,
         Math.min(first + count, getFiltered().size()))
        .iterator();
    }

    public int size() {
```

```
        return getFiltered().size();
    }
    public IModel<Contact> model(Contact object) {
        return Model.of(object);
    }
}
```

How it works...

In step 1 and 2, we have implemented both the DataTable to display contacts as well as the form used to filter them. In order to enable filtering, we must connect our form to the data provider.

As we are working with an in-memory list of contacts, let's implement a method in data provider which will return a list of contacts that matches the filter selected in the form. The form will store the filter in the HomePage's filter field, courtesy of the following property model:

```
form.add(new TextField<String>("filter",
    new PropertyModel<String>(this, "filter")));
```

We can use this field to filter the contact list:

```
private class ContactsProvider extends SortableDataProvider<Contact> {
    private List<Contact> filter() {
        List<Contact> filtered=new ArrayList<Contact>(contacts);
        if (filter != null) {
            String upper = filter.toUpperCase();
            Iterator<Contact> it = filtered.iterator();
            while (it.hasNext()) {
                Contact contact = it.next();
                if (contact.name.toUpperCase().indexOf(upper) < 0
                && contact.email.toUpperCase().indexOf(upper) < 0)
                {
                    it.remove();
                }
            }
        }
        return filtered;
    }
}
```

The filter method itself needs no explanation. As both `IDataProvider#iterator()` and `IDataProvider#size()` need to access the filtered list, lets cache it for the duration of the request so we are not calculating it needlessly:

```
private class ContactsProvider extends SortableDataProvider<Contact> {
    private transient List<Contact> filtered;
    private List<Contact> getFiltered() {
        if (filtered == null) {
            filtered = filter();
        }
        return filtered;
    }

    public void detach() {
        filtered = null;
        super.detach();
    }
}
```

In the preceding code, we cache the result of the `ContactsProvider#filter()` method until the `IDataProvider#detach()` method is called. This method, like `Imodel#detach()` and `Component#detach()` will be called at the end of the request, at which point we no longer need the cached value.

> Notice that we declared the `ContactsProvider#filtered` field as transient. This is because this field serves only as a cache and we do not need to serialize it. Although not strictly necessary, as it is cleared in the `detach()` method, this is a nice safeguard in case we forget to clear the cache in some scenario. It also helps clarify the intent of the field by making it obvious that the value of this field is not persisted across requests.

Now that we have an efficient method of accessing the filtered list we use it to implement the rest of the data provider:

```
private class ContactsProvider extends SortableDataProvider<Contact> {
    public Iterator<? extends Contact> iterator(int first, int count) {
        return getFiltered().subList(first,
            Math.min(first + count, getFiltered().size())).iterator();
    }

    public int size() {
        return getFiltered().size();
    }
}
```

There's more...

Unlike our example, which stores its data in a memory list, most real world applications access data stored in a database. In the next section, we will see how to support sorting of such data.

Sorting database data

Below is a sample implementation of the data provider that filters data coming from a database:

```
private class DatabaseContactsProvider extends
SortableDataProvider<Contact> {
    public Iterator<? extends Contact> iterator(int first, int
      count) {
        return getApplication().getDatabase().query(first, count,
          getSort().getProperty(), getSort().isAscending());
    }
    public int size() {
        return getApplication().getDatabase().count(getSort().
          getProperty(), getSort().isAscending());
    }
    public IModel<Contact> model(Contact object) {
        return new EntityModel<Contact>(object);
    }
}
```

As we can see from the highlighted lines, the data provider delegates the filtering and sorting to the database by passing in all necessary parameters for the database to be able to build a proper query.

Making cells clickable

A common requirement, when presenting tabular data, is to put links into the cells so that the user can interact with the rows in the table. In this recipe, we will create a column that, instead of simply displaying a property of the row object, will allow the user to click the property. When we are done, we will have a table where one column consists of links:

Name	Email	Phone
Homer Simpson	homer@fox.com	555-1211
Charles Montgomery Burns	cmb@fox.com	555-5322
Ned Flanders	green@fox.com	555-9732

click

- You clicked: Charles Montgomery Burns

Name	Email	Phone
Homer Simpson	homer@fox.com	555-1211
Charles Montgomery Burns	cmb@fox.com	555-5322
Ned Flanders	green@fox.com	555-9732

Getting ready

To get started see the *Getting Ready* section of the first recipe in this chapter.

How to do it...

1. Implement a column that will allow cells to be clicked:

```
ClickablePropertyColumn$LinkPanel.html
<wicket:panel>
    <a wicket:id="link"><span wicket:id="label"></span></a>
</wicket:panel>
ClickablePropertyColumn.java
public abstract class ClickablePropertyColumn<T> extends
AbstractColumn<T> {

    private final String property;
```

```java
public ClickablePropertyColumn(IModel<String> displayModel,
    String property) {
  this(displayModel, property, null);
}
public ClickablePropertyColumn(IModel<String> displayModel,
      String property, String sort) {
  super(displayModel, sort);
  this.property = property;
}
public void populateItem(Item<ICellPopulator<T>> cellItem,
      String componentId, IModel<T> rowModel) {
    cellItem.add(new LinkPanel(componentId, rowModel,
      new PropertyModel<Object>(rowModel, property)));
}
protected abstract void onClick(IModel<T> clicked);
private class LinkPanel extends Panel {
    public LinkPanel(String id, IModel<T> rowModel, IModel<?>
      labelModel) {
      super(id);
      Link<T> link = new Link<T>("link", rowModel) {
          @Override
          public void onClick() {
            ClickablePropertyColumn.this.onClick(getModel());
          }
      };
      add(link);
      link.add(new Label("label", labelModel));
    }
}
```

2. Replace the standard name column with the clickable one:

HomePage.java

```java
List<IColumn<Contact>> columns = new
ArrayList<IColumn<Contact>>();
  columns.add(new ClickablePropertyColumn<Contact>(Model.
    of("Name"),
        "name") {
      @Override
      protected void onClick(IModel<Contact> clicked) {
        info("You clicked: " + clicked.getObject().getName());
      }
```

```
        });
            columns.add(new PropertyColumn<Contact>(Model.of("Email"),
        "email"));
            columns.add(new PropertyColumn<Contact>(Model.of("Phone"),
        "phone"));
```

How it works...

What we want to do is to wrap the property string that is used to populate the cell with an anchor tag and react to the click on the anchor tag. We are going to achieve this by implementing a custom DataTable column. We begin by extending `AbstractColumn`, which is the base class for most column implementations:

```
public abstract class ClickablePropertyColumn<T> extends
AbstractColumn<T> {
    private final String property;
    public ClickablePropertyColumn(IModel<String> displayModel, String
      property) {
      super(displayModel,  null);
      this.property=property;
    }
    public void populateItem(Item<ICellPopulator<T>> cellItem,
        String componentId, IModel<T> rowModel) {
    }

}
```

Now it is time to populate each cell inside the `populateItem()` method. We want to populate the cell with markup that looks like this:

```
<a href="..."><span>property value</span></a>
```

To accomplish this we will create a panel that contains the anchor and the span, and populate the cell with this panel. Because this panel will only really be useful inside our custom column we will create it as an inner class:

ClickablePropertyColumn$LinkPanel.html

```
    <wicket:panel>
      <a wicket:id="link"><span wicket:id="label"></span></a>
    </wicket:panel>
```
ClickablePropertyColumn.java

```
    public abstract class ClickablePropertyColumn<T> extends
    AbstractColumn<T> {
        protected abstract void onClick(IModel<T> clicked);
        private class LinkPanel extends Panel {
```

```
      public LinkPanel(String id, IModel<T> rowModel, IModel<?>
labelModel) {
          super(id);
          Link<T> link = new Link<T>("link", rowModel) {
              @Override
              public void onClick() {
              }
          };
          add(link);
          link.add(new Label("label", labelModel));
      }
   }
```

 The markup file for the panel is named: `ClickablePropertyColumn$Li`
`nkPanel.html`, this is because `ClickablePropertyColumn$LinkPa`
`nel` is the qualified name of the `LinkPanel` class. This can be observed by
printing out the value of `LinkPanel.class.getName()`

Now that we have the panel, let's populate the cell with it:

```
public abstract class ClickablePropertyColumn<T> extends
AbstractColumn<T> {
   public void populateItem(Item<ICellPopulator<T>> cellItem,
          String componentId, IModel<T> rowModel) {
      cellItem.add(new LinkPanel(componentId, rowModel,
            new PropertyModel<Object>(rowModel, property)));
   }
}
```

Our custom column is almost functional. All that is left is to forward the click event from the
Link component inside the `LinkPanel` to the column so we can react to it:

```
public abstract class ClickablePropertyColumn<T> extends
AbstractColumn<T> {
   protected abstract void onClick(IModel<T> clicked);
   private class LinkPanel extends Panel {
      public LinkPanel(String id, IModel<T> rowModel, IModel<?>
        labelModel) {
        super(id);
        Link<T> link = new Link<T>("link", rowModel) {
            @Override
            public void onClick() {
               ClickablePropertyColumn.this.onClick(getModel());
            }
        };
      }
   }
}
```

Notice that we pass in the rowModel into the onClick() method of the column; this is so that the user knows which row was clicked.

With our custom column now fully functional let's see how we can use it to display the name of the contact that was clicked:

```
List<IColumn<Contact>> columns = new ArrayList<IColumn<Contact>>();
    columns.add(new ClickablePropertyColumn<Contact>(Model.
    of("Name"),
        "name") {
    @Override
    protected void onClick(IModel<Contact> clicked) {
        info("You clicked: " + clicked.getObject().getName());
    }
});
```

Making rows selectable with checkboxes

A common requirement, when working with tables, is to allow the user to select one or more rows by clicking on checkboxes located in a column. In this recipe, we will build such a column:

	Name	Email	Phone
☑	Homer Simpson	homer@fox.com	555-1211
☑	Charles Montgomery Burns	cmb@fox.com	555-5322
☐	Ned Flanders	green@fox.com	555-9732

[Submit]

click

- Selected Homer Simpson
- Selected Charles Montgomery Burns

	Name	Email	Phone
☑	Homer Simpson	homer@fox.com	555-1211
☑	Charles Montgomery Burns	cmb@fox.com	555-5322
☐	Ned Flanders	green@fox.com	555-9732

[Submit]

Getting ready

Let's get started by creating the page that lists contacts without any selectable rows.

Create the `Contact` bean:

```
Contact.java
public class Contact implements Serializable {
    public String name, email, phone;
    // getters, setters, constructors
}
```

Create the page to display the list of contacts:

```
HomePage.html
<html>
    <body>
      <div wicket:id="feedback"></div>
            <table wicket:id="contacts" class="contacts"></table>
    </body>
</html>
```

```
HomePage.java
public class HomePage extends WebPage {
    private static List<Contact> contacts = Arrays.asList(new Contact[]
{
        new Contact("Homer Simpson", "homer@fox.com", "555-1211"),
        new Contact("Charles Montgomery Burns", "cmb@fox.com", "555-
            5322"),
        new Contact("Ned Flanders", "green@fox.com", "555-9732") });

    private Set<Contact> selected = new HashSet<Contact>();

    public HomePage(final PageParameters parameters) {
        add(new FeedbackPanel("feedback"));

        List<IColumn<Contact>> columns = new
          ArrayList<IColumn<Contact>>();
        columns.add(new PropertyColumn<Contact>(Model.of("Name"),
          "name"));
        columns.add(new PropertyColumn<Contact, String>(Model.
          of("Email"),
              "email"));
        columns.add(new PropertyColumn<Contact>(Model.of("Phone"),
          "phone"));

        DefaultDataTable<Contact> table = new DefaultDataTable<Contact>(
```

```
            "contacts", columns, new ContactsProvider(), 10);
        add(table);
    }

    private static class ContactsProvider extends
       SortableDataProvider<Contact> {

       public Iterator<? extends Contact> iterator(int first, int
          count) {
          return contacts.subList(first,
                Math.min(first + count, contacts.size()))).iterator();
       }

       public int size() {
          return contacts.size();
       }

       public IModel<Contact> model(Contact object) {
          return Model.of(object);
       }

    }

}
```

How to do it...

1. Implement a custom column that will contain the checkboxes:

    `CheckBoxColumn$CheckPanel.html`

    ```html
    <wicket:panel>
       <input wicket:id="check" type="checkbox"/>
    </wicket:panel>
    ```

    `CheckBoxColumn.java`

    ```java
    public abstract class CheckBoxColumn<T> extends AbstractColumn<T>
    {
        public CheckBoxColumn(IModel<String> displayModel) {
           super(displayModel);
        }

        public void populateItem(Item<ICellPopulator<T>> cellItem,
              String componentId, IModel<T> rowModel) {
           cellItem.add(new CheckPanel(componentId,
              newCheckBoxModel(rowModel)));
        }

        protected CheckBox newCheckBox(String id, IModel<Boolean>
           checkModel) {
           return new CheckBox("check", checkModel);
    ```

```
    }
    protected abstract IModel<Boolean> newCheckBoxModel(IModel<T>
      rowModel);
    private class CheckPanel extends Panel {
        public CheckPanel(String id, IModel<Boolean> checkModel) {
            super(id);
            add(newCheckBox("check", checkModel));
        }
    }
}
```

2. Add the custom column to the DataTable:

HomePage.java

```
    List<IColumn<Contact>> columns = new
      ArrayList<IColumn<Contact>>();
        columns.add(new CheckBoxColumn<Contact>(Model.of("")) {
            @Override
            protected IModel<Boolean> newCheckBoxModel(
                    final IModel<Contact> rowModel) {
                return new AbstractCheckBoxModel() {
                    @Override
                    public void unselect() {
                        selected.remove(rowModel.getObject());
                    }
                    @Override
                    public void select() {
                        selected.add(rowModel.getObject());
                    }
                    @Override
                    public boolean isSelected() {
                        return selected.contains(rowModel.getObject());
                    }
                    @Override
                    public void detach() {
                        rowModel.detach();
                    }
                };
            }
        });
        columns.add(new PropertyColumn<Contact>(Model.of("Name"),
            "name"));
```

3. Put the DataTable into a form:

`HomePage.html`

```html
<body>
    <div wicket:id="feedback"></div>
      <form wicket:id="form">
         <table wicket:id="contacts" class="contacts"></table>
         <input type="submit" value="Submit"/>
      </form>
   </body>
```

`HomePage.java`

```java
Form<?> form = new Form<Void>("form") {
        @Override
        protected void onSubmit() {
            for (Contact contact : selected) {
                info("Selected " + contact.getName());
            }
        }
    };
    add(form);
    form.add(new DefaultDataTable<Contact>("contacts", columns,
        new ContactsProvider(), 10));
```

How it works...

The first thing we have to do is to create a custom column for our table that will contain
CheckBoxes. We start by subclassing AbstractColumn, which is a common base class
for DataTable columns:

```java
public abstract class CheckBoxColumn<T> extends AbstractColumn<T> {
    public CheckBoxColumn(IModel<String> displayModel) {
        super(displayModel);
    }
    public void populateItem(Item<ICellPopulator<T>> cellItem,
        String componentId, IModel<T> rowModel) {
    }
}
```

Next, we create a panel that will contain the CheckBox which will be inserted into the cell.
We have to create a panel because whatever component we use to populate the cell will be
attached to a span tag, and we cannot attach a CheckBox directly to a span. So, we will put
the CheckBox into a panel and attach that to the span instead, which is perfectly valid.

When allowing the user to populate predefined placeholders, it is common to use a `<div>` or a `<span>` as the markup tag and allow the user to create a panel to populate the placeholder. Using a `<span>` or a `<div>` allows the most flexibility, and the user may always remove it from generated markup by calling `setRenderBodyOnly(true)` on the instance of the panel they attach to the placeholder tag.

`CheckBoxColumn$CheckColumn.html`

```
<wicket:panel>
   <input wicket:id="check" type="checkbox"/>
</wicket:panel>
```

`CheckBoxColumn.java`

```java
public abstract class CheckBoxColumn<T> extends AbstractColumn<T> {
   protected abstract IModel<Boolean> newCheckBoxModel(IModel<T>
     rowModel);

   protected CheckBox newCheckBox(String id, IModel<Boolean>
     checkModel) {
     return new CheckBox("check", checkModel);
   }

   private class CheckPanel extends Panel {

      public CheckPanel(String id, IModel<Boolean> checkModel) {
         super(id);
         add(newCheckBox("check", checkModel));
      }

   }

}
```

Notice that we delegate the creation of the checkbox to the `newCheckBox()` method, and doing so will allow the user to override the creation of the `CheckBox` and either replace it with a custom instance or modify the instance created by the default implementation.

The `CheckBox` we create is set up with a model that the user will have to specify by implementing the abstract `newCheckBoxModel()` method. This will allow us total control over how we keep track of which rows are selected.

Next, we wire in the panel into the cell:

```java
public abstract class CheckBoxColumn<T> extends AbstractColumn<T> {
   public void populateItem(Item<ICellPopulator<T>> cellItem,
         String componentId, IModel<T> rowModel) {
```

```
        cellItem.add(new CheckPanel(componentId,
    newCheckBoxModel(rowModel)));
    }
}
```

The CheckBox column is now complete. Let's see how we can use it to keep track of the selected contacts. If we look at step 1 where we created the page we will notice a set field:

HomePage.java

```
    private Set<Contact> selected = new HashSet<Contact>();
```

We will use this set to keep track of the contacts that are selected. If we look at the CheckBoxColumn's newCheckBoxModel() method we will notice that it returns a model of type Boolean; this is because the CheckBox component only works with this model. When the model contains true, the check box is selected, and when it contains false the check box is unselected. In order to keep track of which contacts are selected we will somehow have to map a Boolean of each contact to our Set. Wicket provides a helper model that makes implementing this mapping easier called an AbstractCheckBoxModel, and this model requires us to implement three abstract methods:

```
public abstract class AbstractCheckBoxModel implements IModel<Boolean>
{
    public abstract boolean isSelected();
    public abstract void select();
    public abstract void unselect();
}
```

When the CheckBox renders it will call getObject() on the model, which will pass the call onto isSelected(). When the CheckBox is submitted, AbstractCheckBoxModel will either call select() or unselect() based on whether or not the CheckBox was selected. Let's see how we can use this to implement a column to track which contacts are selected:

HomePage.java

```
    columns.add(new CheckBoxColumn<Contact>(Model.of("")) {
            @Override
            protected IModel<Boolean> newCheckBoxModel(
                final IModel<Contact> rowModel) {
              return new AbstractCheckBoxModel() {
                  @Override
                  public boolean isSelected() {
                      return selected.contains(rowModel.getObject());
                  }
                  @Override
                  public void unselect() {
                      selected.remove(rowModel.getObject());
                  }
```

```
            @Override
            public void select() {
                selected.add(rowModel.getObject());
            }
            @Override
            public void detach() {
                rowModel.detach();
            }
        };
    }
});
```

 Notice that we chain the detach call on our anonymous implementation of `AbstractCheckBoxModel` to `rowModel.detach()` because we access it directly. This is an important practice when creating models that use other models because it ensures all models in the chain are detached at the end of the request.

Now, when the table is submitted, all selected contacts will be placed into the selected `Set`, but before we can submit the check boxes inside the table we need to make sure they are in a form. What we do is modify our page and put the DataTable inside a form we create:

HomePage.html

```html
<body>
    <div wicket:id="feedback"></div>
    <form wicket:id="form">
        <table wicket:id="contacts" class="contacts"></table>
        <input type="submit" value="Submit"/>
    </form>
</body>
```

HomePage.java

```java
Form<?> form = new Form<Void>("form") {
        @Override
        protected void onSubmit() {
            for (Contact contact : selected) {
                info("Selected " + contact.getName());
            }
        }
    };
    add(form);
    form.add(new DefaultDataTable<Contact>("contacts", columns,
            new ContactsProvider(), 10));
```

There's more...

In the next section, we will see how to add more usability to our checkbox column.

Adding select/deselect all checkbox

Let's take a look at how to modify `CheckBoxColumn` to implement select/deselect all checkboxes in the header of the column. As this will be a client-side behavior we will use jQuery to implement the necessary JavaScript.

The complete code listing for the new `CheckBoxColumn` follows:

CheckBoxColumn.java

```java
public abstract class CheckBoxColumn<T> extends AbstractColumn<T> {
    private final String uuid = UUID.randomUUID().toString().
        replace("-", "");
    public CheckBoxColumn() {
        super(null);
    }
    public void populateItem(Item<ICellPopulator<T>> cellItem,
            String componentId, IModel<T> rowModel) {
        cellItem.add(new CheckPanel(componentId,
            newCheckBoxModel(rowModel)));
    }
    protected CheckBox newCheckBox(String id, IModel<Boolean>
        checkModel) {
        return new CheckBox("check", checkModel) {
            @Override
            protected void onComponentTag(ComponentTag tag) {
                super.onComponentTag(tag);
                tag.append("class", uuid, " ");
            }
        };
    }
    protected abstract IModel<Boolean> newCheckBoxModel(IModel<T>
        rowModel);

    @Override
    public Component getHeader(String componentId) {
        CheckPanel panel = new CheckPanel(componentId, new
            Model<Boolean>());
        panel.get("check").add(new AbstractBehavior() {
            @Override
```

```
        public void onComponentTag(Component component, ComponentTag
          tag) {
            tag.put("onclick", "var val=$(this).attr('checked'); $('."
              + uuid
                + "').each(function() { $(this).attr('checked',
                  val); });");
          }
        });
        return panel;
    }

    private class CheckPanel extends Panel {
        public CheckPanel(String id, IModel<Boolean> checkModel) {
            super(id);
            add(newCheckBox("check", checkModel));
        }
    }
}
```

The first change we make is to add a `uuid` field to the column:

```
private final String uuid = UUID.randomUUID().toString().replace("-",
"");
```

We will need this field to uniquely identify check boxes generated by this column on the client side so we can select/deselect them all. We will do this by appending a unique CSS class to all of them:

```
protected CheckBox newCheckBox(String id, IModel<Boolean> checkModel)
{
        return new CheckBox("check", checkModel) {
            @Override
            protected void onComponentTag(ComponentTag tag) {
                super.onComponentTag(tag);
                tag.append("class", uuid, " ");
            }
        };
    }
```

Lastly, we override the column's header component and replace it with a checkbox which contains the onclick jQuery trigger that selects/deselects the checkboxes in the column:

```
private final String js="var val=$(this).attr('checked'); $('." + uuid
+ "').each(function() { $(this).attr('checked', val); });";

    public Component getHeader(String componentId) {
```

```
CheckPanel panel = new CheckPanel(componentId, new
   Model<Boolean>());
panel.get("check").add(new AbstractBehavior() {
   public void onComponentTag(Component component, ComponentTag
      tag) {
      tag.put("onclick", js);
   }
});
return panel;
}
```

Exporting data to CSV

Even though web applications have come a long way, they are still not as good at quickly hacking and slashing tabular data as most desktop spreadsheet processors. But, in order to get the data into the desktop software we need to be able to export it from the web application. In this recipe we will build a reusable way to export data, in CSV format, from DataTable components:

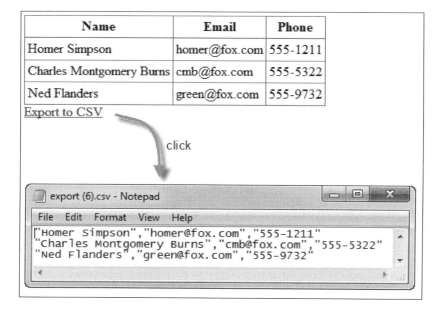

Getting ready

To get started, see the *Getting Ready* section of the first recipe in this chapter.

Create various utility classes:

```java
Pager.java
public class Pager {
    private final int p;
    private final int t;

    public Pager(int perPage, int total) {
        this.p = perPage;
        this.t = total;
    }
    public int pages() {
        return t / p + ((t % p > 0) ? 1 : 0);
    }
    public int offset(int page) {
        return p * page;
    }
    public int count(int page) {
        return Math.min(offset(page) + p, t);
    }
}

    CsvWriter.java
public class CsvWriter {
    private final PrintWriter out;
    private boolean first = true;

    public CsvWriter(OutputStream os) {
        out = new PrintWriter(os);
    }
    public CsvWriter write(Object value) {
        if (!first) {
            out.append(",");
        }
        out.append("\"");
        if (value != null) {
            out.append(value.toString().replace("\"", "\"\"")
                    .replace("\n", " "));
        }
        out.append("\"");
```

Handwritten annotation:

$$1 + (t-1)/p$$

t	p	pages
100	50	2
101	50	3
149	50	3
150	50	3
151	50	4
2	50	1
1	50	1
0	50	1

```
        first = false;
        return this;
    }
    public CsvWriter endLine() {
        out.append("\r\n");
        first = true;
        return this;
    }
    public CsvWriter flush() {
        out.flush();
        return this;
    }
    public void close() {
        out.close();
    }
}
```

How to do it...

1. Create a IColumn mixin that will mark columns as exportable:

    ExportableColumn.java

    ```java
    public interface ExportableColumn<T> extends IColumn<T> {
        void exportCsv(T object, CsvWriter writer);
    }
    ```

2. Implement an exportable property column:

    ExportablePropertyColumn.java

    ```java
    public class ExportablePropertyColumn<T> extends PropertyColumn<T>
    implements
            ExportableColumn<T> {
        public ExportablePropertyColumn(IModel displayModel,
            String propertyExpression) {
            super(displayModel, propertyExpression);
        }
        public void exportCsv(final T object, CsvWriter writer) {
            IModel<?> textModel = createLabelModel(new
                AbstractReadOnlyModel<T>() {
                @Override
                public T getObject() {
                    return object;
                }
            });
    ```

```
            writer.write(textModel.getObject());
            textModel.detach();
        }
    }
```

3. Create a link that will perform the CSV export:

CsvExportLink.java

```
public class CsvExportLink<T> extends Link<Void> {
    private final DataTable<T> table;

    public CsvExportLink(String id, DataTable<T> table) {
        super(id);
        this.table = table;
    }

    @Override
    public void onClick() {
        WebResponse response = (WebResponse) getResponse();

        response.setAttachmentHeader("export.csv");
        response.setContentType("text/csv");

        OutputStream out = getResponse().getOutputStream();
        CsvWriter writer = new CsvWriter(out);

        List<ExportableColumn<T>> exportable =
          getExportableColumns();

        Pager pager = new Pager(100, table.getDataProvider().
          size());
        for (int i = 0; i < pager.pages(); i++) {

            Iterator<? extends T> it = table.getDataProvider().
              iterator(
                pager.offset(i), pager.count(i));

            while (it.hasNext()) {
                T object = it.next();
                for (ExportableColumn<T> col : exportable) {
                    col.exportCsv(object, writer);
                }
                writer.endLine();
            }
        }

        writer.close();

        throw new AbortException();
    }

    private List<ExportableColumn<T>> getExportableColumns() {
```

```
        List<ExportableColumn<T>> exportable = new
          ArrayList<ExportableColumn<T>>(
              table.getColumns().length);
        for (IColumn<?> column : table.getColumns()) {
          if (column instanceof ExportableColumn<?>) {
              exportable.add((ExportableColumn<T>) column);
          }
        }
        return exportable;
    }
}
```

4. Change the table to use exportable columns:

```
List<IColumn<Contact>> columns = new
ArrayList<IColumn<Contact>>();
        columns.add(new ExportablePropertyColumn<Contact>(Model.
          of("Name"),
              "name"));
        columns.add(new ExportablePropertyColumn<Contact>(Model.
          of("Email"),
              "email"));
        columns.add(new ExportablePropertyColumn<Contact>(Model.
          of("Phone"),
              "phone"));
```

5. Add the export link:

```
HomePage.html

    <body>
        <table wicket:id="contacts" class="contacts"></table>
        <a wicket:id="csv">Export to CSV</a>
    </body>
```

```
HomePage.java

add(new CsvExportLink("csv", contacts));
```

How it works...

What we want to happen is that when the export link is clicked, the user is prompted to download a file that contains an export of all the rows in the DataTable in CSV format. As we want this to be reusable across DataTables and across various types of objects, the DataTable displays, ideally, the columns that we want to know how to export data. This way we can iterate the columns and build each CSV record. In order to do this, we first define a mixin interface that columns that know how to export their content into a CSV will implement:

```
public interface ExportableColumn<T> extends IColumn<T> {
    void exportCsv(T object, CsvWriter writer);
}
```

The interface adds a single method that allows the column to contribute to the CSV record that represents an object in one of the rows of the DataTable.

Next, let's build an actual implementation of an `ExportableColumn` we will use in our example. To keep things simple we will extend the columns we used in the *Getting Started* section:

```
public class ExportablePropertyColumn<T> extends PropertyColumn<T> implements
        ExportableColumn<T> {
    public ExportablePropertyColumn(IModel displayModel,
            String propertyExpression) {
        super(displayModel, propertyExpression);
    }
    public void exportCsv(final T object, CsvWriter writer) {
        IModel<?> textModel = createLabelModel(new
          AbstractReadOnlyModel<T>() {
          @Override
          public T getObject() {
              return object;
          }
        });
        writer.write(textModel.getObject());
        textModel.detach();
    }
}
```

Our implementation piggy-backs on `PropertyColumn`'s `createLabelModel()` method to create a model that is used to populate the cells, and writes the value of that model into the CSV writer.

With the basics out of the way, it is time to get down and dirty and create the link that will create the CSV export.

We begin by creating a subclass of Link and passing in the DataTable the link will create the export for:

```
public class CsvExportLink<T> extends Link<Void> {
    private final DataTable<T> table;
    public CsvExportLink(String id, DataTable<T> table) {
        super(id);
        this.table = table;
```

```
        }
    }
```

As the export has to iterate only over columns that implement `ExportableColumn` interface, we create a helper method to retrieve only those columns:

```
public class CsvExportLink<T> extends Link<Void> {
    private List<ExportableColumn<T>> getExportableColumns() {
    List<ExportableColumn<T>> exportable = new
      ArrayList<ExportableColumn<T>>(
          table.getColumns().length);
    for (IColumn<?> column : table.getColumns()) {
       if (column instanceof ExportableColumn<?>) {
          exportable.add((ExportableColumn<T>) column);
       }
    }
    return exportable;
    }
}
```

Now we are ready to implement the export code which will be placed inside the `onClick()` method. We begin by setting the necessary headers on the response object:

```
        WebResponse response = (WebResponse) getResponse();
        response.setAttachmentHeader("export.csv");
        response.setContentType("text/csv");
```

`setAttachmentHeader()` method will cause the browser to prompt the user to download a file.

Next, we create the `CsvWriter` helper and connect it to the response's output stream:

```
        WebResponse response = (WebResponse) getResponse();
        OutputStream out = getResponse().getOutputStream();
        CsvWriter writer = new CsvWriter(out);
```

Finally, it's the actual export loop, which we perform in chunks of 100 records at a time:

```
        List<ExportableColumn<T>> exportable = getExportableColumns();
        Pager pager = new Pager(100, table.getDataProvider().size());
        for (int i = 0; i < pager.pages(); i++) {
           Iterator<? extends T> it = table.getDataProvider().iterator(
                  pager.offset(i), pager.count(i));
           while (it.hasNext()) {
              T object = it.next();
              for (ExportableColumn<T> col : exportable) {
                 col.exportCsv(object, writer);
```

```
        }
      writer.endLine();
    }
  }
```

After we have written the entire CSV content into the response we close the writer and abort any further Wicket-related processing:

```
  writer.close();
  throw new AbortException();
```

There's more...

DataTable comes with support for toolbars. Toolbars are specialized `Panels` that can be easily added to the top or the bottom of the table. In the next section, we will see how to create a reusable toolbar that contains various export options.

Moving data export to a toolbar

Toolbars make it convenient to customize DataTables. For example, the table headers are generated by the `HeadersToolbar`, while paging is generated by the `NavigationToolbar`. Likewise, it makes sense to create an `ExportToolbar` that will contain all the export-related functionality and can be easily added to any DataTable.

Let's create such a toolbar and put our `CsvExportLink` into it.

`ExportToolbar.html`

```html
<wicket:panel>
  <tr class="export">
    <td wicket:id="span">
      <a wicket:id="csv">Export to CSV</a>
    </td>
  </tr>
</wicket:panel>
```

`ExportToolbar.java`

```java
public class ExportToolbar<T> extends AbstractToolbar {
  public ExportToolbar(final DataTable<T> table) {
    super(table);
    WebMarkupContainer span = new WebMarkupContainer("span") {
      @Override
      protected void onComponentTag(ComponentTag tag) {
        tag.put("colspan", table.getColumns().length);
      }
```

```
                };
                add(span);

                span.add(new CsvExportLink<T>("csv", table));
            }

        }
```

With the toolbar complete we can add it to our `DataTable`:

`HomePage.java`

```
    contacts.addBottomToolbar(new ExportToolbar(contacts));
```

6
Enhancing your UI with Tabs and Borders

In this chapter, we will cover:

- ► Creating tabs with dynamic titles
- ► Making a tabbed panel play nice with forms
- ► Creating a client-side JavaScript tabbed panel
- ► Using borders to decorate components
- ► Creating a collapsible border

Introduction

Large applications usually contain complex user interfaces. In this chapter, we will see how to simplify the construction of such user interfaces using tabbed panels and borders. We will see how to use tabbed panels to break up large interfaces into smaller chunks and still present them to the user in the same place. We will also see how to use borders to factor out common repeating pieces of user interface related functionality.

Creating tabs with dynamic titles

A good usecase for a tabbed panel is to present similar, yet slightly different information in a way where tabs act as a means to view disjointed subsets of information. For example, in an online store, a tabbed panel can be used to allow the user to browse through orders in different stages of their fulfillment workflow. Each screen is similar, in that its main content is a list of orders, yet slightly different – perhaps offering different actions or different columns in the table. A very useful feature of such a system would be an item count shown next to the tabs; this way a user will immediately know how many orders are in each tab and which tabs they need to bother looking at. The tabbed panel can look as shown in the following screenshot:

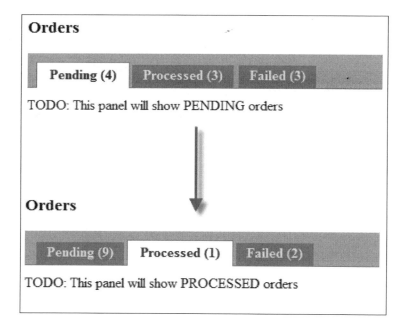

In this recipe, we will see how to create a tabbed panel that allows the developer to easily add the count shown to the right of the tab name.

Getting ready

Let's get started by creating the tabs without dynamic titles.

Create dummy panels to represent the tabs and the page that will host the tabbed panel. Refer to HomePage, PendingOrdersPanel, ProcessedOrdersPanel, and FailedOrdersPanel in the code bundle.

How to do it...

1. Create a helper `ITab` implementation:

`AbstractTabWithCount.java`

```java
public abstract class AbstractTabWithCount implements ITab {
    private final IModel<String> title;
    public AbstractTabWithCount(IModel<String> title) {
        this.title = new TitleModel(title);
    }
    public IModel<String> getTitle() {
        return title;
    }
    public boolean isVisible() {
        return true;
    }
    protected abstract int getCount();
    private class TitleModel extends
      LoadableDetachableModel<String> {
        private final IModel<String> delegate;
        public TitleModel(IModel<String> delegate) {
            this.delegate = delegate;
        }
        protected String load() {
            return delegate.getObject()+" ("+getCount()+")";
        }
        public void detach() {
            super.detach();
            delegate.detach();
        }
    }
}
```

2. Modify the page to use it:

`HomePage.java`

```java
public class HomePage extends WebPage {
    public HomePage(final PageParameters parameters) {
        List<ITab> tabs = new ArrayList<ITab>();
        tabs.add(new AbstractTabWithCount(new Model("Pending")){
            public Panel getPanel(String panelId) {
```

```
                    return new PendingOrdersPanel(panelId);
                }
                protected int getCount() {
                    return new Random().nextInt(10);
                }
            });
            // sample code adds two more tabs
            add(new TabbedPanel("tabs", tabs));
        }
    }
```

How it works...

We begin by creating an implementation of ITab interface that has an additional method for
retrieving the count:

AbstractTabWithCount.java

```
    public abstract class AbstractTabWithCount implements ITab {
        protected abstract int getCount();
        public boolean isVisible() { return true; }
    }
```

As the most common way to provide tab titles is via localized strings using a ResourceModel
or a StringResourceModel, we create a model that will tack on the count to the end of
a string provided by another model. This way we do not lose the ability to feed titles out of
localized resources or via any other model we may choose:

AbstractTabWithCount.java

```
    public abstract class AbstractTabWithCount implements ITab {
        protected abstract int getCount();
        public boolean isVisible() { return true; }
        private class TitleModel
                extends LoadableDetachableModel<String> {
            private final IModel<String> delegate;
            public TitleModel(IModel<String> delegate) {
                this.delegate = delegate;
            }
            protected String load() {
                return delegate.getObject() + " (" + getCount() + ")";
            }
            public void detach() {
                super.detach();
```

```
            delegate.detach();
        }
    }
}
```

 Notice that we detach the delegate model when the model that uses it is detached. Chaining the detach call is very important because it makes sure that all models are detached and helps keep the session footprint small.

The last step is to wire our `TitleModel` to `ITab`'s `getTitle()` method:

AbstractTabWithCount.java

```java
public abstract class AbstractTabWithCount implements ITab {
    private final IModel<String> title;
    public AbstractTabWithCount(IModel<String> title) {
        this.title = new TitleModel(title);
    }
    public IModel<String> getTitle() {
        return title;
    }
    protected abstract int getCount();
}
```

Lastly, we replace the old usage of `AbstractTab`:

HomePage.java

```java
        tabs.add(new AbstractTab(new Model("Pending")) {
            public Panel getPanel(String panelId) {
                return new PendingOrdersPanel(panelId);
            }
        });
```

We replace it with our new `ITab` implementation:

HomePage.java

```java
    tabs.add(new AbstractTabWithCount(new Model("Pending")) {
        public Panel getPanel(String panelId) {
            return new PendingOrdersPanel(panelId);
        }
        protected int getCount() {
            return new Random().nextInt(10);
        }
    });
```

Notice that the implementation is identical with the exception of the new `getCount()` method. This will allow us to easily replace existing tabs with the new implementation.

There's more...

Wicket's models provide a layer of indirection between Wicket and the data it needs to access. This allows us to easily perform tasks like caching retrieval of expensive data.

Optimizing retrieval of item count

Often retrieving counts is not cheap. Let's modify our recipe to build a tabbed panel that will retrieve the counts lazily.

The first thing we do is rewrite our `AbstractTabWithCount` class like this:

```
public abstract class AbstractTabWithCount extends AbstractTab {
    public AbstractTabWithCount(IModel<String> title) {
        super(title);
    }
    protected abstract int getCount();
}
```

This class is no longer responsible for concatenating the count to the title; this will now be done by a specialized Label subclass in an AJAX request. Let's begin by creating a basic Label subclass:

```
public class LazyCountLabel extends Label {
    private final IModel<?> title;
    private String count;
    public LazyCountLabel(String id, IModel<?> model, final int index)
    {
        super(id);
        this.title = model;
    }
    protected void onDetach() {
        title.detach();
        super.onDetach();
    }
}
```

Now let's set a model that will concatenate the count to the title, but only once we have retrieved the count:

```
public class LazyCountLabel extends Label {
    private final IModel<?> title;
```

```
    private String count;

    public LazyCountLabel(String id, IModel<?> model, final int index)
{
        super(id);
        this.title = model;
        setDefaultModel(new LoadableDetachableModel<String>() {
            protected String load() {
                if (count == null) {
                    return "" + title.getObject();
                } else {
                    return title.getObject() + " (" + count + ")";
                }
            }
        });
    }
}
```

With the concatenation of the count taken care of we add the AJAX behavior that will retrieve the count and repaint the label:

```
public class LazyCountLabel extends Label {

    private final IModel<?> title;

    private String count;

    public LazyCountLabel(String id, IModel<?> model, final int index)
{
        super(id);
setDefaultModel(new LoadableDetachableModel<String>() {
            protected String load() {
                if (count == null) {
                    return "" + title.getObject();
                } else {
                    return title.getObject() + " (" + count + ")";
                }
            }
        });
        add(new AbstractAjaxTimerBehavior(Duration.milliseconds(100)) {
            protected void onTimer(AjaxRequestTarget target) {
                TabbedPanel panel = findParent(TabbedPanel.class);
                ITab tab = panel.getTabs().get(index);
                if (tab instanceof AbstractTabWithCount) {
                    count = "" + ((AbstractTabWithCount) tab).getCount();
                }
```

```
                target.addComponent(LazyCountLabel.this);
                stop();
            }
        });
    }
}
```

Lastly we subclass `TabbedPanel` and make sure it uses our special `LazyCountLabel`:

```
public class LazyCountTabbedPanel extends TabbedPanel {
    public LazyCountTabbedPanel(String id, List<ITab> tabs) {
        super(id, tabs);
    }
    protected Component newTitle(String titleId, IModel<?> titleModel,
        int index) {
        if (getTabs().get(index) instanceof AbstractTabWithCount) {
            return new LazyCountLabel(titleId, titleModel, index);
        } else {
            return super.newTitle(titleId, titleModel, index);
        }
    }
}
```

We are now done. Using this tabbed panel variant is the same as using a regular tabbed panel, as long as our tabs are created using the new `AbstractTabWithCount`. When this parent renders, it will issue AJAX callbacks that will retrieve the counts and update them on the fly.

Making a tabbed panel play nice with forms

Often we wish to break up a large form into parts with tabs; this makes the form easier to digest. However, as the tabbed panel's tabs do not submit the form, the form values will be lost when the user switches tabs. In this recipe, we will see how to modify the tabbed panel so that it submits the form it is in, allowing the user to preserve form values from tab to tab:

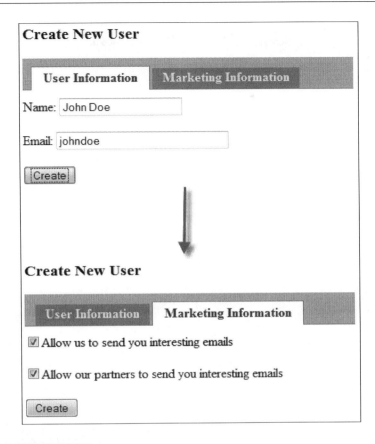

Let's get started by creating our tabs without proper support for form processing.

Create dummy tab panels and a page to host the tabbed panel. Refer to `HomePage`, `UserPanel`, and `MarketingPanel` in the code bundle.

How to do it...

1. Create a `TabbedPanel` subclass that works with forms:

   `FormTabbedPanel.java`

   ```java
   public class FormTabbedPanel extends TabbedPanel {
       public FormTabbedPanel(String id, List<ITab> tabs) {
           super(id, tabs);
       }
   ```

```
protected WebMarkupContainer newLink(String linkId, final int
    index) {
  return new SubmitLink(linkId) {
    public void onSubmit() {
      setSelectedTab(index);
    }
  };
}
}
```

2. Modify our page to use it:

   HomePage.java

   ```
   form.add(new FormTabbedPanel("tabs", tabs));
   ```

How it works...

The problem we are trying to solve is that whenever a tab is switched all form values of components inside it are lost. This is because each tab switch is accomplished via a standard anchor tag. What we need, instead, is a link that will submit and validate the form.

We begin by subclassing the TabbedPanel component:

FormTabbedPanel.java

```
public class FormTabbedPanel extends TabbedPanel {
  public FormTabbedPanel(String id, List<ITab> tabs) {
    super(id, tabs);
  }
}
```

Next, we override the factory method responsible for producing the link components used to switch tabs, and return a SubmitLink:

FormTabbedPanel.java

```
public class FormTabbedPanel extends TabbedPanel {
  protected WebMarkupContainer newLink(String linkId, final int
      index) {
    return new SubmitLink(linkId) {
      public void onSubmit() {
      }
    };
  }
}
```

Replacing the default Link component used by `TabbedPanel` with a `SubmitLink` will get us most of what we need. When the user switches a tab the form will be submitted and validated. The only missing piece is the switching of the actual tab if there are no errors:

`FormTabbedPanel.java`

```
public class FormTabbedPanel extends TabbedPanel {
    protected WebMarkupContainer newLink(String linkId, final int
      index) {
      return new SubmitLink(linkId) {
         public void onSubmit() {
            setSelectedTab(index);
         }
      };
    }
}
```

Our `FormTabbedPanel` is now complete. In order to use it we simply swap the old usage:

`HomePage.java`

```
form.add(new TabbedPanel("tabs", tabs));
```

We swap it with the new one:

`HomePage.java`

```
form.add(new FormTabbedPanel("tabs", tabs));
```

There's more...

In this section we see how to take advantage of factory methods to change behaviors of existing components.

Making TabbedPanel more form friendly

If we wanted this panel to submit the form via AJAX we would override the `newLink()` method like this instead:

```
protected WebMarkupContainer newLink(String linkId, final int
  index) {
  return new AjaxSubmitLink(linkId) {
     public void onSubmit(AjaxRequestTarget target, Form<?> form)
{
        setSelectedTab(index);
        target.addComponent(AjaxTabbedPanel.this);
     }
     public void onError(AjaxRequestTarget target, Form<?> form) {
```

```
            // TODO handle form errors
        }
    };
}
```

Notice that we use the `AjaxSubmitLink` instead of an `AjaxLink`, and doing so will cause the tabbed panel to submit the form via AJAX any time tabs are switched. Also, notice that we must take care to handle errors by implementing the `onError()` method and adding any relevant feedback panels to the `AjaxRequestTarget` to keep them up to date.

Creating a client-side JavaScript tabbed panel

There are various drawbacks when putting parts of a form into a tabbed panel. One such drawback is that every tab switch will usually validate the entire form and will flood the user with errors for unrelated tabs. One way to deal with this is to create the tabs using JavaScript and delay form validation until the user is ready to submit the form. In this recipe, we will see how to utilize jQuery to break a Wicket form into parts hidden behind tabs:

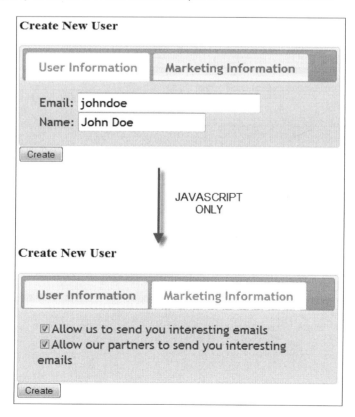

Let's get started by creating the page without any tabs on it.

Create the page with a plain form that contains contents of both tabs. Refer to `HomePage.html` and `HomePage.java` in the code bundle.

1. Modify the markup to create tabs via jQuery:

   `HomePage.html`

```html
<html>
<head>
    <link href="/css/ui-lightness/jquery-ui-1.8.4.custom.css"
rel="stylesheet" type="text/css" />
<script type="text/javascript" src="/js/jquery-1.4.2.min.js"></
script>
<script type="text/javascript" src="/js/jquery-ui-1.8.4.custom.
min.js"></script>
<script type="text/javascript">
$(function() {$("#formbody").tabs();});
</script>
</head>
<body>
    <h3>Create New User</h3>
    <div wicket:id="feedback"></div>
        <form wicket:id="form">
            <div id="formbody">
                <ul>
                    <li><a href="#user"><span>User Information</span></
                      a></li>
                    <li><a href="#marketing"><span>Marketing
                      Information</span></a></li>
                </ul>
                <div id="user">
                    Email: <input wicket:id="email" type="text"
                      size="30"/><br/>
                    Name: <input wicket:id="name" type="text"
                      size="20"/><br/>
                </div>
                <div id="marketing">
                <input wicket:id="company" type="checkbox">Allow us to
                  send you interesting emails<br/>
```

```
            <input wicket:id="partners" type="checkbox">Allow our
                partners to send you interesting emails<br/>
            </div>
        </div>
        <input wicket:id="create" type="submit" value="Create"/>
    </form>
</body>
</html>
```

How it works...

In order to create the tabs completely on the client we are going to use the jQuery UI's excellent `Tabs` plugin.

The first thing we must do is link to jQuery libraries. As our example keeps the libraries in the application's root context we can simply link to them without any help from Wicket:

HomePage.html

```
<script type="text/javascript" src="/js/jquery-1.4.2.min.js"></script>
<script type="text/javascript" src="/js/jquery-ui-1.8.4.custom.min.
js"></script>
```

Next we modify the markup to conform to the format the `Tabs` plugin expects. Namely:

```
<div id="container">
    <ul>
        <li><a href="#tab1"><span>Tab 1 Title</span></a></li>
        <li><a href="#tab2"><span>Tab 2 Title</span></a></li>
        ...
    </ul>
    <div id="tab1">tab 1 contents</div>
    <div id="tab2">tab 2 contents</div>
    ...
</div>
```

We can see the modified markup in Step 2.

The last step is to trigger the actual creation of the tabs. We accomplish this by adding a bit of JavaScript that activates the plugin:

HomePage.html

```
<script type="text/javascript">$(function() {$("#formbody").
tabs();});</script>
```

Using borders to decorate components

As applications get larger and larger we notice more and more places where functionality tends to repeat itself or work in similar ways. One such area where this happens often is markup used for decorating pats of UI; a common use case, for example, is adding rounded corners around some portion of UI. In this recipe, we will see how to factor out this common markup into a Wicket border. Specifically, we are going to create a border that surrounds whatever is inside it with rounded corners:

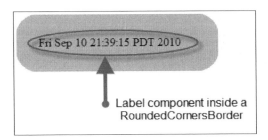

Label component inside a
RoundedCornersBorder

Getting ready

Let's begin by creating a page with the time component not yet decorated:

HomePage.java

```
// for markup refer to HomePage.html in the code bundle
public class HomePage extends WebPage {

    public HomePage(final PageParameters parameters) {
        add(new Label("time", Model.of(new Date().toString())));
    }
}
```

How to do it...

1. Create a border component that wraps others in rounded corners:

   RoundedCornersBorder.html

   ```
   <html xmlns:wicket>
   <wicket:head>
      <wicket:link>
         <link href="style.css" rel="stylesheet"/>
      </wicket:link>
   </wicket:head>
   <wicket:border>
   ```

```
<div class="rc_box">
<div class="rc_top"><div></div></div>
<div class="rc_content">
      <wicket:body/>
</div>
<div class="rc_bottom"><div></div></div>
</div>
</wicket:border>
</html>
```

RoundedCorndersBorder.java

```
public class RoundedCornersBorder extends Border {
    public RoundedCornersBorder(String id) {
        super(id);
    }
}
```

2. Modify the page to wrap the time component in the border:

HomePage.html

```
<html>
<body>
<div wicket:id="border">
      <div wicket:id="time"></div>
</div>
</body>

</html>
```

HomePage.java

```
public class HomePage extends WebPage {

    public HomePage() {

        RoundedCornersBorder border =
          new RoundedCornersBorder("border");
        add(border);

        border.getBodyContainer().add(
            new Label("time",
              Model.of(new Date().toString())));
    }
}
```

How it works...

We begin by creating an empty border implementation:

RoundedCornersBorder.html

```
<wicket:border>
    <wicket:body/>
</wicket:border>
```

RoundedCorndersBorder.java

```
public class RoundedCornersBorder extends Border {
    public RoundedCornersBorder(String id) {
        super(id);
    }
}
```

Next we link to the stylesheet. As we keep the stylesheet in the same package as the border, we can use `wicket:link` to create the link for us.

> We keep the images in the same package as the stylesheet; this allows the stylesheet to reference images using relative urls.

RoundedCornersBorder.html

```
<html xmlns:wicket>
<wicket:head>
    <wicket:link>
        <link href="style.css" rel="stylesheet"/>
    </wicket:link>
</wicket:head>
<wicket:border>
    <wicket:body/>
</wicket:border>
</html>
```

> The `wicket:body` tag above marks where the border's body will be inserted into border's markup. Border's body is everything in between the markup tag the border is bound to. In our specific case it is the output of rendering`<div wicket:id="time"></div>` markup.

Lastly we apply the necessary markup around the wicket:body tag to create the rounded corners:

RoundedCornersBorder.html

```html
<html xmlns:wicket>
<wicket:head>
   <wicket:link>
      <link href="style.css" rel="stylesheet"/>
   </wicket:link>
</wicket:head>
<wicket:border>
<div class="rc_box">
<div class="rc_top"><div></div></div>
<div class="rc_content">
     <wicket:body/>
</div>
<div class="rc_bottom"><div></div></div>
</div>
</wicket:border>
</html>
```

The border is now complete. We install it by adding the components we wish decorated into the border instead of to the page directly:

HomePage.java

```java
RoundedCornersBorder border =
    new RoundedCornersBorder("border");
add(border);
border.getBodyContainer().add(
    new Label("time", Model.of(new Date().toString())));
```

Notice that we add components using `border.getBodyContainer().add()` instead of `border.add()`. We do this because often the `border:body` tag is placed inside another wicket component and so adding components that need to appear in the border's body directly to the border would cause a component hierarchy mismatch. While Wicket has some hacks to deal with this because they make borders easier to use by downstream developers doing so is not recommended. Using `border.getBodyContainer().add()` is the correct form when adding components to border's body.

There's more...

In this section, we examine how introducing factory methods can make the components we create more customizable.

Making stylesheets configurable

To make this component more customizable, we can introduce an easy way to switch out which stylesheet the component uses instead of hard-coding it in the markup:

```
public class RoundedCornersBorder extends Border implements
IHeaderContributor {

    public RoundedCornersBorder(String id) {
        super(id);
    }
    protected ResourceReference getCssReference() {
        return new ResourceReference(RoundedCornersBorder.class, "style.
            css");
    }
    public void renderHead(IHeaderResponse response) {
        response.renderCSSReference(getCssReference());
    }
}
```

Now a subclass may override the `getCssReference()` method and provide its own stylesheet.

> While similar functionality could be provided by assigning different CSS classes it is still nice to have the ability to specify the stylesheet as it may allow reuse of the stylesheet itself.

Creating a collapsible border

A common piece of functionality in a lot of web applications is a section of UI that can be expended or collapsed. These sections usually serve to hide non-critical information so the user does not have to waste time parsing it. In this recipe we will build a reusable `CollapsibleBorder` which will encapsulate this functionality and will allow us to expend and collapse anything we put inside it:

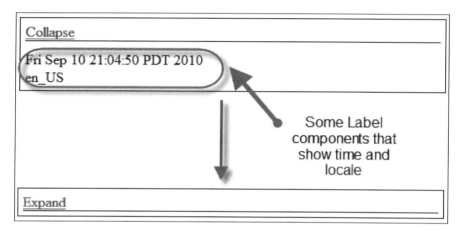

Getting ready

Let's begin by creating a page with the time component not yet decorated:

HomePage.java

```
// for markup refer to HomePage.html in the code bundle
public class HomePage extends WebPage {
    public HomePage() {
        add(new Label("time", Model.of(new Date())));
        add(new Label("locale", Model.of(getLocale())));
    }
}
```

How to do it...

1. Create the border component that can collapse and expand:

CollapsibleBorder.html

```html
<html xmlns:wicket>
<wicket:border>
<div style="border: 1px solid black; padding: 5px">
    <div style="border-bottom: 1px solid black;">
        <a wicket:id="toggle">
            <span wicket:id="caption">expand/collapse</span>
        </a>
    </div>
    <div wicket:id="body" style="padding-top: 10px;">
        <wicket:body/>
    </div>
</div>
</wicket:border>
</html>
```

CollapsibleBorder.java

```java
public class CollapsibleBorder extends Border {

    public CollapsibleBorder(String id,
      IModel<String> collapse,IModel<String> expand) {
        super(id, new Model<Boolean>());
        setCollapsed(false);

        WebMarkupContainer body = new WebMarkupContainer("body")
    {
            protected void onConfigure() {
                setVisible(!isCollapsed());
            }
        };
        add(body);
        body.add(getBodyContainer());

        Link toggle = new Link("toggle") {
            public void onClick() {
                setCollapsed(!isCollapsed());
            }
        };
        add(toggle);

        toggle.add(new Label("caption",
          new ExpandCollapseModel(collapse,expand)));
```

```
        }
        public void setCollapsed(boolean collapsed) {
            setDefaultModelObject(collapsed);
        }
        public boolean isCollapsed() {
            return Boolean.TRUE.equals(getDefaultModelObject());
        }
        private class ExpandCollapseModel extends
          AbstractReadOnlyModel<String> {
          private final IModel<String> collapse;
          private final IModel<String> expand;

          public ExpandCollapseModel(IModel<String> collapse,
                IModel<String> expand) {
            this.collapse = collapse;
            this.expand = expand;
          }

          public String getObject() {
            if (isCollapsed()) {
                return expand.getObject();
            } else {
                return collapse.getObject();
            }
          }

          public void detach() {
            collapse.detach();
            expand.detach();
          }

        }
    }
```

2. Modify page to wrap components in the border:

```
HomePage.html
<html>
<body>
        <div wicket:id="border">
            <div wicket:id="time"></div>
            <div wicket:id="locale"></div>
        </div>
</body>
</html>
```

```
HomePage.java
// sample code puts the two labels into the border
```

How it works...

We begin by creating an empty border:

```
CollapsibleBorder.html
```

```
<wicket:border>
    <wicket:body/>
</wicket:border>
```

```
CollapsibleBorder.java
```

```java
public class CollapsibleBorder extends Border {
    public CollapsibleBorder(String id) {
    }
}
```

Next we define the markup we will need:

```
CollapsibleBorder.html
```

```html
<wicket:border>
<div style="border: 1px solid black; padding: 5px">
    <div style="border-bottom: 1px solid black;">
        <a wicket:id="toggle"><span wicket:id="caption">expand/
collapse</span></a>
    </div>
    <div wicket:id="body" style="padding-top: 10px;">
        <wicket:body/>
    </div>
</div>
</wicket:border>
```

Our border is going to need two models for providing the "expand" and "collapse" text; let's let our border take those via the constructor.

```java
public class CollapsibleBorder extends Border {
    public CollapsibleBorder(String id, IModel<String> collapse,
        IModel<String> expand) {
        super(id);
        };
}
```

Our border will also keep an internal state of whether it is expanded or collapsed by keeping a Boolean as the model object. Let's add methods to manage this state:

CollapsibleBorder.java

```java
public class CollapsibleBorder extends Border {
    public CollapsibleBorder(String id, IModel<String> collapse,
            IModel<String> expand) {
        super(id, new Model<Boolean>());
        setCollapsed(false);
    }
    public void setCollapsed(boolean collapsed) {
        setDefaultModelObject(collapsed);
    }
    public boolean isCollapsed() {
        return Boolean.TRUE.equals(getDefaultModelObject());
    }
}
```

Next let's implement the model that will return the collapse/expand string based on the state of the border and the two models we pass in the constructor. This model will later be used by the label inside the expand/collapse link:

```java
public class CollapsibleBorder extends Border {
    private class ExpandCollapseModel extends
AbstractReadOnlyModel<String> {
        private final IModel<String> collapse;
        private final IModel<String> expand;

        public ExpandCollapseModel(IModel<String> collapse,
                IModel<String> expand) {
            this.collapse = collapse;
            this.expand = expand;
        }

        public String getObject() {
            if (isCollapsed()) {
                return expand.getObject();
            } else {
                return collapse.getObject();
            }
        }

        public void detach() {
            collapse.detach();
            expand.detach();
        }

    }
}
```

Notice that we detach the delegate model when the model that uses it is detached. Chaining the detach call is very important because it makes sure that all models are detached and helps keep the session footprint small.

In order to collapse and expand the border body we must put it inside a container. To collapse the body we will simply set the visibility of this container to false; to expend it again we will set it to true:

```java
public class CollapsibleBorder extends Border {

    public CollapsibleBorder(String id, IModel<String> collapse,
            IModel<String> expand) {
        super(id, new Model<Boolean>());
        setCollapsed(false);

        WebMarkupContainer body=new WebMarkupContainer("body") {
            protected void onConfigure() {
                setVisible(!isCollapsed());
            }
        };
        add(body);
        body.add(getBodyContainer());
    }
}
```

Notice that we reparent the border's body container with: body.add(getBodyContainer()). Because the border:body tag in our border is inside the "body" markup container we must reparent border's body (which is by default added directly to border). Doing so helps us maintain component nesting in-sync between code and markup.

Lastly we implement the link which will toggle the state of the border:

```java
public class CollapsibleBorder extends Border {
    public CollapsibleBorder(String id, IModel<String> collapse,
            IModel<String> expand) {
        super(id, new Model<Boolean>());
        setCollapsed(false);

        Link toggle = new Link("toggle") {
            public void onClick() {
                setCollapsed(!isCollapsed());
            }
```

```
    };
    add(toggle);

    toggle.add(new Label("caption", new
ExpandCollapseModel(collapse,
        expand)));
  }
}
```

There's more...

Wicket comes with great AJAX support. In this section, we will examine how to apply this support to our border.

Collapsing the border with AJAX

If we want our `CollapsibleBorder` to work via AJAX instead of regular requests we can easily modify it:

```
public class CollapsibleBorder extends Border {
    public CollapsibleBorder(String id, IModel<String> collapse,
            IModel<String> expand) {
        super(id, new Model<Boolean>());
        setCollapsed(false);
        final WebMarkupContainer body = new WebMarkupContainer("body") {
            protected void onConfigure() {
                setVisible(!isCollapsed());
            }
        };
        body.setOutputMarkupPlaceholderTag(true);
        add(body);
        body.add(getBodyContainer());

        AjaxLink toggle = new AjaxLink("toggle") {
            public void onClick(AjaxRequestTarget target) {
                setCollapsed(!isCollapsed());
                target.addComponent(body);
                target.addComponent(this);
            }
        };
        add(toggle);

        toggle.add(new Label("caption", new
          ExpandCollapseModel(collapse,
              expand)));
    }
}
```

Notice we use `setOutputMarkupPlaceholderTag(true)` on the
body container instead of the `setOutputMarkupId(true)`. This is
because we will be AJAX-updating this tag when it is in an invisible state,
which means we will be removing it from the markup. However, if we remove
it from the markup completely we will not be able to make it visible again
since Wicket will not know where to insert the markup. To work around
this we can update the body container's parent, but this is clumsy as it
requires an extra nesting of markup containers. Instead, Wicket provides
the `setOutputMarkupPlaceholderTag()` method, which when set
to `true` and the component is invisible Wicket will leave behind a `<tag
id="markup-id"></tag>` markup so that it may locate the place where
the component's markup should be placed on a further update; tag being the
name of the markup tag the component is attached to.

7
Deeper into Ajax

In this chapter, we will cover:

- ▶ Adding Ajax validation to individual form components
- ▶ Blocking until an Ajax request is complete
- ▶ Providing Ajax feedback automatically

Introduction

Ajax has become a very popular technology for building web applications. It allows developers to build applications that respond faster to user input and make overall user experience better. In this chapter, we will examine some ways to make integrating Ajax into Wicket applications easier. A lot of the recipes in this chapter can be combined to create a great user experience with minimal coding effort.

Adding Ajax validation to individual form components

As the technology for building web applications improves, the applications are able to respond quicker to the user's input. Whereas before it was acceptable to delay validation until the user has submitted the form, by today's standards it is considered an arcane practice. Today's web applications validate user input as soon as the user leaves the field, to provide a more immediate feedback cycle. In this recipe, we will see how to implement such behavior using Wicket's Ajax facilities. We will build a simple User Registration Form that will provide feedback to the user as soon as they leave the field. This is especially useful for validating highly contested values, such as usernames, because the user is able to find an acceptable value much quicker:

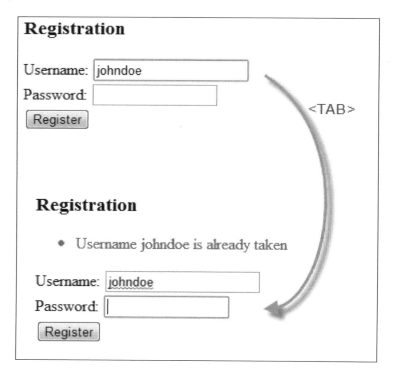

Getting ready

Let's begin by creating the form without Ajax validation:

1. Create a custom user name validator:

   ```
   UserNameValidator.java
   ```

```
public class UsernameValidator implements IValidator<String> {
    public void validate(IValidatable<String> validatable) {
        final String value = validatable.getValue();
        if (value.equalsIgnoreCase("johndoe")) {
            ValidationError error = new ValidationError();
            error.setMessage("Username "+value+" is already taken");
            validatable.error(error);
        }
    }
}
```

2. Create the page that will host the form as shown in the previous screenshot. Refer to `HomePage.html` and `HomePage.java` in the code bundle.

How to do it...

1. Add an Ajax behavior that will validate form components when the user tabs out of them:

`HomePage.java`

```
username.add(new AjaxFormComponentUpdatingBehavior("onblur") {
    protected void onUpdate(AjaxRequestTarget target) {
        target.addComponent(feedback);
    }
    protected void onError(AjaxRequestTarget target,
      RuntimeException e) {
        target.addComponent(feedback);
    }
});
```

How it works...

Wicket's Ajax support is built on top of the behavior concept, and so Wicket ships with a lot of Ajax-related behaviors.

 Behaviors are component plugins which can be used to extend or enrich functionality of Wicket components. Typically, behaviors encapsulate cross-component concerns; one such concern is Ajax.

Such cross-component concerns vary widely and include trivial functionality such as modifying component's tag attributes (`AttributeModifier`, `AttributeAppender`), to transforming component's markup (`XsltTransformerBehavior`), to advanced functionality such as Ajax. Implementing a custom behavior is as easy as extending the `AbstractBehavior` class and adding it to the component using `Component#add(IBehavior)` method.

In this example, we wish to validate a form component every time it loses focus. For this we are going to use the `AjaxFormComponentUpdatingBehavior`. This behavior can be attached to a DOM event, in our case we will use `onblur`, and process the form component when that event occurs via Ajax.

Let's begin by adding the behavior to our user name field:

```
username.add(new AjaxFormComponentUpdatingBehavior("onblur") {
    protected void onUpdate(AjaxRequestTarget target) {
    }
});
```

Now whenever the textfield receives the `onblur` event its value will be sent to the server via Ajax and processed. If the processing is successful (the required check, type conversion, and validation steps all pass), the `onUpdate` method will be called. However, if a validation error occurs, the `onError` method will be called instead. When the error occurs we wish to repaint the `FeedbackPanel` to display the error, this is what the `onError` method implementation will look like:

```
username.add(new AjaxFormComponentUpdatingBehavior("onblur") {
    protected void onUpdate(AjaxRequestTarget target) {
    }
    protected void onError(AjaxRequestTarget target, RuntimeException
      e) {
      target.addComponent(feedback);
    }
});
```

Now imagine the situation where the user first enters an invalid value, receives the error, and corrects the input. In this case, we too, need to repaint the `FeedbackPanel` so the previous error, which has been corrected, disappears. In order to do this we add the repainting logic to the `onUpdate` method as well. The complete implementation of the behavior then looks like this:

```
username.add(new AjaxFormComponentUpdatingBehavior("onblur") {
    protected void onUpdate(AjaxRequestTarget target) {
       target.addComponent(feedback);
    }
    protected void onError(AjaxRequestTarget target, RuntimeException
       e) {
```

```
        target.addComponent(feedback);
    }
});
```

We now have a form field which can be validated using Ajax and a `FeedbackPanel` which will correctly display errors to the user.

There's more...

In the next section we will see how to specialize the AJAX behavior for updating feedback panels to make code simpler.

Simplifying AJAX validation

We can remove some code-noise by creating a subclass of `AjaxFormComponentUpdatingBehavior` suitable for validation:

`AjaxFieldValidator.java`

```java
public class AjaxFieldValidator extends
AjaxFormComponentUpdatingBehavior {
    private final Component feedback;
    public AjaxFieldValidator(Component feedback) {
        super("onblur");
        this.feedback = feedback;
    }
    protected void onUpdate(AjaxRequestTarget target) {
        target.addComponent(feedback);
    }
    protected void onError(AjaxRequestTarget target, RuntimeException
      e) {
        target.addComponent(feedback);
    }
}
```

Now the code to add validation to a field would be a one-liner:

```java
username.add(new AjaxFieldValidator(feedback));
```

Blocking until an Ajax request is complete

Ajax requests are not immune to the double-submit problem. While usually harmless, sometimes double-submits can lead to serious consequences such as the user's credit card being charged two or more times for the same product. In this recipe, we will build a reusable solution that will prevent double-clicks and double-submits in Wicket Ajax requests. To demonstrate the solution, we will build a fake order confirmation page with a fake place order link. We will make sure this link cannot be clicked while an Ajax request it already initiated is still running.

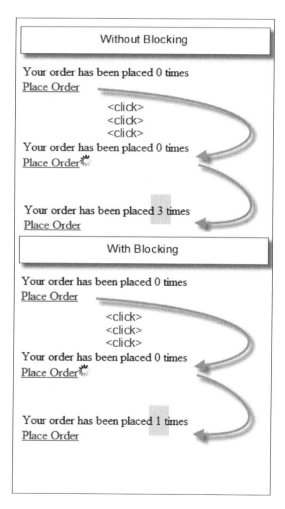

Getting ready

Let's begin by creating the page without worrying about multiple clicks to the Place Order Ajax link.

Create the page with the Ajax link:

```java
HomePage.java
// for markup refer to HomePage.html in the code bundle
public class HomePage extends WebPage {

    private int counter = 0;

    public HomePage() {

        final Component label = new Label("counter",
            new PropertyModel<Integer>(this, "counter"))
          .setOutputMarkupId(true);
        add(label);
        add(new IndicatingAjaxLink<Void>("buy") {
            public void onClick(AjaxRequestTarget target) {
                counter++;
                target.addComponent(label);
                try {
                    Thread.sleep(2000);
                } catch (InterruptedException e) {}
            }
        });
    }
}
```

How to do it...

1. Create a reusable `IAjaxCallDecorator` that will block clicks while an Ajax request is already in progress:

   ```java
   BlockingDecorator.java

   public class BlockingDecorator implements IAjaxCallDecorator
   {
       private static final String latch=
           "var locked=this.hasAttribute('data-wicket-blocked');" +
           "if (locked) { return false; }"+
           "this.setAttribute('data-wicket-blocked','data-wicket-
               blocked');";

       private static final String reset="this.removeAttribute('data-
           wicket-blocked');";
   ```

```
    public CharSequence decorateScript(CharSequence script) {
        return latch + script;
    }

    public CharSequence decorateOnSuccessScript(CharSequence
        script) {
        return reset + script;
    }

    public CharSequence decorateOnFailureScript(CharSequence
        script) {
        return reset + script;
    }
}
```

2. Install the decorator in the Ajax link:

```
HomePage.java
add(new IndicatingAjaxLink<Void>("buy") {
    public void onClick(AjaxRequestTarget target) {
        counter++;
        target.addComponent(label);
        try {
            Thread.sleep(2000);
        } catch (InterruptedException e) {}
    }
    protected IAjaxCallDecorator getAjaxCallDecorator() {
        return new BlockingDecorator();
    }
});
```

How it works...

The way we are going to block multiple clicks is to modify the JavaScript used to initiate the Ajax request so it adds a markup attribute to the link's tag before the call is initiated and removes it when the call is done. It will also ignore clicks while this markup attribute is present.

Because it would be nice to have this functionality reusable we are going to implement it by creating an IAjaxCallDecorator. Ajax call decorators are used in Wicket to modify or decorate Ajax-related JavaScript that triggers the Ajax calls and, much like behaviors, can be reused across components. Let's begin by implementing the skeleton decorator:

BlockingDecorator.java

```
public class BlockingDecorator implements IAjaxCallDecorator{
    public CharSequence decorateScript(CharSequence script) {
        return script;
    }
    public CharSequence decorateOnSuccessScript(CharSequence script) {
        return script;
    }
    public CharSequence decorateOnFailureScript(CharSequence script) {
        return script;
    }
}
```

Now let's implement the JavaScript that will add the attribute and ignore any calls while the attribute is present:

BlockingDecorator.java

```
public class BlockingDecorator implements IAjaxCallDecorator
{
    private static final String latch=
        "var locked=this.hasAttribute('data-wicket-blocked');" +
        "if (locked) { return false; }"+
        "this.setAttribute('data-wicket-blocked','data-wicket-
          blocked');";
    public CharSequence decorateScript(CharSequence script) {
        return latch + script;
    }
}
```

The preceding JavaScript aborts any duplicate calls by returning false from the script, which causes all further processing to stop. Now we must implement the part of the code that removes the attribute after the processing of the request is finished:

BlockingDecorator.java

```
public class BlockingDecorator implements IAjaxCallDecorator
{
    private static final String latch=
        "var locked=this.hasAttribute('data-wicket-blocked');" +
        "if (locked) { return false; }"+
        "this.setAttribute('data-wicket-blocked','data-wicket-
          blocked');";
    private static final String reset="this.removeAttribute('data-
      wicket-blocked');";
    public CharSequence decorateScript(CharSequence script) {
        return latch + script;
```

```
        }
        public CharSequence decorateOnSuccessScript(CharSequence script) {
            return reset + script;
        }
        public CharSequence decorateOnFailureScript(CharSequence script) {
            return reset + script;
        }
    }
```

Note that we clear the attribute whether the request has succeeded or failed. The decorator is now complete, and all that is left is to install it in our `IndicatingAjaxLink`. All Ajax components and behaviors in Wicket provide a method that can be used to install the decorator; this method is called `getAjaxCallDecorator`:

HomePage.java

```
    add(new IndicatingAjaxLink<Void>("buy") {
        public void onClick(AjaxRequestTarget target) {
            //...
        }
        protected IAjaxCallDecorator getAjaxCallDecorator() {
            return new BlockingDecorator();
        }
    });
```

There's more...

JavaScript allows us almost unlimited options when it comes to manipulating the browser's DOM. Let's explore another way to block user interactions.

Using a mask to visibly block the UI

While the implementation above is definitely functional it might be nice to have something a bit prettier. jQuery has a great plugin called **blockUI** which can be used to smoothly dim the screen for a period of time and prevent the user from clicking anything. While achieving the same as above it does so it a much more pleasant way. Let's see how we can implement an `IAjaxCallDecorator` that will leverage this jQuery plugin:

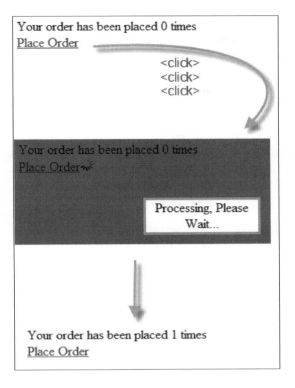

We begin by augmenting our page to include all the necessary JavaScript:

HomePage.html

```
<html>
<head>
<wicket:link>
        <script type="text/javascript" src="jquery.js"></script>
        <script type="text/javascript" src="jquery.blockui.js"></script>
        </wicket:link>
</head>
<body>
        Your order has been placed <span wicket:id="counter">x</span>
times<br/>
<a wicket:id="buy">Place Order</a>
</body>
</html>
```

Then we build the decorator that adds the necessary Javascript to trigger and dismiss the blocking overlay:

`BlockUIDecorator.java`

```java
public class BlockUIDecorator implements IAjaxCallDecorator {
    public CharSequence decorateScript(CharSequence script) {
        return "$.blockUI({message: 'Processing, Please Wait...'});" +
            script;
    }

    public CharSequence decorateOnSuccessScript(CharSequence script) {
        return "$.unblockUI();" + script;
    }

    public CharSequence decorateOnFailureScript(CharSequence script) {
        return "$.unblockUI();" + script;
    }
}
```

Finally, we install the decorator into our `IndicatingAjaxLink`:

`HomePage.java`

```java
add(new IndicatingAjaxLink<Void>("buy") {
    public void onClick(AjaxRequestTarget target) {
        counter++;
        target.addComponent(label);
        try {
            Thread.sleep(2000);
        } catch (InterruptedException e) {}
    }
    protected IAjaxCallDecorator getAjaxCallDecorator() {
        return new BlockUIDecorator();
    }
});
```

We now have a much more pleasant way to disable the UI while an Ajax request is executing.

Providing Ajax feedback automatically

Whenever we use Ajax in Wicket, we must always take care to include the feedback panels in the Ajax response so the user sees any errors or other feedback messages as part of Ajax request's response. However, doing so can get quite tedious. In this recipe, we will see how to automate the process of including feedback panels into the Ajax response while building a simple User Registration Form.

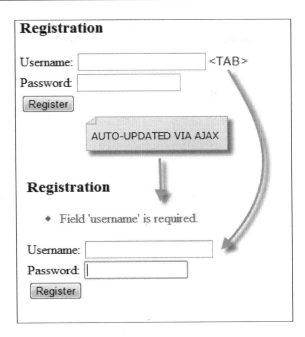

Let's begin by creating the form with manual feedback repainting.

1. Create the page and form:

HomePage.html

```
<html>
<body>
<h3>Registration</h3>
<div wicket:id="feedback"></div>
<form wicket:id="form">
    Username: <input type="text" wicket:id="username"
      size="20"/><br/>
    Password: <input type="password" wicket:id="password"
      size="15"/><br/>
    <input type="submit" value="Register"/>
</form>
</body>
</html>
```

HomePage.java

```
public class HomePage extends WebPage {
```

```
public HomePage(final PageParameters parameters) {
    final Component feedback=new FeedbackPanel("feedback").setOu
      tputMarkupPlaceholderTag(true);
    add(feedback);

    Form<?> form = new Form<Void>("form");
    add(form);

    Component username = new TextField<String>("username",
      Model.of(""))
          .setRequired(true).add(StringValidator.
            minimumLength(6));
    username.add(new AjaxFormComponentUpdatingBehavior("onblur")
    {
        protected void onUpdate(AjaxRequestTarget target) {
            target.addComponent(feedbacK);
        }
        protected void onError(AjaxRequestTarget target) {
            target.addComponent(feedbacK);
        }
    });

    form.add(username);

    Component password = new PasswordTextField("password",
      Model.of(""))
          .setRequired(true);

    password.add(new AjaxFormComponentUpdatingBehavior("onblur")
    {
        protected void onUpdate(AjaxRequestTarget target) {
            target.addComponent(feedback);
        }
        protected void onError(AjaxRequestTarget target) {
            target.addComponent(feedbacK);
        }
    });
    form.add(password);
    }
}
```

How to do it...

1. Remove the noise caused by having to manually repaint feedback panels from the page code:

```java
HomePage.java
public class HomePage extends WebPage {
    public HomePage(final PageParameters parameters) {
        final Component feedback=new FeedbackPanel("feedback").
          setOutputMarkupPlaceholderTag(true);
        add(feedback);
        Form<?> form = new Form<Void>("form");
        add(form);
        Component username = new TextField<String>("username",
          Model.of(""))
                .setRequired(true).add(StringValidator.
                  minimumLength(6));

        username.add(new AjaxFormComponentUpdatingBehavior("onblur")
          {
            protected void onUpdate(AjaxRequestTarget target) {}
        });

        form.add(username);

        Component password = new PasswordTextField("password",
          Model.of(""))
                .setRequired(true);


        password.add(new AjaxFormComponentUpdatingBehavior("onblur")
          {
            protected void onUpdate(AjaxRequestTarget target) {}
        });


        form.add(password);
    }
}
```

2. Create an `AjaxRequestTarget` listener which will automatically update feedback panels:

```java
AjaxFeedbackUpdater.java
public class AjaxFeedbackUpdater implements AjaxRequestTarget.
IListener {
    public void onBeforeRespond(Map<String, Component> map,
            final AjaxRequestTarget target) {
```

```
                target.getPage().visitChildren(FeedbackPanel.class,
                    new IVisitor<FeedbackPanel>() {
                        public Object component(FeedbackPanel component) {
                        if (component.getOutputMarkupId()) {
                            target.addComponent(component);
                        }
                            return CONTINUE_TRAVERSAL_BUT_DONT_GO_DEEPER;
                        }
                    });
            }
        public void onAfterRespond(Map<String, Component> map,
                IJavascriptResponse response) {
            }
        }
    }
```

3. Install the listener in every `AjaxRequestTarget`:

    ```
    WicketApplicaiton.java
    public class WicketApplication extends WebApplication {
        public Class<HomePage> getHomePage() {
            return HomePage.class;
        }
        public AjaxRequestTarget newAjaxRequestTarget(Page page) {
            AjaxRequestTarget target = super.newAjaxRequestTarget(page);
            target.addListener(new AjaxFeedbackUpdater());
            return target;
        }
    }
    ```

How it works...

We begin by removing the code we used to manually keep the `FeedbackPanel` in sync with Ajax validation of form components. This involves simplifying code from:

```
HomePage.java
    username.add(new AjaxFormComponentUpdatingBehavior("onblur") {
        protected void onUpdate(AjaxRequestTarget target) {
            target.addComponent(feedbacK);
        }
        protected void onError(AjaxRequestTarget target) {
            target.addComponent(feedbacK);
        }
    });
```

Down to the following:

`HomePage.java`

```
username.add(new AjaxFormComponentUpdatingBehavior("onblur") {
    protected void onUpdate(AjaxRequestTarget target) {}
});
```

That is a major saving if you consider we save for every field in a form. Next, we implement an `AjaxRequestTarget.IListener` that will find and update all `FeedbackPanel` components in our page. The `IListener` can be used to post-process the request target by either adding additional components to it or adding more JavaScript to the response. It is the former functionality we are after. Let's begin by implementing the skeleton of the listener:

`AjaxFeedbackUpdater.java`

```
public class AjaxFeedbackUpdater implements AjaxRequestTarget.
IListener {
    public void onBeforeRespond(Map<String, Component> map,
            final AjaxRequestTarget target) {

    }
    public void onAfterRespond(Map<String, Component> map,
            IJavascriptResponse response) {

    }
}
```

As we want to add more components to the target we will flush out the `onBeforeRespond` method. We will use a visitor to find all `FeedbackPanel` components in the page and add them to the request target:

```
public class AjaxFeedbackUpdater implements AjaxRequestTarget.
IListener {
    public void onBeforeRespond(Map<String, Component> map,
            final AjaxRequestTarget target) {
        target.getPage().visitChildren(FeedbackPanel.class,
            new IVisitor<FeedbackPanel>() {
                public Object component(FeedbackPanel component) {
                    if (component.getOutputMarkupId()) {
                        target.addComponent(component);
                    }
                    return CONTINUE_TRAVERSAL_BUT_DONT_GO_DEEPER;
                }
            });
    }
}
```

Readers who pay close attention may have noticed that the listener skips feedback panels that are not configured to output their markup ids. If the panel was not initially rendered with its markup id it will not be update-able via Ajax and adding it to the `AjaxRequestTarget` will cause an exception. As we are doing all these updates automatically and the existing code in our application may have created feedback panels without the markup ids, we simply skip them without causing an error. Depending on your application it may or may not make sense to add a WARN-level log statement that will point out feedback panels rendered without their markup ids.

Now that the listener is complete we have to add it to our `AjaxRequestTarget` so it is invoked. We can add the listener like this:

```
username.add(new AjaxFormComponentUpdatingBehavior("onblur") {
    protected void onUpdate(AjaxRequestTarget target) {
        target.addListener(new AjaxFeedbackUpdater());
    }
    protected void onError(AjaxRequestTarget target) {
        target.addListener(new AjaxFeedbackUpdater());
    }
});
```

And while doing so will afford us not having to know where our `FeedbackPanels` are located it is still too noisy. As we want the entire system to work automatically, we also have to register the listener automatically. To do this we override the method responsible for creating new instances of the `AjaxRequestTarget` and add the listener there:

`WicketApplicaiton.java`

```
public class WicketApplication extends WebApplication {
    public AjaxRequestTarget newAjaxRequestTarget(Page page) {
        AjaxRequestTarget target = super.newAjaxRequestTarget(page);
        target.addListener(new AjaxFeedbackUpdater());
        return target;
    }
}
```

We now have fully automated updates to `FeedbackPanels` during Ajax requests.

There's more...

In this section, we will see how to fine-tune the work performed by our AJAX submit.

Limiting form processing to validation only

With the current approach, only a message from a single field will be displayed. This is because feedback messages from the previous request are discarded after render, and only one field is submitted and validated at a time. To avoid this problem, we can submit the entire form every time the user leaves the field by adding AjaxFormValidatingBehavior instead of AjaxFormComponentUpdatingBehavior to fields instead:

```
username.add(new AjaxFormValidatingBehavior(form, "onblur") {
    protected void onSubmit(AjaxRequestTarget target, Form<?> form) {}

});
```

However, the drawback will be that all required fields will present their errors, even the ones the user did not yet have a chance to fill out.

8

Visualizing Data with Charts

In this chapter, we will cover:

- ► Charting with Open Flash Chart
- ► Feeding chart data using a SharedResource
- ► Responding to clicks
- ► Responding to clicks using Ajax

Introduction

In this chapter, we are going to learn how to integrate the great **Open Flash Charts** (**OFC**) library into Wicket to display charts in Wicket applications. We are going to see how to wrap the OFC object into a Wicket component to make working with it easier.

Even though we will focus exclusively on working with the OFC library, the techniques learned in this chapter can be applied to integrate any kind of client-side technology into Wicket.

Charting with Open Flash Chart

In this recipe, we will see how to wrap the OFC Flash component into a Wicket component in order to display a stock chart like the one as follows:

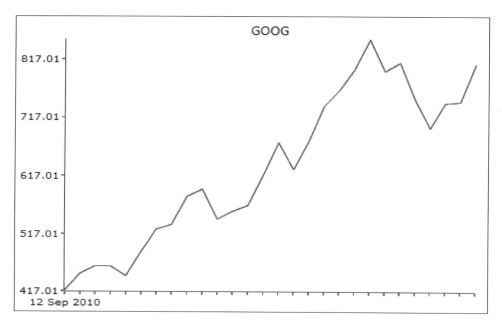

Getting ready

Create a StockService class which we will use to retrieve stock data:

StockService.java

```
public class StockService {
   public Data getData(String symbol) {
      // sample code creates random data
   }
   public static class Data {
      public Point[] points;
      public double min, max;
   }
   public static class Point {
      public Date date;
      public double value;
   }
}
```

How to do it...

1. Create the chart component:

Chart.java

```java
public class Chart extends WebComponent implements
IHeaderContributor,
        IResourceListener {
    private static final ResourceReference OFC = new
      ResourceReference(Chart.class, "open-flash-chart.swf");
    private static final ResourceReference SWF = new
      ResourceReference(Chart.class, "swfobject.js");
    public Chart(String id, IModel<String> symbol) {
        super(id, symbol);
        setOutputMarkupId(true);
    }
    protected boolean getStatelessHint() {
        return false;
    }
    public final void onResourceRequested() {
        String data = getData();
        IRequestTarget response = new StringRequestTarget(data);
        getRequestCycle().setRequestTarget(response);
    }
    private String getData() {
        Data data =
            new StockService()
            .getData(getDefaultModelObjectAsString());

        String json = "{ "
        += "\"bg_colour\": \"#FFFFFF\",\"title\":{\"text\":\""
        + getDefaultModelObjectAsString() + "\"}";

        // sample code appends further configuration options to the
           json string

        json += "\"values\": [ ";

        for (int i = 0; i < data.points.length; i++) {
            if (i > 0) { json += ","; }
            json += "{\"x\":"+data.points[i].date.getTime()/1000;
            json += ",\"y\":" + data.points[i].value + "}";
```

```
        }
        json += "]}]}";
        return json;
    }

    public void renderHead(IHeaderResponse response) {
        response.renderJavascriptReference(SWF);

        final CharSequence swf = urlFor(OFC);
        String dataUrl = urlFor(IResourceListener.INTERFACE).
            toString();
        dataUrl = RequestUtils.toAbsolutePath(dataUrl);

        String script = "swfobject.embedSWF(\"" + swf + "\",\"" +
            getMarkupId();
        markup += "\",\"500\",\"300\"";
        markup += ",\"9.0.0\",\"expressInstall.swf\"";
        markup += ",{\"data-file\":\"" + dataUrl + "\"});";

        response.renderOnDomReadyJavascript(script);
    }
}
```

2. Create the page that will display the chart:

    HomePage.java

    ```
    // for markup refer to HomePage.html in the code bundle
    public class HomePage extends WebPage {
        public HomePage() {
            add(new Chart("chart", Model.of("GOOG")));
        }
    }
    ```

How it works...

Let's start by creating a shell component for our chart. As the chart will not contain any other Wicket components inside it we extend the WebComponent class, and as we will be contributing to the head of the page, we also implement the IHeaderContributor interface:

Chart.java

```
public class Chart extends WebComponent
    implements IHeaderContributor
{
```

```
    public Chart(String id, IModel<String> symbol) {
        super(id, symbol);
        setOutputMarkupId(true);
    }
    public void renderHead(IHeaderResponse response) {    }
}
```

As the OpenFlashChart library we are using is based on Flash, we need to add it to the markup. To do this, we are going to use the SWFObject JavaScript library which will create the markup needed to embed the Flash component for us. But, first things first, we need to be able to serve and build URLs to both the Flash and JavaScript resources. To keep things simple we are going to drop both resources into the same package as our Chart component and let Wicket serve them. We can easily reference packaged resources using ResourceReference objects, so let's construct the two resource references:

Chart.java

```
public class Chart extends WebComponent implements IHeaderContributor
{
    private static final ResourceReference OFC = new
ResourceReference(Chart.class, "open-flash-chart.swf");

    private static final ResourceReference SWF = new
ResourceReference(Chart.class, "swfobject.js");

    public Chart(String id, IModel<String> symbol) {
        super(id, symbol);
        setOutputMarkupId(true);
    }

}
```

Now let's output the necessary JavaScript to allow SWFObject to embed the OpenFlashChart component into our page:

Chart.java

```
public class Chart extends WebComponent implements IHeaderContributor
{
    private static final ResourceReference OFC = new
      ResourceReference(Chart.class, "open-flash-chart.swf");
    private static final ResourceReference SWF = new
      ResourceReference(Chart.class, "swfobject.js");

    public Chart(String id, IModel<String> symbol) {
        super(id, symbol);
        setOutputMarkupId(true);
    }
```

```
    public void renderHead(IHeaderResponse response) {
        response.renderJavascriptReference(SWF);
    final CharSequence swf = urlFor(OFC);
        String dataUrl = urlFor(IResourceListener.INTERFACE).toString();
        dataUrl = RequestUtils.toAbsolutePath(dataUrl);

        String script = "swfobject.embedSWF(\"" + swf + "\",\"" +
    getMarkupId();
        markup += "\",\"500\",\"300\"";
        markup += ",\"9.0.0\",\"expressInstall.swf\"";
        markup += ",{\"data-file\":\"" + dataUrl + "\"});";

        response.renderOnDomReadyJavascript(script);
    }
}
```

The preceding code will end up outputting JavaScript similar to this:

```
Wicket.Event.add(window, "domready", function(event) {
    swfobject.embedSWF(
        "resources/cookbook.chart.Chart/open-flash-chart.swf"
        ,"chart14","500","100" ,"9.0.0","expressInstall.swf");
});
```

The JavaScript snippet will cause SWFObject to embed the Flash component in our page. As the chart component does not yet have any data, the page will look like this:

```
Open Flash Chart
IO ERROR
Loading test data
Error #2032

This is the URL that I tried to open: ../../data-files/y-axis-auto-steps.txt
```

Now that the OpenFlashChart component is properly embedded in our page we are ready to feed it data. We need a way to construct a URL that the Flash component can use to retrieve chart data. We will do this by allowing our Chart component to implement a IResourceListener interface and feed the callback URL to the chart:

Chart.java

```
    public void renderHead(IHeaderResponse response) {
        response.renderJavascriptReference(SWF);
    final CharSequence swf = urlFor(OFC);
        String dataUrl = urlFor(IResourceListener.INTERFACE).toString();
        dataUrl = RequestUtils.toAbsolutePath(dataUrl);
```

```
        String script = "swfobject.embedSWF(\"" + swf + "\",\"" +
getMarkupId();
        markup += "\",\"500\",\"300\"";
        markup += ",\"9.0.0\",\"expressInstall.swf\"";
        markup += ",{\"data-file\":\"" + dataUrl + "\"});";

        response.renderOnDomReadyJavascript(script);
    }
}
```

Note that we take care to convert the relative URL Wicket generates to its absolute form using `RequestUtils` helper class. Flash components do not usually like to work with relative URLs.

Wicket has a very simple way to generate callback URLs. Each callback URL links to a callback method, which is defined as any `void` method that takes no parameters and is the only method in an interface. Let's take a look at the `IResourceListener` interface we are using:

```
public interface IResourceListener extends
IRequestListener
{
    void onResourceRequested();
}
```

However, having the interface itself is not enough to generate a URL. The interface specifies what method to invoke, but not how to invoke it. In order to specify how the method should be invoked Wicket uses a `RequestListenerInterface` object. Usually each interface with a callback method defines an implementation of a `RequestListenerInterface`. For example, here is one defined by `IResourceListener`:

```
public interface IResourceListener extends
IRequestListener
{
    public static final RequestListenerInterface
INTERFACE = new RequestListenerInterface(
IResourceListener.class)
    {
        public IRequestTarget newRequestTarget(
Page page,
            Component component,
RequestListenerInterface listener,
            RequestParameters requestParameters)
        {
            return new ComponentResourceRequestTarget(
                page, component, listener);
        }
    };
    void onResourceRequested();
}
```

Once a component implements a callback interface a URL to it can be built by calling the `RequestCycle# urlFor(Component component, RequestListenerInterface listener)` method. All such URLs are stateful in the sense that they point to a specific instance of a component.

Because we are constructing stateful URLs back to our component it is a good idea to tell Wicket that our component is stateful. This way Wicket will always make sure the URLs point to the correct instance of the component:

```
public class Chart extends WebComponent implements IHeaderContributor,
IResourceListener {
    protected boolean getStatelessHint() {
        return false;
    }
}
```

Now when the Chart is ready for data it will call the URL we have generated for it using the `urlFor(IResourceListener.INTERFACE).toString()` code, which will in turn call `IResourceListener`'s callback method `onResourceRequested` in our component. As the OpenFlashChart component expects chart data in a JSON formatted string let's get our callback ready to serve it by putting the JSON string into a new `IRequestTarget` that will stream it to the client:

Chart.java

```
public class Chart extends WebComponent implements IHeaderContributor,
IResourceListener {
    public final void onResourceRequested() {
        String data = getData();
        IRequestTarget response = new StringRequestTarget(data);
        getRequestCycle().setRequestTarget(response);
    }
    private String getData() {
    }
}
```

The last order of business to get our Chart component working is to generate the chart data itself; to keep things simple we do it via simple string concatenation:

Chart.java

```
public class Chart extends WebComponent implements IHeaderContributor,
IResourceListener {

    private String getData() {
        String symbol=getDefaultModelObjectAsString();
        Data data = new StockService().getData(symbol);

        String json=//refer to code in the How to do it Section
        return json;
    }
}
```

The `Chart` component is now ready to serve stock charts, we just have to put it on our page and give it the stock symbol in a model:

`HomePage.java`

```
add(new Chart("chart", Model.of("GOOG")));
```

There's more...

In this section, we will take a look at some common issues that come up when integrating Wicket with client-side technologies.

A better way to write strings

The code for our Chart component contains a lot of noisy string manipulation; let's take a look at how we can externalize it as much as possible to make the code cleaner.

Wicket provides support for `TextTemplates` which support variable interpolation using the `${var}` placeholder syntax. Let's cleanup our `renderHead` method which currently looks like this:

```java
public class Chart extends WebComponent implements IHeaderContributor,
IResourceListener {

    public void renderHead(IHeaderResponse response) {
        response.renderJavascriptReference(SWF);

        final CharSequence swf = urlFor(OFC);
        String dataUrl = urlFor(IResourceListener.INTERFACE).toString();
        dataUrl = RequestUtils.toAbsolutePath(dataUrl);

        String markup = "swfobject.embedSWF(\"" + swf + "\",\"" +
          getMarkupId();
        markup += "\",\"500\",\"300\"";
        markup += ",\"9.0.0\",\"expressInstall.swf\"";
        markup += ",{\"data-file\":\"" + dataUrl + "\"});";

        response.renderOnDomReadyJavascript(markup);
    }
}
```

Begin by externalizing the string data into a `Chart.template` file located in the same package as the `Chart` component:

`Chart.template`

```
swfobject.embedSWF("${swf}","${id}","${width}","${height}"
    ,"9.0.0","expressInstall.swf"
    ,{"data-file":"${data}"}
);
```

Templates stored in the Java packages can be easily accessed using the
`PackagedTextTemplate` class. Let's rewrite the `renderHead()` method to use the
template:

Chart.java

```
public class Chart extends WebComponent implements IheaderContributor,
IResourceListener {
    public void renderHead(IHeaderResponse response) {
        response.renderJavascriptReference(SWF);

        final CharSequence swf = urlFor(OFC);
        String dataUrl = urlFor(IResourceListener.INTERFACE).toString();
        dataUrl = RequestUtils.toAbsolutePath(dataUrl);

        Map params = new HashMap();
        params.put("id", getMarkupId());
        params.put("width", 500);
        params.put("height", 300);
        params.put("swf", swf);
        params.put("data", dataUrl);

        String decl = new PackagedTextTemplate(
            Chart.class, "Chart.template").asString(params);

        response.renderOnDomReadyJavascript(decl);
    }
}
```

We can use the same technique to significantly clean up the `getData()` method:

Chart.data.template

```
{
    "bg_colour": "#FFFFFF", "title":{"text":"${title}"}
    ,"x_axis": { "steps":"86400","stroke":"1","colour":"#0000FF","grid-
      colour":"#FFFFFF",
        "labels":{"text":"#date:d M Y#"}}
    ,"y_axis": { "stroke":"1","colour":"#0000FF","grid-
      colour":"#FFFFFF","min": "${min}", "max":"${max}", "steps":"100"}
    ,"elements": [
        { "type": "line",
            "dot-style":{"tip":"#date:d M Y# - #y#"},
            "width":"1", "values": [ ${values} ]}]
}
```

```
Chart.java
```

```java
public class Chart extends WebComponent implements IHeaderContributor,
        IResourceListener {

    private String getData() {
        String symbol=getDefaultModelObjectAsString();
        String values = new String();
        Data data = new StockService().getData(symbol);
        for (int i = 0; i < data.points.length; i++) {
            if (i > 0) {values += ",";}
            values+="{\"x\":"+data.points[i].date.getTime()/1000;
            values+=",\"y\":" + data.points[i].value + "}";
        }
        Map params = new HashMap();
        params.put("min", data.min - 1);
        params.put("max", data.max + 1);
        params.put("values", values);
        params.put("title", symbol);
        return new PackagedTextTemplate(Chart.class, "Chart.data.
template").asString(params);
    }
}
```

Extracting useful code into reusable blocks

It seems that the SWFObject library is useful for any Flash component, not just
OpenFlashChart. Let's see how we can factor it out and make it reusable. As the bulk of code
needed to set up SWFObject is written into the head of the page, we can implement it using a
behavior. Let's begin by creating the template and a shell behavior:

```
SWFObject.template
```

```java
swfobject.embedSWF("${swf}","${id}","${width}","${height}"
    ,"9.0.0","expressInstall.swf"
    ,{${params}}
);
```

```
SWFObject.java
```

```java
public abstract class SWFObject extends AbstractBehavior {
    private static final TextTemplate DECL = new PackagedTextTemplate(
            Chart.class, "SWFObject.template");
    private static final ResourceReference SWF = new ResourceReference(
            Chart.class, "swfobject.js");
}
```

As our SWFObject will require some configuration, Let's create an object to encapsulate it:

```
public abstract class SWFObject extends AbstractBehavior {

    protected abstract Config getConfig();

    public static class Config {
        private ResourceReference swf;
        private int width, height;
        private String params;

        public Config(ResourceReference swf, int width, int height,
          String params) {
          this.swf = swf;
          this.width = width; this.height = height;
          this.params = params;
        }

    }

}
```

A curious reader might pose the question as to why SWFObject behavior does not provide a setter for the Config object, as after all, using a setter is simpler than creating an anonymous class that overrides the abstract getConfig() method. In fact, the pattern of providing abstract getters is prevalent throughout the Wicket codebase. The reason is simple; having a setter would require a field to store the Config object, which means the Config instance would be serialized with the behavior, which in turn means the behavior would have a much larger memory and serialization footprint. It would also require the Config object to be serializable, while not a problem for the current use case it may be a problem for others. So, not having setters in Wicket components and behaviors is an optimization which has a large effect on the memory and serialization footprint of the application.

As we need a reference to the component to which the behavior is attached in order to generate the URL to the swf reference we need a way to find it:

```
public abstract class SWFObject extends AbstractBehavior {
    private Component parent;

    public void bind(Component component) {
        parent = component;
        parent.setOutputMarkupId(true);
    }

}
```

Now we are ready to write out the JavaScript necessary to activate the SWFObject, much like before we do this in the `renderHead()` method:

```java
public abstract class SWFObject extends AbstractBehavior {

    private static final TextTemplate DECL = new PackagedTextTemplate(
            Chart.class, "SWFObject.template");
    private static final ResourceReference SWF = new ResourceReference(
            Chart.class, "swfobject.js");

    public void renderHead(IHeaderResponse response) {
        response.renderJavascriptReference(SWF);

        Config config = getConfig();
        Map<String, Object> params = new HashMap<String, Object>();
        params.put("id", parent.getMarkupId());
        params.put("width", config.width);
        params.put("height", config.height);
        params.put("swf", parent.urlFor(config.swf));
        String extra = (config.params != null)?config.params:"";
        params.put("params", extra);

        String decl = DECL.asString(params);
        response.renderOnDomReadyJavascript(decl);
    }
}
```

We now have a reusable SWFObject behavior; let's see how we can use it in our `Chart`:

`Chart.java`

```java
public class Chart extends WebComponent implements IResourceListener {

    private static final ResourceReference OFC = new ResourceReference(
            Chart.class, "open-flash-chart.swf");

    private static final TextTemplate DATA = new PackagedTextTemplate(
            Chart.class, "Chart.data.template");

    public Chart(String id, IModel<String> symbol) {
        super(id, symbol);
        add(new SWFObject() {
            protected Config getConfig() {
                String params = String.format(
                    "\"data-file\":\"%s\"",
                    RequestUtils.toAbsolutePath(
                    urlFor(IResourceListener.INTERFACE)
                        .toString()));
                return new Config(OFC, 500, 300, params);
            }
```

```
        });
    }
    protected boolean getStatelessHint() {
        return false;
    }
    public final void onResourceRequested() {
        String data = getData();
        IRequestTarget response = new StringRequestTarget(data);
        getRequestCycle().setRequestTarget(response);
    }
    private String getData() {
        // unchanged
    }
}
```

Feeding chart data using a SharedResource

In this recipe, we will see how to feed data to the OFC chart using a `SharedResource`. The advantage of this technique, over using a component-callback, is that all charts on the page can get their data asynchronously because access to SharedResources is not synchronized to a single thread per page. This will reduce the total time to load the page and make the application feel more responsive. This will make a big difference when we have multiple charts on the page as follows:

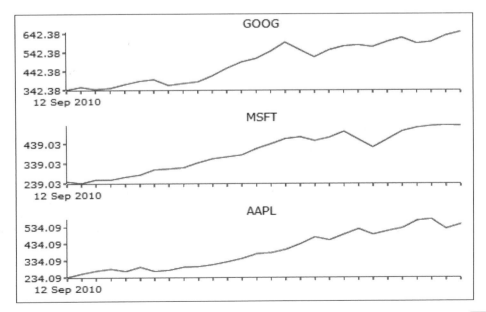

Getting ready

Let's get started by implementing the chart by using a component callback to retrieve the data.

1. Implement StockService that will feed us chart data; see the first recipe for code listing.

2. Implement the Chart component. Refer to Chart.template and Chart.data. template in the code bundle for the data setup of the chart.

Chart.java

```
public class Chart extends WebComponent
        implements IHeaderContributor, IResourceListener {

    public Chart(String id, IModel<String> symbol) {
        super(id, symbol);
        setOutputMarkupId(true);
    }

    protected boolean getStatelessHint() {
        return false;
    }

    public final void onResourceRequested() {
        String data = getData();
        IRequestTarget response = new StringRequestTarget(data);
        getRequestCycle().setRequestTarget(response);
    }

    public void renderHead(IHeaderResponse response) {
        response.renderJavascriptReference(SWF);

        String dataUrl=
            urlFor(IResourceListener.INTERFACE).toString();

        // sample code sets up the chart to get data using dataUrl
            which in turn retrieves data using getData() method

    }

    private String getData() {
        // sample code generates the data string using the
            StockService() and the DATA template
    }
}
```

3. Add three instances of the `Chart` component to a page:

HomePage.java

```java
// for markup refer to HomePage.html in the code bundle
public class HomePage extends WebPage {
    public HomePage() {
        add(new Chart("chart1", Model.of("GOOG")));
        add(new Chart("chart2", Model.of("MSFT")));
        add(new Chart("chart3", Model.of("AAPL")));
    }
}
```

How to do it...

1. Create a `Resource` to serve stock data:

StockResource.java

```java
public class StockResource extends Resource {
    private static final String KEY = StockResource.class.
        getName();
    private static final String PARAM = "symbol";
    private static final TextTemplate DATA = new
        PackagedTextTemplate(
            Chart.class, "Chart.data.template");
    public static String urlFor(String symbol) {
        return RequestCycle.get().urlFor(
            new ResourceReference(KEY)) + "?"
            + PARAM + "=" + symbol;
    }
    public static void register(WebApplication application) {
        application.getSharedResources().add(KEY, new
            StockResource());
    }
    public StockResource() {
        setCacheable(false);
    }
    public IResourceStream getResourceStream() {
        Request request = RequestCycle.get().getRequest();
        String symbol = request.getParameter(PARAM);
```

```
        return new StringResourceStream(getData(symbol));
}

    private String getData(String symbol) {
        // sample code generates the data string using StockService
            and DATA tempalte
    }
}
```

2. Modify the `Chart` component to use the resource instead of a callback:

```
public class Chart extends WebComponent implements
IHeaderContributor {
    private static final ResourceReference OFC = new
        ResourceReference(
            Chart.class, "open-flash-chart.swf");
    private static final TextTemplate DECL = new
        PackagedTextTemplate(
            Chart.class, "Chart.template");
    private static final ResourceReference SWF = new
        ResourceReference(
            Chart.class, "swfobject.js");

    public Chart(String id, IModel<String> symbol) {
        super(id, symbol);
        setOutputMarkupId(true);
    }

    protected boolean getStatelessHint() {
        return false;
    }

    public void renderHead(IHeaderResponse response) {
        response.renderJavascriptReference(SWF);

        final CharSequence swf = urlFor(OFC);
        String dataUrl = StockResource.urlFor(getDefaultModelObjectA
            sString());
        dataUrl = RequestUtils.toAbsolutePath(dataUrl);

        Map<String, Object> params = new HashMap<String, Object>();
        params.put("id", getMarkupId());
        params.put("width", 500);
        params.put("height", 100);
        params.put("swf", swf);
        params.put("data", dataUrl);
        String decl = DECL.asString(params);
```

```
      response.renderOnDomReadyJavascript(decl);
    }
  }
```

3. Register `StockResource` as a SharedResource in our application:

```
public class WicketApplication extends WebApplication {
  protected void init() {
    super.init();
    StockResource.register(this);
  }
}
```

How it works...

We begin by creating a shell implementation of our `StockResource` by extending Wicket's `Resource` class – the most basic base class for all resources:

```
public class StockResource extends Resource {
  public IResourceStream getResourceStream() {
  }
}
```

SharedResources in Wicket are identified by a simple name; this name becomes part of the resource's URL and is how Wicket maps back to the resource. As our resource is a single-purpose resource (meaning it can only be used to do one thing) we can define the name we wish to use for it as a constant. To avoid any collisions with other resource names we will use the class name as the resource name:

```
public class StockResource extends Resource {

  private static final String KEY =
    StockResource.class.getName();
}
```

By default in Wicket all resources are marked cacheable – meaning Wicket will output headers that will cause the browser to cache the data. As stock data is not cacheable we disable the caching:

```
public class StockResource extends Resource {
  public StockResource() {
    setCacheable(false);
  }
  public IResourceStream getResourceStream() {
  }
}
```

Because resources do not have access to component state the only way to pass data to them is via a URL. Let's create a helper method to construct a URL to our resource:

```
public class StockResource extends Resource {

    private static final String KEY = StockResource.class.getName();

    private static final String PARAM = "symbol";

    public static String urlFor(String symbol) {
        return RequestCycle.get().urlFor(new ResourceReference(KEY)) +
        "?"
            + PARAM + "=" + symbol;
    }
}
```

All SharedResources in Wicket have to be registered, much like servlets have to be registered in web.xml. The SharedResources object in Wicket acts as a registry for all SharedResources in the application, and this is where we must register our resource. Let's add a helper method that will take care of the registration:

```
public class StockResource extends Resource {

    private static final String KEY = StockResource.class.getName();

    public static void register(WebApplication application) {
        application.getSharedResources()
            .add(KEY, new StockResource());
    }
}
```

We are done building out the miscellaneous infrastructure for our resource class; now let's build out the part that serves the data. When the resource is requested, its getResourceStream() method will be called. The return value of this method is a IResourceStream implementation which will be used by Wicket to construct the response that will go back to the browser. Wicket contains an implementation of the IResourceStream for serving back string data called the StringResourceStream; we can use it to easily send the JSON-formatted chart data:

```
public class StockResource extends Resource {

    public IResourceStream getResourceStream() {
        Request request = RequestCycle.get().getRequest();
        String symbol = request.getParameter(PARAM);
        return new StringResourceStream(getData(symbol));
    }

    private String getData(String symbol) {
    }
}
```

All that is left is to implement the `getData()` method. We already have this method implemented in the `Chart` component above, so we will not list it here for brevity.

Now that our resource is complete we have to register it with the application and modify our Chart component to use it. Let's take care of registering it with the application first:

```
public class WicketApplication extends WebApplication {
    protected void init() {
        super.init();
        StockResource.register(this);
    }
}
```

Finally, let's modify the `Chart` to use a URL that points to our resource in order to retrieve the data. The old URL was constructed like this:

`Chart.java`

```
String dataUrl = urlFor(IResourceListener.INTERFACE).toString();
dataUrl = RequestUtils.toAbsolutePath(dataUrl);
```

While the new URL will be constructed like this:

```
String dataUrl = StockResource.urlFor(getDefaultModelObjectAsStri
ng());
dataUrl = RequestUtils.toAbsolutePath(dataUrl);
```

We now have a `Chart` component that will pull its data from a SharedResource.

There's more...

Wicket has a rich infrastructure for serving non-page related data. In the next section, we will see how to leverage it to make our code cleaner.

Using DynamicWebResource to serve data

In this recipe, we have used a `Resource` subclass to serve the JSON data. While working well, the Resource itself is not really well suited for serving web resources. For example, it does not set any headers such as `Content-Type` and `Content-Length`. To make our resource more web-friendly we can instead subclass the `DynamicWebResource`, which will automatically set all the required headers for us.

Begin by subclassing `DynamicWebResource`:

`StockResource.java`

```
public class StockResource extends DynamicWebResource {

}
```

Now let's add the code necessary to generate the JSON string:

```
public class StockResource extends DynamicWebResource
{

   private String getData(String symbol) {
      // same as original
   }
}
```

Unlike `Resource`, `DynamicWebResource` uses the `getResourceState()` callback to serve the data, so let's implement it:

```
public class StockResource extends DynamicWebResource {

   private String getData(String symbol) {
      // same as original
   }

   protected ResourceState getResourceState() {
      Request request = RequestCycle.get().getRequest();
      final String symbol = request.getParameter(PARAM);
      return new ResourceState() {

         public byte[] getData() {
            return StockResource.this.getData(symbol)
               .getBytes();
         }

         public String getContentType() {
            return "application/json";
         }
      };
   }
}
```

Notice that we are now able to specify the content type of our data, and `DynamicWebResource` will take care of setting all the right headers for us.

Responding to clicks

Displaying a nice flash chart is great, but allowing the user to interact with it is even better. In this recipe, we will see how to integrate the OFC and Wicket so that the Wicket component knows when the chart has been clicked:

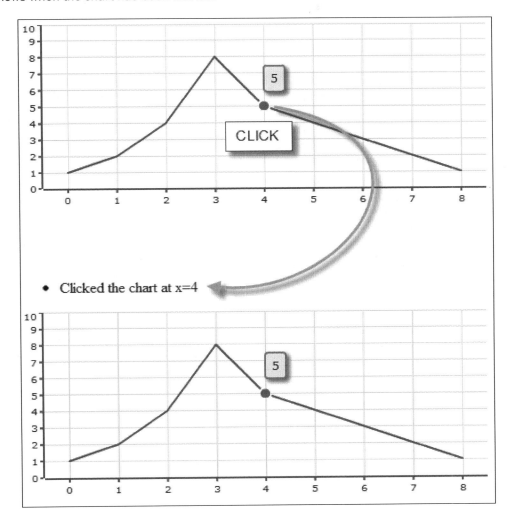

Getting ready

Let's get started by implementing the basic chart component. To keep things simple the Chart will serve static data defined in the `Chart.data.template` file.

1. Implement the `Chart` component. Refer to `Chart.java` in the code bundle and to the first recipe in this chapter.

2. Add the `Chart` component to a page:

    `HomePage.java`

    ```
    // for markup see HomePage.html in the code bundle
    public class HomePage extends WebPage {
        public HomePage() {
            add(new Chart("chart);    }
    }
    ```

How to do it...

1. Tell the chart to invoke a specific JavaScript function when the chart is clicked:

    `Chart.data.template`

    ```
    {
        "bg_colour": "#FFFFFF"
        ,"elements": [
            { "type": "line",
            "dot-style":{ "on-click":"${onclick}" },
                "values": [ 1,2,4,8,5,4,3,2,1 ]}]
    }
    ```

2. Provide the JavaScript function that will act as a click handler:

    ```
    public class Chart extends WebComponent implements
    IHeaderContributor, IResourceListener
    , ILinkListener
    {
        public void renderHead(IHeaderResponse response) {

            // sample code sets up the chart

            response.renderJavascript(
                String.format(
                "function chart_%s(x) { window.location='%s&x='+x;}",
                id,
                urlFor(ILinkListener.INTERFACE)),
    ```

```
            "chart_" + id);
    }
    private String getData() {
        return DATA.asString(
            new MicroMap("onclick", "chart_" + getMarkupId()));
    }
    public final void onLinkClicked() {
        int x = Integer.parseInt(getRequest().getParameter("x"));
        onClick(x);
    }
    protected void onClick(int x) {}
}
```

3. Modify the page to output where the chart was clicked:

HomePage.java

```
public class HomePage extends WebPage {
    public HomePage() {
        add(new FeedbackPanel("feedback"));
        add(new Chart("chart", Model.of("GOOG")) {
        protected void onClick(int x) {
            info("Clicked at x=" + x);
        }
        });
    }
}
```

How it works...

The first thing we must be able to do in order to handle clicks is to be able to construct a URL that will invoke some callback method on our `Chart` component. We do this by allowing our `Chart` to implement the `ILinkListener` request interface that is bundled with Wicket; this is the same interface used by Link components to implement their `onClick()` callbacks:

```
public class Chart extends WebComponent implements IHeaderContributor,
IResourceListener
, ILinkListener
{
    public void onLinkClicked() {}
}
```

Now that our component implements `ILinkListener` we can construct a URL to it by calling `urlFor(ILinkListener.INTERFACE)` method, the generated URL will call our `Chart`'s `onLinkClicked()` method.

OpenFlashChart API allows us to specify a JavaScript function that will be invoked whenever a point on the chart is clicked. The function will be passed in an argument which is the x-coordinate of the clicked point. In order to handle the click, therefore, we can write out a JavaScript function like this:

```
function <some-unique-name>(x) {
    window.location='<callback-url>'+'&x='+x;
}
```

We already have the callback URL, so the only remaining piece of the puzzle is to come up with a unique name for the function. Wicket already generates unique markup ids for our components, so we can simply use this unique markup id as the function name. We are now ready to write out the function:

`Chart.java`

```
public class Chart extends WebComponent implements IHeaderContributor,
IResourceListener, ILinkListener
{
    public void renderHead(IHeaderResponse response) {

        response.renderJavascript(
            String.format(
            "function chart_%s(x) { window.location='%s&x='+x;}",
            id,
            urlFor(ILinkListener.INTERFACE)),
            "chart_" + id);
    }
}
```

The last argument to `IHeaderResponse#renderJavascript()` method is a uniqueness key. If two calls to `renderJavascript()` are made with the same key, only the output of the first will be rendered. This is how Wicket allows developers to make sure that a specific piece of JavaScript is output only once even though it may be written out from multiple places in code. In our case, we make sure that our function definition is only contributed once.

Now that we have our function we have to let our Flash component know what it is; we modify the `Chart.data.template` to include the necessary `onclick` placeholder:

Chart.data.template

```
{
    "bg_colour": "#FFFFFF"
    ,"elements": [
        { "type": "line",
            "dot-style":{ "on-click":"${onclick}" },
            "values": [ 1,2,4,8,5,4,3,2,1 ]}]
}
```

And pass in the function name when we render the template:

```
public class Chart extends WebComponent implements IHeaderContributor,
IResourceListener, ILinkListener
{
    private String getData() {
        return DATA.asString(
            new MicroMap("onclick", "chart_" + getMarkupId()));
    }
}
```

Now, whenever a user clicks a dot on the chart our JavaScript function will be called and it will in turn call our callback URL passing in the x-coordinate along with it. The remaining part is to implement the handling of the URL:

```
public class Chart extends WebComponent implements IHeaderContributor,
IResourceListener, ILinkListener
{
    public final void onLinkClicked() {
        int x=Integer.parseInt(getRequest().getParameter("x"));
        onClick(x);
    }
    protected void onClick(int x) {}
}
```

The `Chart` component's click handling is now complete, so let's see how we can use it to output the x-coordinate of the point clicked:

HomePage.java

```
public class HomePage extends WebPage {
    public HomePage() {
        add(new FeedbackPanel("feedback"));
        add(new Chart("chart", Model.of("GOOG")) {
```

```
        protected void onClick(int x) {
            info("Clicked at x=" + x);
        }
    });
  }
}
```

There's more...

OpenFlashChart library supports multiple graphs on the same chart. In the following section, we will see how to add this support into our component.

Adding support for multiple graphs

First let's modify our `Chart.data.template` to display two line graphs instead of one:

`Chart.data.template`

```
{
    "bg_colour": "#FFFFFF"
    ,"elements": [
        { "type": "line", "colour":"#00ff00",
          "dot-style":{ "on-click":"${onclick1}" },
          "values": [ 1,2,4,8,5,4,3,2,1 ]},
        { "type": "line", "colour":"#ff0000",
          "dot-style":{ "on-click":"${onclick2}" },
          "values": [ 5,4,3,3,4,5,6,7,7 ]}
    ]
}
```

With this JSON fed to the chart it will now look like this:

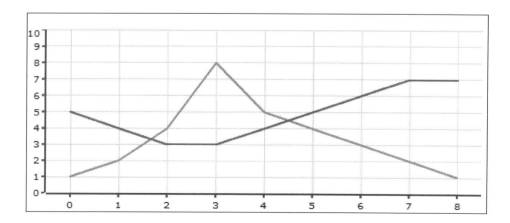

Each graph in the chart requires its own JavaScript callback function. We are going to modify our original callback function that looked like this:

```
function chart_<markup-id>(x) {
    window.location='<callback-url>'+'&x='+x;
}
```

So it will also take the chart index parameter:

```
function chart_<markup-id>(chart, x) {
    window.location='<callback-url>'+'&chart='+chart+'&x='+x;
}
```

And then we are going to create a callback for each chart which will delegate to our new method; for example a callback might look like this:

```
function chart_chart1_1(x) { chart_chart1(1,x); }
```

There will be as many callbacks as there are graphs in the chart. As in our example we have two graphs we will need to generate two such callbacks:

```
Chart.java
public class Chart extends WebComponent implements IheaderContributor,
IResourceListener, ILinkListener {
    public void renderHead(IHeaderResponse response) {
        final String func = "chart_" + getMarkupId();
        response.renderJavascript(
            String.format(
            "function %s(chart,x) { window.location='%s&chart='+chart+'&
              x='+x; }",
            func, urlFor(ILinkListener.INTERFACE)), func);
        for (int i = 0; i < 2; i++) {
            response.renderJavascript(String.format(
            "function %s_%d(x) { %s(%d,x); }", func, i, func, i),
              func + "_" + i);
        }
    }
}
```

The only part left is to hook the two new callbacks into the Flash component when we generate the data JSON string:

```
public class Chart extends WebComponent implements IheaderContributor,
IResourceListener, ILinkListener {
    private String getData() {
        Map<String, Object> params =
            new MiniMap<String, Object>(2);
        params.put("onclick1", "chart_" + getMarkupId() + "_1");
```

```
            params.put("onclick2", "chart_" + getMarkupId() + "_2");
            return DATA.asString(params);
    }
}
```

We now have a chart that can respond to clicks on both line graphs:

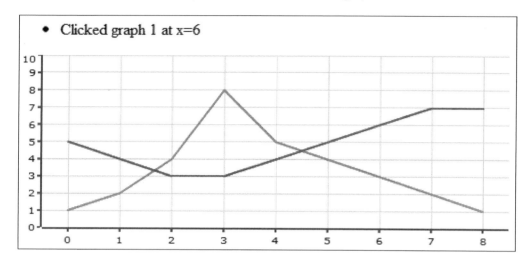

9
Building Dynamic and Rich UI

In this chapter, we will cover:

- ► Swapping components using a select box
- ► Creating dynamic forms
- ► Creating a Dynamic Portal Layout

Introduction

In this chapter, we are going to look at use cases that require the user interface to be highly dynamic. This is probably one of the biggest strengths of Wicket; it makes it very simple to change the component hierarchy at runtime. The recipes presented in this chapter show us different ways we can create and change Wicket's component hierarchy on the fly.

Swapping components using a select box

A common pattern in building web applications is to change the user interface based on some selection the user made. In this recipe, we will see how to change the interface when the user changes a value of a select box. The specific example we will be looking at is how to change the form to collect appropriate payment information when the user changes the payment type:

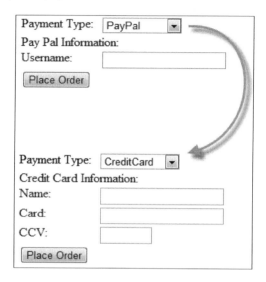

Getting ready

Let's begin by implementing some of the miscellaneous classes we will need to model the different payments.

Create the `Payment` and `Order` classes:

`Payment.java`

```
public abstract class Payment implements Serializable {}
```

`Order.java`

```
public class Order implements Serializable {
   public Payment payment;
}
```

Create classes to model different types of payments we will be accepting:

CreditCardPayment.java

```
public class CreditCardPayment extends Payment {
    public String name, card, ccv;
}
```

PayPalPayment.java

```
public class PayPalPayment extends Payment {
    public String username;
}
```

How to do it...

1. Create Wicket panels to model form fragments that will collect information for different payment types. Please refer to CreditCardPanel.java and PayPalPanel.java in the code bundle.

2. Create the page that wires everything together:

```
HomePage.java
// refer to the code bundle for markup
public class HomePage extends WebPage {
    private Order order = new Order();
    private Component paymentPanel;
    public HomePage(final PageParameters parameters) {
        Form<?> form = new Form<Void>("form") {
            protected void onSubmit() {
                info(order.toString());
            }
        };
        add(form);
        form.add(new DropDownChoice<PaymentType>("type",
          new Model<PaymentType>(null), Arrays.asList(PaymentType.
          values())) {
            protected boolean
                wantOnSelectionChangedNotifications() {
                return true;
            }
            protected void onSelectionChanged(PaymentType
              newSelection) {
                setupPayment(newSelection);
            }
        });
        paymentPanel = new EmptyPanel("payment");
        form.add(paymentPanel);
    }
```

```
private void setupPayment(PaymentType type) {
    IModel<Payment> paymentModel =
     new PropertyModel<Payment>(this,"order.payment");
    String id = paymentPanel.getId();
    Component replacement = null;
    switch (type) {
    case CreditCard:
       replacement = new CreditCardPanel(id, paymentModel);
       break;
    case PayPal:
       replacement = new PayPalPanel(id, paymentModel);
       break;
    }
    paymentPanel.replaceWith(replacement);
    paymentPanel = replacement;
}
    public static enum PaymentType { CreditCard, PayPal; }
}
```

How it works...

We began by implementing the data model in steps 1 and 2.

In step 3, we start implementing user interface fragments that represent each different payment type; these are the fragments we will be swapping when the user changes the payment type in the select box. To represent each fragment we use a `FormComponentPanel` instead of just `Panel` because doing so gives us an easy way to push the proper `Payment` instance into the model:

```
public class PayPalPanel extends FormComponentPanel<Payment> {
    private final PayPalPayment bean = new PayPalPayment();
    public PayPalPanel(String id, IModel<Payment> model) {
       super(id, model);
       add(new TextField("username",
          new PropertyModel(this, "bean.username")));
    }
    protected void convertInput() {
       setConvertedInput(bean);
    }
}
```

When the form is submitted our `FormComponentPanel`'s `convertInput()` method will be called, and in it we set our `bean` field as the converted value of the panel. Wicket will later run this value through validation and if there are no errors it will push this into the model. This is an easy way to work with objects whose values are edited by multiple fields.

Now that we have all the necessary pieces to represent the user interface it is time to put it all together. The markup for our form is simple:

```
<form wicket:id="form">
    <label>Payment Type:</label>
  <select wicket:id="type"></select><br/>
    <div wicket:id="payment"></div>
  <input type="submit" value="Place Order"/>
</form>
```

We have the `select` box with wicket id "type" and a `div` that will contain the different variants of payment interfaces with id "payment". Our goal is to wire this so that when the user changes the value of the "type" `select` box the "payment" `div` is replaced with the proper instance of `FormComponentPanel`- in our specific example either the `PayPalPanel` or `CreditCardPanel`.

In order to know what payment type is selected we will create a simple `enum` whose values will represent all possible payment types:

```
public static enum PaymentType { CreditCard, PayPal; }
```

We will use the values of this enum as possible choices for our payment type select box:

```
form.add(
    new DropDownChoice<PaymentType>("type",
        new Model<PaymentType>(null),
        Arrays.asList(PaymentType.values()))
);
```

Next, we will tell Wicket that we want to know when the user changes the selection:

```
form.add(
    new DropDownChoice<PaymentType>("type",
        new Model<PaymentType>(null),
        Arrays.asList(PaymentType.values())) {

        protected boolean wantOnSelectionChangedNotifications()
{ return true;    }

    }
);
```

Now we can implement the code to handle swapping of the different payment panels:

```
form.add(
    new DropDownChoice<PaymentType>("type",
        new Model<PaymentType>(null),
        Arrays.asList(PaymentType.values())) {
```

```
            protected boolean wantOnSelectionChangedNotifications()
    { return true;    }

        protected void onSelectionChanged(
            PaymentType newSelection) {
                setupPayment(newSelection);
            }
    }
);
    private void setupPayment(PaymentType type) {
        IModel<Payment> paymentModel =
            new PropertyModel<Payment>(this, "order.payment");
        String id = paymentPanel.getId();

        Component replacement = null;

        switch (type) { // 1
        case CreditCard:
            replacement = new CreditCardPanel(id, paymentModel);
            break;
        case PayPal:
            replacement = new PayPalPanel(id, paymentModel);
            break;
        }

        paymentPanel.replaceWith(replacement); // 2
        paymentPanel = replacement; // 3
    }
```

Swapping of the payment panel consists of three steps:

1. Create a replacement panel.

2. Replace the current panel with the replacement.

3. Update the reference to the current panel with the replacement.

It is a common mistake to forget step 3 when performing component replacement. Doing so will result in an exception with the message that states that replacement was attempted on a component that is not part of page's component hierarchy when performing the second replacement.

Let's look at the flow of two replacements without step 3:

```
Component replacement=new Replacement();
current.replaceWith(replacement);
```

```
replacement=new Replacement();
current.replaceWith(replacement);
```

When we call `replaceWith()` method on line 4 we do so on the `current` component that was removed from the page hierarchy's when we replaced it on line 2. This is why it is important to update the `current` reference to the component that replaced the old instance.

We now have a working form that will present the correct payment type interface to the user when they make a change to the select box.

There's more...

In this section, we are going to see how to make the select box in our recipe swap our panels with AJAX.

Swapping panels with AJAX

We can easily change the interaction to work via Ajax; there are only two small changes that we need to make:

1. Make sure the div being replaced has its markup id output so it can be found in markup.

2. Add an Ajax behavior to the select box that will trigger an Ajax request when the selection changes, instead of using the more conventional `wantOnSelectionChangedNotifications()` method.

Both of these changes are highlighted in the code snippet as follows:

HomePage.java

```
final DropDownChoice<PaymentType> switcher =
    new DropDownChoice<PaymentType>(
        "type", new Model<PaymentType>(null),
        Arrays.asList(PaymentType.values()));

    switcher.add(
        new AjaxFormComponentUpdatingBehavior("onchange") {
        protected void onUpdate(AjaxRequestTarget target) {
            setupPayment(switcher.getModelObject());
            paymentPanel.setOutputMarkupId(true);
            target.addComponent(paymentPanel);
        }
    });
```

Creating dynamic forms

It is not too uncommon to have to have a portion of a user interface defined completely at runtime. Even though Wicket requires the developer to provide both the markup and the code for defining the user interface, it is still possible to build the interface completely at runtime. In this recipe, we will look at how to build survey forms whose fields are defined at runtime by a string. If the string looks like this:

```
Name:string:name,
Age:integer:age,
Favorite Color:string:favcolor
```

Then the survey form should look like this:

In this recipe, we will create a `DynaForm` component that will take a string in the format specified previously and will create the form at runtime.

Getting ready

Create the skeleton page to house our `DynaForm` component. The page contains a form with a submit button. For complete listing, please refer to `HomePage.java` and `HomePage.html` in the code bundle.

How to do it...

1. Create the `DynaForm` component:

   `DynaForm.html`

   ```html
   <wicket:panel>
      <div wicket:id="fields">
         <label wicket:id="label"></label>
         <input wicket:id="fc" type="text" />
      </div>
   </wicket:panel>
   ```

   `DynaForm.java`

   ```java
   public class DynaForm extends Panel {
   ```

```java
private static final String FCID = "fc";

private final IModel<String> definition;

public DynaForm(String id, IModel<Map<String, Object>>
        model,IModel<String> definition) {
    super(id, model);
    this.definition = definition;
}

protected void onInitialize() {
    super.onInitialize();

    RepeatingView fields = new RepeatingView("fields");
    add(fields);

    String[] parts = definition.getObject().split(",");
    for (String part : parts) {
        String[] segments = part.split(":");
        String label = segments[0];
        String type = segments[1];
        String key = segments[2];
        addComponent(fields, label, type, key);
    }
}

private void addComponent(RepeatingView fields,
     String label, String type, String key) {
    WebMarkupContainer field =
        new WebMarkupContainer(fields.newChildId());
    fields.add(field);

    field.add(new Label("label", label));

    FormComponent<?> fc = null;

    if (type.equals("string")) {
        IModel<String> model = new PropertyModel<String>(
                getDefaultModel(), key);
        fc=new TextField<String>(FCID, model);
    } else if (type.equals("integer")) {
        IModel<Integer> model = new PropertyModel<Integer>(
                getDefaultModel(), key);
        fc=new TextField<Integer>(FCID, model,Integer.class);
    }

    field.add(fc);
    fc.setLabel(Model.of(label));
}

protected void onDetach() {
    definition.detach();
```

```
            super.onDetach();
        }
    }
```

2. Install the `DynaForm` into the page:

    `HomePage.java`

    ```
    // for a complete listing please refer to the code bundle
    String def = "Name:string:name,Age:integer:age,Favorite
        Color:string:favcolor";
    form.add(new DynaForm("dynaform",
    new PropertyModel<Map<String,Object>>(this, "data"),
    Model.of(def)));
    ```

How it works...

Let's begin by looking at some basic ideas for the implementation:

  ▶ Our component has to be a panel because its inner markup is not defined in the
     component that uses it

  ▶ Our component has to take two models: the string defining a form and the map
     containing the results

From these two ideas we can construct the basic shell:

```java
public class DynaForm extends Panel {
    private final IModel<String> definition;
    public DynaForm(String id,
        IModel<Map<String, Object>> model,
        IModel<String> definition)
    {
        super(id, model);
        this.definition = definition;
    }
    protected void onDetach() {
        definition.detach();
        super.onDetach();
    }
}
```

Notice that because our component takes two models we have to manually detach the one we do not pass to the `Component(String, IModel)` constructor.

If we look closer at our example survey form, we notice that it consists of a field label and field tuple repeated a number of times. Given this we can come up with the basic markup for our component:

`DynaForm.html`

```
<wicket:panel>
    <div wicket:id="fields">
        <label wicket:id="label"></label>
        <input wicket:id="fc" type="text" />
    </div>
</wicket:panel>
```

The "fields" `div` in the preceding markup will have to be attached to some sort of a repeater component that will be responsible for creating all the fields. As the fields will not change past the initial form render we can use the `RepeatingView`, which is one of the most basic repeaters in Wicket:

`DynaForm.java`

```
public class DynaForm extends Panel {
    protected void onInitialize() {
        super.onInitialize();

        RepeatingView fields = new RepeatingView("fields");
        add(fields);
        }
    }
}
```

Now we have to parse the definition string and build the component hierarchy:

```
    protected void onInitialize() {
        super.onInitialize();

        RepeatingView fields = new RepeatingView("fields");
        add(fields);
        String[] parts = definition.getObject().split(",");
        for (String part : parts) {
            String[] segments = part.split(":");
            String label = segments[0];
            String type = segments[1];
```

```
        String key = segments[2];
        addComponent(fields, label, type, key);
    }
}
```

With the parsing out of the way, we can begin adding components to the repeater. We begin by adding a `WebMarkupContainer` that will act as a parent for the field label and the field components. This is something we need to do every time a repeater's markup contains more than one direct child component and something that higher level repeaters such as `ListView` and `DataView` do for us:

```
private void addComponent(RepeatingView fields,
    String label, String type,    String key) {
        WebMarkupContainer field = new WebMarkupContainer(
            fields.newChildId());
        fields.add(field);
    }
```

Notice that each direct child of a repeater has to have a unique component id. In the example above we use `RepeatingView#newChildId()` method to generate a unique component id for each item we add to the repeater.

Now that we have the base structure in place, it is time to add components that represent the fields in our survey. We will add different components to represent different types of fields:

```
private void addComponent(RepeatingView fields,
    String label, String type,    String key) {
        WebMarkupContainer field = new WebMarkupContainer(
            fields.newChildId());
        fields.add(field);
        field.add(new Label("label", label));
        FormComponent<?> fc = null;
        if (type.equals("string")) {
            IModel<String> model = new PropertyModel<String>(
                getDefaultModel(), key);
            fc = new TextField<String>(FCID, model);
        } else if (type.equals("integer")) {
            IModel<Integer> model = new PropertyModel<Integer>(
                getDefaultModel(), key);
            fc = new TextField<Integer>(FCID, model, Integer.class);
        }
        field.add(fc);
        fc.setLabel(Model.of(label));
    }
```

Each form component we add has to place its value into the specified key of the `DynaForm`'s model map. This is easily accomplished by chaining a `PropertyModel` to the model containing the map and using the needed key as the `PropertyModel`'s expression:

```
IModel<String> model = new PropertyModel<String>(
    getDefaultModel(), key);
```

The `DynaForm` is now complete; it is time to wire it into our page:

```
public class HomePage extends WebPage {
    public HomePage(final PageParameters parameters) {
        add(new FeedbackPanel("feedback"));

        Form<?> form = new Form<Void>("form") {};
        add(form);

        String def = "Name:string:name,Age:integer:age,Favorite
         Color:string:favcolor";

        form.add(new DynaForm("dynaform", new PropertyModel<Map<String,
          Object>>(this,
                "data"), Model.of(def)));

    }
}
```

Our recipe is now complete; we have built a component capable of displaying forms defined at runtime.

There's more...

In this section, we will see how to extend our `DynaForm` to support more input types.

Adding select box support to DynaForm

So far our `DynaForm` is only capable of displaying string and integer textfields, but what if we wanted to support other types of components such as select boxes? In this recipe, we will see how to enhance our `DynaForm` to do just that:

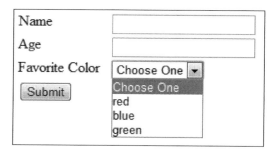

As different component types are represented by different markup tags, we will have to create panels for different component types:

`TextFieldPanel.html`

```
<wicket:panel><input wicket:id="field" type="text" size="20"/></
wicket:panel>
```

`TextFieldPanel.java`

```java
public class TextFieldPanel<T> extends Panel {
    public TextFieldPanel(String id, IModel<T> model) {
        super(id, model);
    }
    protected void onInitialize() {
        super.onInitialize();
        TextField<T> field = new TextField<T>("field",
                (IModel<T>) getDefaultModel());
        add(field);
        onCustomize(field);
    }

    protected void onCustomize(TextField<T> field) {
    }
}
```

Notice that because we are providing the `onCustomize(Component)` callback so that the text field component can be customized further we are using the `onInitialize()` method to avoid calling an overridable method from a constructor.

ChoiceFieldPanel.html

```
<wicket:panel><select wicket:id="field"></select></wicket:panel>
```

ChoiceFieldPanel.java

```
public class ChoiceFieldPanel<T> extends Panel {
    private final IModel<List<? extends T>> choices;
    public ChoiceFieldPanel(String id, IModel<T> model,
            IModel<List<? extends T>> choices) {
        super(id, model);
        this.choices = choices;
    }
    protected void onInitialize() {
        super.onInitialize();
        DropDownChoice<T> field = new DropDownChoice<T>("field",
                (IModel<T>) getDefaultModel(), choices);
        add(field);
        configure(field);
    }
    protected void onCustomize(DropDownChoice<T> field) {
    }
}
```

Now we are ready to modify our `DynaForm` to use the panels:

DynaForm.java

```
public class DynaForm extends Panel {
    private void addComponent(RepeatingView fields,
    String label, String type,   String key) {
        if (type.equals("string")) {
            IModel<String> model = new PropertyModel<String>(
                getDefaultModel(), key);
            fc = new TextFieldPanel<String>(FCID, model) {
                protected void onCustomize(TextField<String> field) {
                    field.setLabel(Model.of(label));
                };
```

```
                };
        } else if (type.equals("integer")) {
            IModel<Integer> model = new PropertyModel<Integer>(
                getDefaultModel(), key);
            fc = new TextFieldPanel<Integer>(FCID, model) {
                protected void onCustomize(TextField<Integer> field) {
                    field.setType(Integer.class);
                    field.setLabel(Model.of(label));
                };
            };
        } else if (type.equals("choice")) {
            List<String> choices = Arrays.asList(segments[3].
                split("-"));
            IModel<String> model = new PropertyModel<String>(
                getDefaultModel(), key);
            fc = new ChoiceFieldPanel<String>(FCID, model,
                Model.ofList(choices)) {
                protected void onCustomize(DropDownChoice<String>
                    field) {
                    field.setLabel(Model.of(label));
                };
            };
        }
        field.add(fc);
    }
}

}
```

Creating a dynamic portal layout

Complex web applications often require a dashboard to make it easy for their users to discover information at a glance. In this recipe, we will see how to build such a dashboard page. A dashboard is a page made out of small panels called portlets that give the user information. The dashboard page also allows the user to rearrange these portlets into a layout that makes sense to the user. The following example shows a dashboard page from a web-shop application:

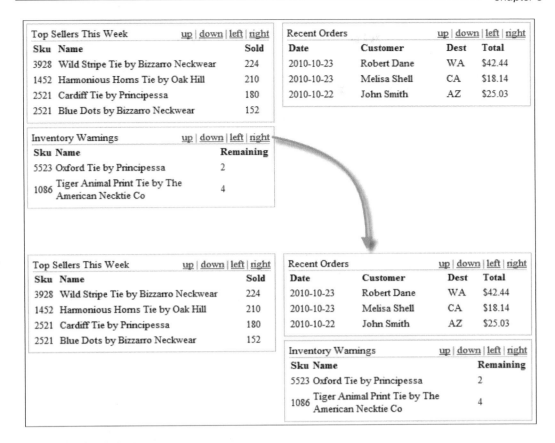

Getting ready

Let's get started by building out the portlets and a layout manager.

Create panels that represent the portlets. For the purposes of this recipe we create panels that display static content. Please refer to `TopSellersPanel`, `RecentOrdersPanel`, and `InventoryWarningsPanel` panels in the code bundle.

Build class that will manage the layout of the dashboard (keep track of which portal is in which column):

`PortalLayout.java`

```java
public class PortalLayout implements Serializable {
    private List<List<String>> columns = new ArrayList<List<String>>();
```

```
// Sample code provides methods to manage the columns list. The
outer list represents the columns, while the inner list represents
portlet ids of portlets in that column.
```

```
}
```

How to do it...

1. Create an interface to represent a portlet:

   ```
   Portlet.java

   public interface Portlet {
       IModel<String> getTitle();
       Component newContentComponent(String id);
   }
   ```

2. Create a border that will provide the title and move links for each portlet:

   ```
   ProtletBorder.java
   // refer to the code bundle for markup
   public class PortletBorder extends Border {
       public PortletBorder(String id,
               final String portletId, IModel<String> title) {
           super(id, Model.of(portletId));
           add(new Label("title", title));
           add(new Link("up") {
               public void onClick() {
                   getPortalContainer().move(portletId, -1);
               }
           });
           // sample code also adds the down, left, right links
       }
       private PortalContainer getPortalContainer() {
           return findParent(PortalContainer.class);
       }
       public String getPortletId() {
           return getDefaultModelObjectAsString();
       }
   }
   ```

3. Create the portal container component:

   ```
   PortalContainer.html
   <wicket:panel>
     <div wicket:id="column" class="column">
       <div wicket:id="portlet" class="portlet">
             <div wicket:id="content"></div>
       </div>
   ```

```
        </div>
    </wicket:panel>
PortalContainer.java
public abstract class PortalContainer extends Panel {
    private RepeatingView cols;
    public PortalContainer(String id, IModel<PortalLayout> model) {
        super(id, model);
    }
    protected void onInitialize() {
        super.onInitialize();
        PortalLayout layout = getLayout();
        cols = new RepeatingView("column");
        add(cols);
        for (int i = 0; i < layout.getColumnCount(); i++) {
            WebMarkupContainer item=new WebMarkupContainer(""+i);
            RepeatingView col =
                new PortletRepeatingView("portlet");
            cols.add(item.add(col));
            for (String portletId : layout.getColumn(i)) {
                Portlet portlet = getPortlet(portletId);
                PortletBorder border =
                  new PortletBorder(cols.newChildId(),
                      portletId, portlet.getTitle());
                col.add(border);
                border.getBodyContainer().add(
                    portlet.newContentComponent("content"));
            }
        }
    }
    protected abstract Portlet getPortlet(String portletId);
    protected PortalLayout getLayout() {
        return (PortalLayout) getDefaultModelObject();
    }
    private RepeatingView getColumn(int i) {
        return (RepeatingView)cols.get(""+ i).get("portlet");
    }
    public void move(String portletId, int delta) {
        getLayout().move(portletId, delta);
    }
    public void slide(final String portletId, int delta) {
```

```
            getLayout().slide(portletId, delta);
            PortletBorder border = findPortletBorder(portletId);
            border.getParent().remove(border);
            getColumn(getLayout().
              getPortletColumn(portletId)).add(border);
        }
        private PortletBorder findPortletBorder(
                final String portletId) {
            return (PortletBorder) cols.visitChildren(
                    PortletBorder.class,
                    new IVisitor<PortletBorder>() {
                        public Object component(
                                PortletBorder component) {
                        if (component.getPortletId()
                            .equals(portletId)) {return component;}
                        return CONTINUE_TRAVERSAL_BUT_DONT_GO_DEEPER;
                    }
            });
        }
        private final class PortletRepeatingView extends RepeatingView
    {
            private PortletRepeatingView(String id) {
                super(id);
            }
            protected Iterator<? extends Component> renderIterator()
            {
                return iterator(new PortletRenderOrderComparator());
            }
        }
        private class PortletRenderOrderComparator implements
                Comparator<Component>, Serializable {
            public int compare(Component o1, Component o2) {
                String lhs = ((PortletBorder) o1).getPortletId();
                String rhs = ((PortletBorder) o2).getPortletId();
                return getLayout().getPortletPosition(lhs)
                        - getLayout().getPortletPosition(rhs);
            }
        }
    }
}
```

4. Add it to the page:

    HomePage.java

```
PortalLayout layout = new PortalLayout(2);
layout.add(0, "1");
layout.add(0, "2");
```

```
        layout.add(1, "3");
        add(new PortalContainer("container", Model.of(layout)) {
            protected Portlet getPortlet(String portletId) {
                if ("1".equals(portletId)) {
                    return new Portlet() {
                        public IModel<String> getTitle() {
                            return Model.of("Top Sellers This Week");
                        }
                        public Component newContentComponent(String id) {
                            return new TopSellersPanel(id);
                        }
                    };
                } else if ("2".equals(portletId)) {
                    // sample code creates InventoryWarningsPanel portlet
                } else {
                    // sample code creates RecentOrdersPanel
                }
            }
        });
```

How it works...

The container will need a way to keep track of which portlet is where; to do this we will identify each portlet with a string id. The layout class we have created in step 2 keeps track of which portlet is in which column by tracking their ids. The Wicket component will need to resolve the portlet id to its title and content; to do this we create the following interface:

Portlet.java

```
    public interface Portlet {
        IModel<String> getTitle();
        Component newContentComponent(String id);
    }
```

This interface will allow our container to create the portlets for display.

Next, we build the component to represent the border around portlets. From our screenshot, we can see that this border consists of the portlet's title and some links to manage its position. The border will not contain the logic to move the portlet, instead it will delegate to the container to do so. The border will also be given the id of the portlet it manages; this is how it will tell the container which portlet needs to be moved.

Let's begin by creating a simple border:

PortletBorder.java

```
public class PortletBorder extends Border {
    public PortletBorder(String id, final String portletId,
      IModel<String> title) {
       super(id, Model.of(portletId));
    }
}
```

As the border needs to talk to the container, let's add the method that will find the container that the border is in:

PortletBorder.java

```
public class PortletBorder extends Border {
    private PortalContainer getPortalContainer() {
       return findParent(PortalContainer.class);
    }
}
```

Now we can add the title and the links that will move the portlet:

PortletBorder.java

```
public class PortletBorder extends Border {
    public PortletBorder(String id, final String portletId,
    IModel<String> title) {
       super(id, Model.of(portletId));
       add(new Label("title", title));
       add(new Link("up") {
          public void onClick() {
             getPortalContainer().move(portletId, -1);
          }
       });

    }
}
```

The border is now complete; let's get started on the main container component.

The basic layout of a container is made up of multiple columns, each column containing zero or more portlets. The layout can be visualized like the following diagram:

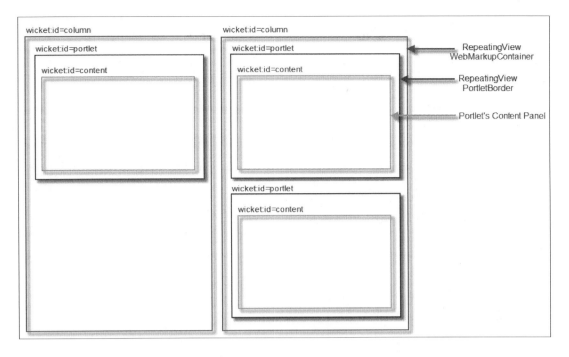

Looking at the diagram, we will need a repeater to model the columns. Each item in the column repeater will also contain a repeater to model the portlets in that column.

If we model the preceding markup, we will have this:

```
<wicket:panel>
    <div wicket:id="column" class="column">
        <div wicket:id="portlet" class="portlet">
            <div wicket:id="content"></div>
        </div>
    </div>
</wicket:panel>
```

Now let's get started on the code-side of things. We begin by creating the shell panel:

```
public abstract class PortalContainer extends Panel {
    public PortalContainer(String id, IModel<PortalLayout> model) {
        super(id, model);
    }
    protected abstract Portlet getPortlet(String portletId);
    protected PortalLayout getLayout() {
        return (PortalLayout) getDefaultModelObject();
    }
}
```

Now let's add the repeater that will represent the columns:

```
public abstract class PortalContainer extends Panel {

    private RepeatingView cols;

    protected void onInitialize() {
        super.onInitialize();

        PortalLayout layout = getLayout();

        cols = new RepeatingView("column");
        add(cols);

    }

}
```

And now let's populate that repeater with a repeater that contains portlets, and the portlets themselves:

```
for (int i = 0; i < layout.getColumnCount(); i++) {
    WebMarkupContainer item = new WebMarkupContainer("" + i);
    RepeatingView col = new RepeatingView("portlet");
    cols.add(item.add(col));

    for (String portletId : layout.getColumn(i)) {
        Portlet portlet = getPortlet(portletId);
        PortletBorder border =
            new PortletBorder(cols.newChildId(),
                portletId, portlet.getTitle());
        col.add(border);
        border.getBodyContainer().add(
            portlet.newContentComponent("content"));
    }
}
```

Notice that we have delegated the creating of portlets themselves to the abstract `getPortlet()` method, this way our component does not have to know where or how the portlets are stored.

We may now define the move methods which will allow us to move the portlets around:

PortalContainer.java

```
public abstract class PortalContainer extends Panel {

    private PortletBorder findPortletBorder(
            final String portletId) {
        return (PortletBorder)
            cols.visitChildren(PortletBorder.class,
            new IVisitor<PortletBorder>() {
```

```
            public Object component(PortletBorder component) {
                if (component.getPortletId().equals(portletId))
                {
                    return component;
                }
                return CONTINUE_TRAVERSAL_BUT_DONT_GO_DEEPER;
                }
            });
    }

    private RepeatingView getColumn(int i) {
        return (RepeatingView) cols.get("" + i).get("portlet");
    }

    public void slide(final String portletId, int delta) {
        getLayout().slide(portletId, delta);
        PortletBorder border = findPortletBorder(portletId);
        border.getParent().remove(border);
        getColumn(getLayout().getPortletColumn(portletId))
            .add(border);
    }

    public void move(String portletId, int delta) {
        getLayout().move(portletId, delta);
    }

}
```

We begin by defining the findPortletBorder() method which can find the portlet border that represents a portlet with the specified id. To do this, we use a visitor that looks for a border with the matching portlet id. Next we define the getColumn() method which allows us to find the portlets repeater for the correct column. Now we can define move() and slide() methods. The slide() method moves the portlet from column to column; to accomplish this we remove the border container from the old column and add it to the new column. The move() method moves the portlet up or down and is slightly more complex to implement. Moving a portlet is not as easy as removing it from the old parent and adding it to the new parent, because the parent is the same repeater. Instead, we need to find a way to specify in which order the repeater will render its children – that way we can move the portlet up or down by changing its render order. Our layout component already keeps track of this order, so we need to wire our "portlets" repeater to match this order. All repeaters in Wicket have a renderIterator() method; this method is used to supply the iterator of children the repeater will render and also provides their order. As the components we are trying to order are our PortletBorder instances let's define a comparator that can compare two borders based on their index in the layout:

```
public abstract class PortalContainer extends Panel {
    private class PortletRenderOrderComparator implements
```

```
        Comparator<Component>, Serializable {
    public int compare(Component o1, Component o2) {
        String lhs = ((PortletBorder) o1).getPortletId();
        String rhs = ((PortletBorder) o2).getPortletId();
        return getLayout().getPortletPosition(lhs)
                - getLayout().getPortletPosition(rhs);
    }
    }
}
```

Now let's create a subclass of `RepeatingView` that will use this comparator to change the render order of its children:

```
public abstract class PortalContainer extends Panel {
    private final class PortletRepeatingView extends
            RepeatingView {
        private PortletRepeatingView(String id) {
            super(id);
        }
        protected Iterator<? extends Component> renderIterator()         {
            return iterator(new PortletRenderOrderComparator());
        }
    }

}
```

We use the `Component#iterator(Comparator)` helper method to create an iterator of children that will be ordered by the comparator. Now we have to use our new `PortletRepeatingView`:

```
protected void onInitialize() {
    super.onInitialize();
    PortalLayout layout = getLayout();
    cols = new RepeatingView("column");
    add(cols);
    for (int i = 0; i < layout.getColumnCount(); i++) {
        WebMarkupContainer item = new WebMarkupContainer(""+i);
        RepeatingView col = newPortletRepeatingView("portlet");
        cols.add(item.add(col));
        for (String portletId : layout.getColumn(i)) {
            Portlet portlet = getPortlet(portletId);
            PortletBorder border = new
                PortletBorder(cols.newChildId(),
                    portletId, portlet.getTitle());
```

```
        col.add(border);

        border.getBodyContainer().add(
            portlet.newContentComponent("content"));
      }
    }
  }
```

The remaining task is to actually use our new `PortletContainer`, which we do in step 6.

There's more...

Our current implementation of the portlet container is very fragile. In this section, we will examine how to make it more bulletproof.

Disabling out-of-bound links

In the recipe above the links used to move the portlet around do not account for whether or not the portlet can actually be moved there. For example, the "up" link is still enabled even though the portlet is at the top of the column, and clicking it will result in an error. Let's look at how we can enable/disable the links so that we can only move a portlet if it can be moved.

We begin by adding methods to `PortalLayout` that can be queried to see if moving or sliding the portal is legal:

PortalLayout.java

```
public class PortalLayout implements Serializable {
    public boolean canMove(String id, int delta) {
        List<String> column = columns.get(getPortletColumn(id));
        int pos = column.indexOf(id);
        int moved = pos + delta;
        return moved >= 0 && moved < column.size();
    }
    public boolean canSlide(String id, int delta) {
        int col = getPortletColumn(id);
        int newCol = col + delta;
        return newCol >= 0 && newCol < columns.size();
    }
}
```

Then in the `PortletBorder` we wire the enabled state of the move links to the new query methods in the layout:

PortletBorder.java

```
public class PortletBorder extends Border {
    public PortletBorder(String id, final String portletId,
IModel<String> title) {
        super(id, Model.of(portletId));
        add(new Label("title", title));

        add(new MoveLink("up", -1));
        add(new MoveLink("down", 1));
        add(new SlideLink("left", -1));
        add(new SlideLink("right", 1));
    }
    public class MoveLink extends Link<Void> {
        private final int delta;
        public MoveLink(String id, int delta) {
            super(id);
            this.delta = delta;
        }
        public void onClick() {
            getPortalContainer().move(getPortletId(), delta);
        }
        protected void onConfigure() {
            super.onConfigure();
            setEnabled(getPortalContainer().getLayout()
                .canMove(getPortletId(), delta));
        }
    }
    public class SlideLink extends Link<Void> {
        private final int delta;
        public SlideLink(String id, int delta) {
            super(id);
            this.delta = delta;
        }
        public void onClick() {
            getPortalContainer().slide(getPortletId(), delta);
        }
        protected void onConfigure() {
            super.onConfigure();
            setEnabled(getPortalContainer().getLayout()
                .canSlide(getPortletId(), delta));
        }
    }
}
```

The links will now be properly enabled or disabled based on portlet's current position.

10

Securing your Application

In this chapter, we will cover:

- ► Creating a login page and forcing the user to log in
- ► Authenticating with `OpenID`
- ► Securing components using `IAuthorizationStrategy`
- ► Securing URLS and protecting against cross-site request forgery
- ► Switching from HTTP to HTTPS and back again

Introduction

This chapter focuses on implementing authentication and authorization in your Wicket applications. Here, we will examine how to log users in and out of the application, as well as how to isolate access to a subset of pages to only users who are logged in. We will also examine how to authorize components based on the user who has logged in, allowing them to respond to the permissions of that user. Finally, we will look at some general ways to secure the application from outside tampering.

Creating a login page and forcing the user to log in

The ability for a user to authenticate with an application is probably the most common requirement shared by all web applications. In this recipe, we will see how to leverage Wicket's security features to force the user to authenticate before they are able to access any page in the application.

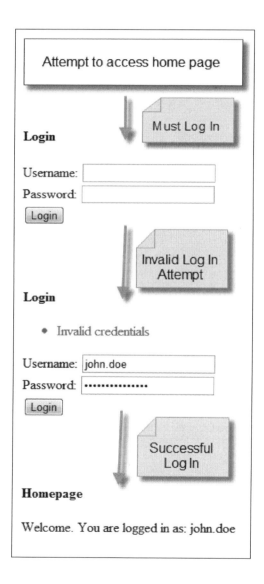

Create a custom `Session` implementation that will track whether the user is logged in or not:

`MySession.java`

```java
public class MySession extends WebSession {
    private String username;
    public MySession(Request request) {
        super(request);
    }
    public boolean login(String username, String password) {
        if (username.equals(password)) {
            this.username = username;
            return true;
        }
        return false;
    }
    public String getUsername() {
        return username;
    }
}
```

 Notice that if we had an object that represented the user we would not store it in session. Access to the session subclass is not synchronized and thus concurrency would have to be taken into account. A much simpler solution is to keep only the id or username of the user in session, and store the user object in a `RequestCycle` subclass.

Configure the application to use our `MySession` subclass:

`WicketApplication.java`

```java
public class WicketApplication extends WebApplication {

    public Session newSession(Request request,
            Response response) {
        return new MySession(request);
    }
}
```

Create the home page for our application. This page will be available only to authenticated users. Refer to `HomePage.html` and `HomePage.java` in the code bundle.

Create the page used by users to log in:

`LoginPage.java`

```java
// refer to the code bundle for markup
public class LoginPage extends WebPage {
```

```
private String username;
private String password;

public LoginPage() {
    // sample code adds a form that collects username and password
        in the fields and calls login() when submitted
}

private void login() {
    MySession session=(MySession)getSession();
    if (session.login(username, password)) {
        if (!continueToOriginalDestination()) {
            setResponsePage(getApplication().getHomePage());
        }
    } else {
        error("Invalid credentials");
    }
}
```

How to do it...

1. Create an implementation of IAuthorizationStrategy that will force users to log in to access any page other then the login page:

    AuthStrategy.java

    ```
    public class AuthStrategy implements IAuthorizationStrategy {

        public <T extends Component> boolean
          isInstantiationAuthorized(Class<T> componentClass) {

            if (!Page.class.isAssignableFrom(componentClass)) {
                return true;
            }

            if (LoginPage.class.isAssignableFrom(componentClass)) {
                return true;
            }

            if (((MySession) Session.get()).getUsername() == null) {
                throw new RestartResponseAtInterceptPageException(LoginPa
                  ge.class);
            }

            return true;
        }
    ```

```
  public boolean isActionAuthorized(Component component, Action
    action) {
    return true;
  }
}
```

2. Configure the application to use our `AuthStrategy`:

    `WicketApplication.java`

    ```
    public class WicketApplication extends WebApplication {

      protected void init() {
        super.init();
        getSecuritySettings().setAuthorizationStrategy(
          new AuthStrategy());
      }

    }
    ```

How it works...

In order to intercept access to pages we must implement our own
`IAuthorizationStrategy` and let Wicket know to use it. Let's begin by letting our class
implement the interface:

```
public class AuthStrategy implements IAuthorizationStrategy {
  public <T extends Component> boolean
    isInstantiationAuthorized(Class<T> componentClass) {
    return true;
  }
  public boolean isActionAuthorized(Component component, Action
    action) {
    return true;
  }
}
```

As we want to intercept instantiation of pages and only allow it if the user is logged in we will
extend the `isInstantiationAuthorized` method.

The first thing we do is filter out all queries to non-page components, as we are only interested
in intercepting instantiation of pages and not components such as labels and text fields:

```
public <T extends Component> boolean
  isInstantiationAuthorized(Class<T> componentClass) {

  if (!Page.class.isAssignableFrom(componentClass)) {
```

```
        return true;
    }

    return true;
}
```

Next, we forbid access to all pages unless the user is logged in:

```
public <T extends Component> boolean
  isInstantiationAuthorized(Class<T> componentClass) {

    if (!Page.class.isAssignableFrom(componentClass)) {
        return true;
    }

    if (((MySession) Session.get()).getUsername() == null) {
        throw new RestartResponseAtInterceptPageException(LoginPage.
class);
    }

    return true;
}
```

Now when the user tries to access a page and Wicket attempts to instantiate it, a RestartResponseAtInterceptPageException will be thrown and the user will be redirected to our login page.

 Here we notice that we are using an exception that redirects to something called an "intercept" page. When we use this exception Wicket will remember the URL that the user tried to access before being redirected. Later, we can return the user to their original URL using Component#continueToOriginalDestination() method (see implementation of LoginPage#login() method in Step 4). This feature allows us to insert a page into user's path without interrupting it.

If we try to execute our application with this authorization strategy we will get an infinite redirect loop. What will happen is that as soon as the user tries to access the home page our strategy will intercept them and redirect them to the login page. However, as soon as they try to access the login page our strategy will intercept them, and you guessed it, redirect them to the login page again. This is a common problem when implementing login page scenarios. What we have to do to fix it is make our strategy allow access to the login page to users who are not logged in:

```
public <T extends Component> boolean
  isInstantiationAuthorized(Class<T> componentClass) {

    if (!Page.class.isAssignableFrom(componentClass)) {
        return true;
    }
```

```
    if (LoginPage.class.isAssignableFrom(componentClass)) {
        return true;
    }
    if (((MySession) Session.get()).getUsername() == null) {
        throw new RestartResponseAtInterceptPageException(LoginPage.
class);
    }
    return true;
}
```

Our strategy is now complete, we just have to install it in our application:

WicketApplication.java

```
public class WicketApplication extends WebApplication {
    protected void init() {
        super.init();
        getSecuritySettings().setAuthorizationStrategy(
            new AuthStrategy());
    }
}
```

There's more...

In the next section, we will see how to make our authorization strategy more flexible and reuse more code to make the implementation simpler.

Securing only subsets of pages

Protecting all pages from anonymous users is great, but usually web applications only protect a subset of their pages. Let us take a look at how we can restrict authorization.

First, we must somehow define the subset of pages we wish to protect. There are many ways to do this: subclasses, tagging interfaces and annotations are only a few ways that come to mind. To keep things simple we will use a tagging interface:

SecurePage.java

```
public interface SecurePage {}
```

Then we can annotate the pages we want secured:

HomePage.java

```
@SecurePage
public class HomePage extends WebPage {...}
```

Now, we can modify our strategy to only require authorization for pages that implement this interface:

```
public <T extends Component> boolean
  isInstantiationAuthorized(Class<T> componentClass) {
    if (!Page.class.isAssignableFrom(componentClass)) {
      return true;
    }
    if (!SecurePage.class.isAssignableFrom(componentClass)) {
      return true;
    }
    if (((MySession) Session.get()).getUsername() == null) {
      throw new RestartResponseAtInterceptPageException(LoginPage.
        class);
    }
    return true;
}
```

Now anonymous users can access any page unless somewhere in its class hierarchy it implements the SecurePage interface.

Taking advantage of a base class

Wicket ships with an abstract implementation of IAuthorizationStrategy that makes implementing the above scenario trivial. Using the SimplePageAuthorizationStrategy as the superclass we can condense our own implementation down to just a few lines of code:

```
SimplifiedAuthStrategy.java
    public class SimplifiedAuthStrategy
        extends SimplePageAuthorizationStrategy{
        public SimplifiedAuthStrategy() {
            super(SecurePage.class, LoginPage.class);
        }
        protected boolean isAuthorized() {
            return ((MySession)Session.get()).getUsername()!=null;
        }
    }
```

We provide the SimplePageAuthorizationStrategy the three key pieces of information that our scenario requires:

1. The tagging interface for pages that require authentication
2. The class of the login page
3. A test that determines if the user is currently logged in

Given this information the implementation of SimplePageAuthorizationStrategy can take care of all the details.

Authenticating with OpenID

Remembering passwords has been a long standing pain point for people, so much so that a lot of people simply use the same password to sign into all of their web applications. This, of course, is a big security problem because if the password is compromised on any site then all of other accounts that use the same password are potentially compromised as well. To help users deal with this problem some sites started offering a "pass-through" authentication mechanism which allows the user to authenticate to sites using the original site as the middle man. This idea was quickly picked up and a couple of standards were created to support it such as `OpenID`, `OAuth`, and others. In this recipe we will see how to integrate a Wicket application with an OpenID provider.

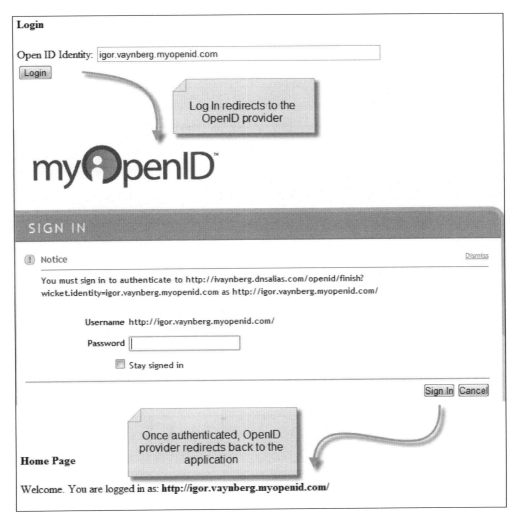

Getting ready

Create a custom `Session` implementation that will track which user is logged in.

MySession.java

```java
public class MySession extends WebSession {
    private String username;
    // getter and setter
}
```

Configure the application to use our `MySession` subclass:

WicketApplication.java

```java
public class WicketApplication extends WebApplication {
    public Session newSession(Request req,Response res) {
        return new MySession(req);
    }
}
```

Create the home page and the login page for our application. Please refer to HomePage.java and HomePage.html in the code bundle for the home page code.

LoginPage.java

```java
public class LoginPage extends WebPage {
    private String identity;

    public LoginPage() {
        // sample code creates a form that collects user's identity into
            the field and calls login() when submitted
    }
    private void login() {
        try {
            OpenIdConsumer consumer =
             OpenIdConsumer.get(getApplication());
            consumer.startLogin(identity);
        } catch (OpenIDException e) {
            error("OpenId Authentication Failed");
        }
    }
}
```

How to do it...

1. Create the class that will encapsulate interactions with the OpenID provider. In this recipe we use the excellent OpenID4Java library to help us get started quickly:

```java
public abstract class OpenIdConsumer {
    private static MetaDataKey<OpenIdConsumer> KEY=
        new MetaDataKey<OpenIdConsumer>() {};

    public static OpenIdConsumer get(Application application) {
        return application.getMetaData(KEY);
    }

    private Map<String, ConsumerManager> consumers;
    private String applicationUrl;

    public OpenIdConsumer(String applicationUrl) {
        this.applicationUrl = applicationUrl;
    }

    public void init(WebApplication application) {
        consumers = new MapMaker()
            .expiration(5, TimeUnit.MINUTES).makeMap();

        application.mountBookmarkablePage("/openid/finish",
            OpenIdCallbackPage.class);

        application.setMetaData(KEY, this);
    }

    public void startLogin(String identity)
            throws OpenIDException {
        consumers.remove(identity);

        String callbackUrl = applicationUrl + "/"
            + RequestCycle.get()
            .urlFor(OpenIdCallbackPage.class, null);
        callbackUrl += callbackUrl.contains("?") ? "&" : "?";
        callbackUrl += "wicket.identity=" + identity;

        String authUrl;
        // sample code constructs an auth url using OpenID4Java
        // the above callbackUrl is encoded in generated authUrl
        throw new RedirectToUrlException(authUrl);
    }

    public void finishLogin(Request req, Page page) {
```

```
        // sample code uses OpenID4Java to validate auth server's
response and either call onLoginSuccessful() or onLoginFailed.
Refer to the code bundle for details
    }

    protected abstract void onLoginSuccessful
        (Identifier identifier, Page page);

    protected abstract void onLoginFailed
        (String identity, OpenIDException cause, Page page);

}
```

2. Create the page which will handle the callback from the OpenID provider:

```
public class OpenIdCallbackPage extends WebPage {
    public OpenIdCallbackPage()
    {
        OpenIdConsumer consumer =
            OpenIdConsumer.get(getApplication());
        consumer.finishLogin(getRequest(), this);
    }
}
```

3. Modify authorization strategy to allow the callback page created in the previous step:

```
public class AuthStrategy implements IAuthorizationStrategy {
    public <T extends Component> boolean
            isInstantiationAuthorized(Class<T> componentClass)
    {
        if (!Page.class.isAssignableFrom(componentClass)) {
            return true;
        }
        if (LoginPage.class.isAssignableFrom(componentClass)) {
            return true;
        }
        if (OpenIdCallbackPage.class.isAssignableFrom(
                componentClass)) {
            return true;
        }
        if (((MySession) Session.get()).getUsername() == null) {
            throw new RestartResponseAtInterceptPageException(
                LoginPage.class);
        }
        return true;
    }
}
```

4. Wire the consumer into our application:

`WicketApplication.java`

```java
public class WicketApplication extends WebApplication {
    protected void init() {
        super.init();
        getSecuritySettings().setAuthorizationStrategy(new
            AuthStrategy());

        OpenIdConsumer consumer = new OpenIdConsumer(
                "http://ivaynberg.dnsalias.com") {

            protected void onLoginSuccessful(
                    Identifier identifier, Page page) {
                MySession session = (MySession) page.getSession();
                session.setUsername(identifier.getIdentifier());
                if (!page.continueToOriginalDestination()) {
                    page.setResponsePage(getHomePage());
                }
            }

            @Override
            protected void onLoginFailed(String identity,
                    OpenIDException cause, Page page) {
                LoginPage login = new LoginPage();
                login.error("OpenID Authentication Failed");
                page.setResponsePage(login);
            }
        };
        consumer.init(this);
    }
}
```

How it works...

OpenID4Java encapsulates all the details of the OpenID protocol inside `ConsumerManager` instances. Each instance represents a conversation between the site to which the user wishes to authenticate and the OpenID provider site. As instances of these managers are not serializable, we have to keep them at the `Application` level in some temporary store. To keep things simple we will keep them in a `Map` implementation which expires its entries every five minutes. To create the map we use the Guava library:

OpenIdConsumer.java

```
public abstract class OpenIdConsumer {
    private Map<String, ConsumerManager> consumers;
    public void init(WebApplication application) {
        consumers = new MapMaker()
            .expiration(5, TimeUnit.MINUTES).makeMap();
    }
}
```

As the OpenID provider needs to redirect back to our application when authentication is complete, we pass that into our consumer:

OpenIdConsumer.java

```
public abstract class OpenIdConsumer {

    private String applicationUrl;

    public OpenIdConsumer(String applicationUrl) {
        this.applicationUrl = applicationUrl;
    }
}
```

As the consumer acts as a global storage for all ongoing authentication attempts we must have an easy way to retrieve it. We can store it as a field in our Application subclass and provide a getter, but to keep things more reusable let's store it in Application's metadata – which will not require any changes to the Application subclass itself:

OpenIdConsumer.java

```
public abstract class OpenIdConsumer {
    private static MetaDataKey<OpenIdConsumer> KEY=
        new MetaDataKey<OpenIdConsumer>() {};
    public static OpenIdConsumer get(Application application) {
        return application.getMetaData(KEY);
    }
    public void init(WebApplication application) {
        consumers = new MapMaker()
            .expiration(5, TimeUnit.MINUTES).makeMap();
        application.setMetaData(KEY, this);
    }
}
```

Now let's implement the first phase of the authentication process—redirecting to the provider site:

OpenIdConsumer.java

```
public abstract class OpenIdConsumer {
    public void startLogin(String identity)
        throws OpenIDException {

        consumers.remove(identity);

        ConsumerManager manager = new ConsumerManager();
        List<?> discoveries = manager.discover(identity);

        String callbackUrl = applicationUrl + "/"
            + RequestCycle.get()
            .urlFor(OpenIdCallbackPage.class, null);
        callbackUrl += callbackUrl.contains("?") ? "&" : "?";
        callbackUrl += "wicket.identity=" + identity;

        DiscoveryInformation discovered =
            manager.associate(discoveries);
        AuthRequest req = manager
            .authenticate(discovered, callbackUrl);

        consumers.put(identity, manager);

        throw new RedirectToUrlException(
            req.getDestinationUrl(true));
    }

}
```

The preceding code leverages OpenID4Java library to do most of the heavy lifting. When the user authenticates on the provider's site the provider will redirect user's browser back to the callback URL we have provided which will hit our `OpenIdCallbackPage` page. This page will complete the authentication process by processing the result the provider sent. All we have to do is retrieve the right consumer, based on the query string parameter we specified in the callback URL:

```
public abstract class OpenIdConsumer {
    public void finishLogin(Request req, Page page) {
        HttpServletRequest request = ((WebRequest) req)
            .getHttpServletRequest();

        String identity=request.getParameter("wicket.identity");
        if (Strings.isEmpty(identity)) {
            throw new AbortWithWebErrorCodeException(500);
        }

        ConsumerManager manager = consumers.get(identity);
```

```
        if (manager == null) {
            throw new AbortWithWebErrorCodeException(500);
        }
        consumers.remove(manager);


    }
}
```

And then allow OpenID4Java to retrieve the credentials of the authenticated user:

```
public abstract class OpenIdConsumer {

    public void finishLogin(Request req, Page page) {

        ParameterList response =
            new ParameterList(request.getParameterMap());

        StringBuffer url = request.getRequestURL();
        if (!Strings.isEmpty(request.getQueryString())) {
            url.append("?").append(request.getQueryString());
        }
        try {
            VerificationResult verification =
                manager.verify(url.toString(),response, null);
            Identifier verified = verification.getVerifiedId();

            if (verified == null) {
                throw new OpenIDException(
                    "Authentication failed");
            }
            onLoginSuccessful(verified, page);
        } catch (OpenIDException e) {
            onLoginFailed(identity, e, page);
        }

    }

    protected abstract void onLoginSuccessful
        (Identifier identifier, Page page);

    protected abstract void onLoginFailed
        (String identity, OpenIDException cause, Page page);

}
```

Based on the result of authentication, we invoke either the success or the failure callback our consumer class provides. The class is now ready to be wired into the application, which is done in Step 7.

Securing components using IAuthorizationStrategy

In this recipe, we are going to examine how to leverage `IAuthorizationStrategy` to secure individual components on a page given the current user's permissions. A specific example we are going to look at is how to secure a form component so that it appears as disabled to some users while being completely invisible to others. Suppose we are building an employee management system. In this system, managers can log in and edit performance reviews for employees, while human resource people can log in and view these reviews. However, when an employee logs in, they cannot see the review:

Edit Employee

Name:

| Bart Simpson |

Email:

| bart@thesimpsons.com |

Review:

| Has a problem with authority |

[Save]

Logged in as manager, can edit employee's review

Edit Employee

Name:

| Bart Simpson |

Email:

| bart@thesimpsons.com |

Review:

| Has a problem with authority |

[Save]

Same form, but logged in as human resources, can only view employee's review

Edit Employee

Name:

| Bart Simpson |

Email:

| bart@thesimpsons.com |

[Save]

Same form, but logged in as employee, can not see review

Getting ready

Create an enum that will model user's permissions:

Permission.java

```java
public enum Permission {
    VIEW_REVIEW, EDIT_REVIEW;
}
```

Create a session that exposes the user's permissions:

MySession.java

```java
public class MySession extends WebSession {
    public boolean hasPermission(Permission permission) {
        switch (permission) {
        case EDIT_REVIEW:
            return "manager".equals(username);
        case VIEW_REVIEW:
            return "manager".equals(username)
                    || "humanresources".equals(username);
        default:
            return false;
        }
    }
}
```

Wire our custom session into the application:

WicketApplication.java

```java
public class WicketApplication extends WebApplication {
    public Session newSession(Request request,
        Response response) {
    return new MySession(request);
    }
}
```

Create the page used to edit the employee. Refer to HomePage.html and HomePage.java in the code bundle.

How to do it...

1. Create the class that will manage component permissions:

```java
public class Permissions {
    private static MetaDataKey<ArrayList<Permission>> RENDER =
        new MetaDataKey<ArrayList<Permission>>() {};
    private static MetaDataKey<ArrayList<Permission>> ENABLE =
        new MetaDataKey<ArrayList<Permission>>() {};

    public static Permissions of(Component c) {
        return new Permissions(c);
    }

    private final Component component;

    private Permissions(Component component) {
        this.component = component;
    }

    public Permissions render(Permission... permissions) {
        set(RENDER, permissions);
        return this;
    }

    public Permissions enable(Permission... permissions) {
        set(ENABLE, permissions);
        return this;
    }

    public boolean canRender() {
        return can(RENDER);
    }

    public boolean canEnable() {
        return can(ENABLE);
    }

    public boolean can(MetaDataKey<ArrayList<Permission>> key) {
        ArrayList<Permission> stored=component.getMetaData(key);
        if (stored == null) { return true; }

        MySession session = (MySession) component.getSession();

        for (Permission permission : stored) {
            if (session.hasPermission(permission)) {
                return true;
            }
```

```
        }
        return false;
    }

    private void set(MetaDataKey<ArrayList<Permission>> key,
            Permission... permissions) {
        if (permissions.length == 0) {
            component.setMetaData(key, null);
        } else {
            ArrayList<Permission> stored =
                component.getMetaData(key);
            if (stored == null) {
                stored = new ArrayList<Permission>();
                component.setMetaData(key, stored);
            }
            stored.clear();
            stored.addAll(Arrays.asList(permissions));
        }
    }
}
```

2. Implement `IAuthorizationStrategy` that will use the stored permissions to authorize components:

`AuthorizationStrategy.java`

```
public class AuthorizationStrategy implements
IAuthorizationStrategy {

    public <T extends Component> boolean
        isInstantiationAuthorized(Class<T> componentClass) {

        // whatever page authorization needs to happen

    }

    public boolean isActionAuthorized(
            Component component, Action action) {
        if (action == Component.RENDER) {
            return Permissions.of(component).canRender();
        } else if (action == Component.ENABLE) {
            return Permissions.of(component).canEnable();
        }
        return true;
    }

}
```

3. Install the authorization strategy into the application:

`WicketApplication.java`

```java
public class WicketApplication extends WebApplication {
    protected void init() {
        getSecuritySettings().setAuthorizationStrategy(
            new AuthorizationStrategy());
    }
}
```

4. Authorize the review textfield on the Home page:

`HomePage.java`

```java
public class HomePage extends WebPage {
    public HomePage() {
        ...
        Component review = new TextArea<String>("review",
            new PropertyModel<String>(this,
                "review")).setRequired(true);

        Permissions.of(review)
            .render(Permission.VIEW_REVIEW)
            .enable(Permission.EDIT_REVIEW);

        form.add(review);
    }
}
```

How it works...

`IAuthorizationStrategy` strategy contains a method called: `isActionAuthorized()`. This method is called whenever a component wants to perform an action such as rendering or enabling itself. We will use this method to override a component's ability to enable or render itself based on our application's permission scheme:

```java
public class AuthorizationStrategy
    implements IAuthorizationStrategy {

    public boolean isActionAuthorized(
            Component component, Action action) {
        if (action == Component.RENDER) {
            return Permissions.of(component).canRender();
        } else if (action == Component.ENABLE) {
            return Permissions.of(component).canEnable();
        }
```

```
        return true;
    }


}
```

In the preceding code we use the `Permissions` class to check if a component has the permission. In order for this to work, we have to be able to associate permissions with component instances. Luckily, components provide a storage mechanism for storing arbitrary objects with the component instance called "metadata".

 In some environments, it is possible to arbitrarily associate data with objects using a `Map` with weak keys; however, such associations will not survive serialization. This is why Wicket provides its own storage mechanism for such data.

Each metadata object is stored by associating it with a key. As we wish to store two sets of permissions: one for enabling the component and one for rendering it, we will need two metadata keys:

`Permissions.java`

```
public class Permissions {
    private static MetaDataKey<ArrayList<Permission>> RENDER = new Meta
DataKey<ArrayList<Permission>>() {};

    private static MetaDataKey<ArrayList<Permission>> ENABLE = new Meta
DataKey<ArrayList<Permission>>() {};
}
```

With the keys ready, we can write the methods to store a list of permissions with a component instance:

`Permissions.java`

```
public class Permissions {
    private void set(MetaDataKey<ArrayList<Permission>> key,
            Permission... permissions) {
        if (permissions.length == 0) {
            component.setMetaData(key, null);
        } else {
            ArrayList<Permission> stored =
                component.getMetaData(key);
            if (stored == null) {
                stored = new ArrayList<Permission>();
                component.setMetaData(key, stored);
            }
```

```
            stored.clear();
            stored.addAll(Arrays.asList(permissions));
        }
    }
}
```

Metadata is read much like it is written, so we are going to skip examining that part in detail. The rest of the methods in the `Permissions` class provide a nice way to associate `Permission` instances with the component.

The system is now complete. The authorization strategy can now veto both ENABLE and RENDER actions of component instances based on permissions associated with those instances. The only remaining piece is to associate some permissions with our review field, which we do in Step 9:

HomePage.java

```
    Permissions.of(review)
        .render(Permission.VIEW_REVIEW)
        .enable(Permission.EDIT_REVIEW);
```

There's more...

In this section, we will see how to make permissions more reusable.

Internalizing permissions in subclasses

The nice thing about binding components to their permissions in code instead of some sort of a meta document is that we can easily internalize permissions. If we had more than one place in the user interface that edited an employee's review, we can create a subclass of `TextField` that would internalize the permissions:

```
    public class ReviewTextArea extends TextArea {
        public ReviewTextArea(String id, IModel model) {
            super(id, model);
            Permissions.of(this).render(Permission.VIEW_REVIEW)
                .enable(Permission.EDIT_REVIEW);
        }
    }
```

Securing URLs and protecting against cross-site request forgery

Some web applications need to be more secure than others. For example, security is much more important in a banking application than it is in a book-marking service. As applications become more and more complex making sure that they are totally secure becomes harder and harder. A class of attacks that takes advantage of this fact is called **Cross-site Request Forgery** (**CSRF**). These attacks have become very popular as of late, and can cause some serious problems for users of vulnerable sites. The attacks are explained in detail elsewhere on the Internet; in this recipe we are going to concentrate on how to prevent them. The short of it is that in order to prevent these attacks all URLs that can execute an action on the site must be signed with some sort of user token; this makes it impossible for the attackers to create a URL that will forge a request for all users. Even better if the token varies from login to login, as this makes it impossible for an attacker to even create a user-specific forged URL. Wicket makes guarding against this class of attacks trivial. URLs in a Wicket application are generated at a single point called `IRequestCodingStrategy`. Most applications out there use the default `WebRequestCodingStrategy`, but Wicket also ships with an implementation called `CryptedUrlWebRequestCodingStrategy`. This strategy encrypts all URLs with a randomly generated key stored in the user's session. Not only can the URLs not be forged, but they are also encrypted – making it even harder for attackers to figure out what is going on in the application. In this recipe, we will see how to install this strategy and make our Wicket web application even more secure.

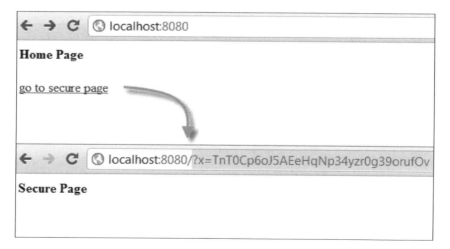

Getting ready

Create some pages that link to each other. We will use them to test the
`CryptedUrlWebRequestCodingStrategy` strategy. Refer to sources of `SecurePage`
and `HomePage` in the code bundle.

How to do it...

1. Install the `CryptedUrlWebRequestCodingStrategy` in the application:

```
public class WicketApplication extends WebApplication {
    public Class<HomePage> getHomePage() {
        return HomePage.class;
    }

    protected IRequestCycleProcessor
        newRequestCycleProcessor() {
      return new WebRequestCycleProcessor() {
        protected IRequestCodingStrategy
            newRequestCodingStrategy() {
          return new CryptedUrlWebRequestCodingStrategy(
              super.newRequestCodingStrategy());
        }
      };
    }
}
```

How it works...

In Wicket, the `IRequestCodingStrategy` instance that will be used for the application
is created as part of the `IRequestCycleProcessor`. In order to switch to another coding
strategy, we must override its creation in the processor and override the creation of the
processor in the application. Let's first override the processor:

```
public class WicketApplication extends WebApplication {
    protected IRequestCycleProcessor
        newRequestCycleProcessor() {
      return new WebRequestCycleProcessor();
    };
}
```

Now let's override the strategy:

```
public class WicketApplication extends WebApplication {
    protected IRequestCycleProcessor
        newRequestCycleProcessor() {
    return new WebRequestCycleProcessor() {
        protected IRequestCodingStrategy
            newRequestCodingStrategy() {
            return new CryptedUrlWebRequestCodingStrategy(
                super.newRequestCodingStrategy());
        }
    };
    }
}
```

Switching from HTTP to HTTPS and back again

SSL is the standard protocol when it comes to securing communication between a browser and a server. All the web application has to do in order to secure its communication is to switch the user from `http` to `https` protocol. Wicket ships with a `HttpsRequestCycleProcessor` class that handles protocol switching for the user based on page annotations. In this recipe we will see how to install and use the processor in our application.

Getting ready

Create two pages that link to each other so we can test the processor. Refer to the sources of `SecurePage` and `HomePage` in the code bundle.

How to do it...

1. Install the `HttpsRequestCycleProcessor` in the application:

    `WicketApplication.java`

    ```
    public class WicketApplication extends WebApplication {
        public Class<HomePage> getHomePage() {
            return HomePage.class;
        }

        protected IRequestCycleProcessor
            newRequestCycleProcessor() {
            return new HttpsRequestCycleProcessor(
    ```

```
            new HttpsConfig(8080, 8443));
        }


    }
```

2. Add the @RequireHttps annotation to pages we want served over https:

   SecurePage.java

   @RequireHttps
   public class SecurePage extends WebPage {}

How it works...

The processor intercepts all incoming requests and checks if the page they are meant for has the @RequireHttps annotation; if it does the processor rewrites the URL to have the https protocol and performs the redirect. Likewise, if the page does not contain the annotation and the URL comes in on the https protocol, the processor will rewrite it to http and perform a redirect; in this way, it is easy to switch back to the http protocol.

The processor also takes the HttpsConfig object. This object allows the developer to specify non-standard ports, which is useful when developing applications. In our example, we specify ports 8080 for unsecure and port 8443 for secure communications:

```
new HttpsConfig(8080, 8443));
```

There's more...

More Info Section 1

While ensuring that certain pages are served over https is great, sometimes we wish to serve a page over http and have a form on it submit to https; this is especially useful for login forms that appear on pages that do not need to be served over https. In order to do this we need to rewrite the form's action attribute to the https protocol. Let's see how we can do that:

```
public class HttpsForm<T> extends Form<T> {
    public HttpsForm(String id, IModel<T> model) {
        super(id, model);
    }
    public HttpsForm(String id) {
        super(id);
    }
    protected void onComponentTag(ComponentTag tag) {
```

```
        super.onComponentTag(tag);
        String action=tag.getAttribute("action");
        String absolute=RequestUtils.toAbsolutePath(action);
        absolute=absolute.replaceFirst("http://", "https://");
        absolute=absolute.replaceFirst(":8080", ":8443");
        tag.put("action", absolute);
    }
}
```

We create a subclass of `Form` that literally rewrites the action attribute. The first step is to translate the original attribute to an absolute URL; we do this with the help of `RequestUtils` class:

```
String absolute=RequestUtils.toAbsolutePath(action);
```

Next, we rewrite the protocol and the port using simple regular expression substitutions:

```
absolute=absolute.replaceFirst("http://", "https://");
absolute=absolute.replaceFirst(":8080", ":8443");
```

Finally, we replace the original value with our rewritten one:

```
tag.put("action", absolute);
```

Our secure form is now complete.

11
Integrating Wicket with Middleware

In this chapter, we will cover:

- ► Integrating with Spring
- ► Integrating with CDI
- ► Populating repeaters from a JPA query
- ► Creating a model for a JPA entity

Introduction

Web applications should not be built with Wicket alone. Wicket is a great place to put your user interface code, but it should not contain any business-related code. Usually the code that makes up Web applications is divided into three layers: the data access layer, the business layer, and the user interface layer. In this chapter, we are going to see how to integrate Wicket with frameworks that are used to build the data access and the business layers.

Integrating with Spring

In this recipe we will see how to integrate Wicket with Spring's popular inversion of control container. We will explore how to enable injection of component classes as well as any Java object with dependencies that come from Spring's contexts. In order to demonstrate the necessary concepts, we are going to build a simple application that displays the current time:

The time will come from a bean managed by Spring, and we will see how to bring it into a Wicket page.

Getting ready

Let's begin by creating the necessary business beans and installing them into the Spring context.

Create the interface for our time service:

`TimeService.java`

```
public interface TimeService {
    String getTime();
}
```

Create a simple implementation:

```
TimeServiceImpl.java
@Service
public class TimeServiceImpl implements TimeService {
    public String getTime() {
        return DateFormat
            .getDateTimeInstance()
            .format(new Date());
    }
}
```

Set up the Spring context:

`applicationContext.xml`

```
<?xml version="1.0" encoding="UTF-8"?>
<beans>
    <context:component-scan base-package="cookbook"/>
</beans>
```

Now, let's create the Wicket page.

Create the page that will display the time using our service:

`HomePage.java`

```
// for markup refer to HomePage.html in the code bundle
public class HomePage extends WebPage {

    private TimeService service;

    public HomePage(final PageParameters parameters) {
        add(new Label("time", new PropertyModel<String>(this, "service.
            time")));
    }

}
```

How to do it...

If we run the application now we will receive a `NullPointerException` when accessing the page because we have not yet set up the mechanism that will inject our `HomePage`'s `service` field with a reference to the `TimeServiceImpl` bean from our context. Let's do that now.

1. Set up the `ComponentInstantiationListener` that will perform the injection:

   `WicketApplication.java`

   ```
   public class WicketApplication extends WebApplication {

       protected void init() {
           super.init();
           addComponentInstantiationListener(
             new SpringComponentInjector(this));
       }

   }
   ```

2. Tell the listener we want the `service` field injected:

   `HomePage.java`

   ```
   public class HomePage extends WebPage {
   ```

```
    @SpringBean
    private TimeService service;

    public HomePage() {
        add(new Label("time",
            new PropertyModel<String>(this, "service.time")));
    }
}
```

How it works...

Wicket contains an extension point called the **component instantiation listener**. This extension point allows developers to install listeners which are notified any time a subclass of Component is instantiated. The listeners are represented by the following trivial interface:

```
public interface IComponentInstantiationListener
{
    void onInstantiation(Component component);
}
```

Any number of such listeners can be installed in the application. One such listener is the SpringComponentInjector. Once installed in the application it will listen to component instantiations and will inject any fields annotated with @SpringBean annotation with beans that come from the Spring context.

 As Wicket serializes the component graph and, by association, all objects the components reference, we may have a problem with Wicket trying to serialize the injected beans. This would be very bad because beans are often very large and have lifecycles that do not match that of components they are injected into. For this reason SpringComponentInjector wraps the injected beans in proxies that can free the reference before the component is serialized, and reinject it when the component is deserialized.

Once we install the injector using the Application# addComponentInstantiationListener() method it will begin injecting our component fields, and this is how our @SpringBean   private TimeService service field gets its value.

There's more...

Wicket provides various hooks for plugins such as the
`IComponentInstantiationListener` to make the framework extensible. However,
because Wicket does not use any byte code-weaving or aspect-oriented magic the places in
code where it can provide the hooks are limited. In the next section, we will see how to make
the injection hook work in standalone classes.

Injecting non-components

In the preceding recipe, we have discussed how to use `SpringComponentInjector`
to inject `Component` subclasses, but what if we wish to inject classes that do not extend
`Component`? For example, what if we wanted to encapsulate the retrieval of current time in
an `IModel` implementation?

Once we install `SpringComponentInjector` in the application it will register itself with
Wicket's `InjectorHolder` object which we can use to retrieve the injector and inject
instances of any class:

TimeModel.java

```java
public class TimeModel extends LoadableDetachableModel<String> {

    @SpringBean
    private TimeService service;

    public TimeModel() {
        InjectorHolder.getInjector().inject(this);
    }

    protected String load() {
        return service.getTime();
    }

}
```

Now that we have the code necessary to retrieve the time encapsulated in a model, we can
make our page code a lot less noisy:

HomePage.java

```java
public class HomePage extends WebPage {

    public HomePage() {
        add(new Label("time", new TimeModel()));
    }

}
```

Integrating with CDI

Context Dependency and Injection (**CDI**) is the new standard for managing dependencies inside Java applications. In this recipe, we will see how to integrate our Wicket application with a CDI implementation so that it can access dependencies managed by the CDI container. In this recipe, we will be working with JBoss Weld, which is the reference implementation of the CDI specification. In order to enable Wicket interoperability, we will be using Seam-Wicket module, which is a portable CDI extension.

Note that we are using Seam-Wicket version 3.0.0-SNAPSHOT as of the writing of this book. The final release of the Seam-Wicket module may differ slightly from the usage demonstrated in this recipe, but the concepts should remain the same.

In order to demonstrate how to integrate Wicket with CDI, we are going to build a simple application that displays the current time which will come from a CDI-managed service bean:

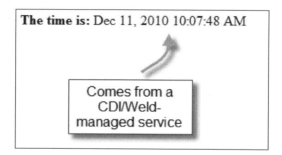

Getting ready

First we will create the service and install it as a CDI bean.

Define the service interface:

TimeService.java

```
public interface TimeService {
    String getTime();
}
```

Create an implementation that is a CDI bean:

TimeServiceImpl.java

```
@ApplicationScoped
public class TimeServiceImpl implements TimeService {
```

```
    public String getTime() {
        return DateFormat
                .getDateTimeInstance()
                .format(new Date());
    }
}
```

Enable CDI by creating a `beans.xml` descriptor:

`META-INF/beans.xml`

```
<?xml version="1.0" encoding="UTF-8"?>
<beans
  xmlns=http://java.sun.com/xml/ns/javaee
  xmlns:xsi=http://www.w3.org/2001/XMLSchema-instance
  xmlns:weld=http://jboss.org/schema/weld/beans
  xsi:schemaLocation="
      http://java.sun.com/xml/ns/javaee
      http://docs.jboss.org/cdi/beans_1_0.xsd
      http://jboss.org/schema/weld/beans
      http://jboss.org/schema/weld/beans_1_1.xsd">
</beans>
```

With our service ready we can build the user interface.

Build the page used to display the time:

`HomePage.html`

```html
<html>
    <body>
        <strong>The time is: </strong>
        <span wicket:id="time"></span>
    </body>
</html>
```

`HomePage.java`

```java
public class HomePage extends WebPage {
    private TimeService service;

    public HomePage() {
        add(new Label("time", new PropertyModel<String>(this,
          "service.time")));
    }
}
```

How to do it...

1. Change the application to extend `SeamApplication` class:

   `WicketApplication.java`

   ```
   public class WicketApplication
           extends SeamApplication {
      public Class<HomePage> getHomePage() {
         return HomePage.class;
      }
   }
   ```

2. Annotate the service field with the `@Inject` annotation:

   `HomePage.java`

   ```
   public class HomePage extends WebPage {
      @javax.inject.Inject
      private TimeService service;

      public HomePage() {
         add(new Label("time",
            new PropertyModel<String>(this, "service.time")));
      }
   }
   ```

How it works...

Seam-Wicket module configures various aspects of Wicket to enable the injection of fields in `Component` subclasses with CDI-managed dependencies. All this configuration magic lives inside the `SeamApplication` class, so the first thing we must do is extend it instead of Wicket's default `WebApplication`; we do this in Step 5. Once Wicket is configured, we must tell Seam-Wicket which fields we want to be injected; this is done just like in any other CDI-bean – by annotating them with the `@Inject` annotation.

There's more...

By default, Seam-Wicket module only supports injection of `Component` subclasses; in the next section we will take a look at how to inject classes that do not extend `Component`, such as models.

Injecting non-component classes

Let's take a look at how to inject instances of classes that do not extend `Component`. Sometimes this can be useful to make code more reusable and isolated, for example we can wrap the usage of `TimeService` in a model which we can then use on any component:

`TimeModel.java`

```
public class TimeModel extends LoadableDetachableModel<String> {
    @Inject
    private TimeService service;

    public TimeModel() {
        BeanManager manager =
new BeanManagerLocator().getBeanManager();
        NonContextual.of(TimeModel.class, manager).
existingInstance(this).inject();
    }
    protected String load() {
        return service.getTime();
    }
}
```

In order to accomplish this we use the `BeanManagerLocator` available in the **Seam-Solder** extension module to locate the current `BeanManager` instance:

```
BeanManager manager =  new BeanManagerLocator().getBeanManager();
```

We then use the `NonContextual` utility class that comes with the Seam-Wicket module to inject our model instance. Now that our model can inject itself and access `TimeService` we can clean up our `HomePage`:

`HomePage.java`

```
public class HomePage extends WebPage {
    public HomePage() {
        add(new Label("time", new TimeModel()));
    }
}
```

Populating repeaters from a JPA query

Every database-driven web application will eventually have to display a list of records from the database, and in this recipe we will look at the best way of accomplishing that in Wicket. Being a component-based framework, Wicket ships with a lot of components capable of displaying a list of data; however, amongst them are a special subset of components designed specifically for working with databases – the components that use `IDataProvider` interface to retrieve data – such as `DataView` and `DataTable`. We are going to examine the use of `IDataProvider` together with a `DataView` to build a simple guestbook application:

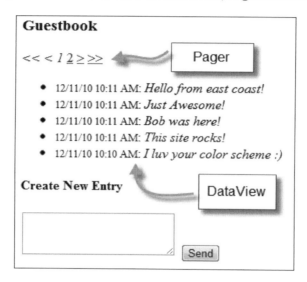

 In this recipe we will use Spring to wire everything together; however, the ideas discussed here apply to any other container.

Getting ready

The best place to get started is to build the business layer of the application first – the entities and the service layer.

Create the guestbook entry entity:

`Entry.java`

```
@Entity
public class Entry {
    @GeneratedValue
```

```
    @Id
    private Long id;
    private String text;
    private Date created;

    // getters and setters
}
```

Create the JPA descriptor:

`META-INF/persistence.xml`

```xml
<?xml version="1.0" encoding="UTF-8"?>
<persistence version="2.0">
    <persistence-unit name="cookbook"
        transaction-type="RESOURCE_LOCAL">
    <provider>org.hibernate.ejb.HibernatePersistence</provider>
    <class>cookbook.Entry</class>
    </persistence-unit>
</persistence>
```

Define the interface for our service layer:

`EntriesDao.java`

```java
public interface EntriesDao {
    List<Entry> list(final int offset, final int count);
    int count();
    void save(Entry entry);
    Entry load(Long id);
}
```

Build the implementation of the service layer:

`EntriesDaoImpl.java`

```java
@Repository
@Transactional
public class EntriesDaoImpl extends JpaDaoSupport
    implements EntriesDao {
    // sample code implements methods using Spring's JpaTemplate
mechanism. Refer to the code bundle for details.
}
```

Wire everything together in a Spring context:

`applicationContext.xml`

```xml
<?xml version="1.0" encoding="UTF-8"?>
<beans>
```

```
<context:component-scan base-package="cookbook" />
<tx:annotation-driven
    transaction-manager="transactionManager" />
<bean id="entityManagerFactory"
  class="org.springframework.orm.jpa.
    LocalEntityManagerFactoryBean">
    <property name="persistenceUnitName" value="cookbook" />
</bean>
<bean id="transactionManager" class="org.springframework.orm.jpa.
  JpaTransactionManager">
    <property name="entityManagerFactory" ref="entityManagerFactory"
/>
</bean>
</beans>
```

Enable Wicket's Spring integration:

WicketApplication.java

```
public class WicketApplication extends WebApplication {
    protected void init() {
        super.init();
        addComponentInstantiationListener(
new SpringComponentInjector(this));
    }
}
```

How to do it...

With the business layer completed, it is time to integrate with Wicket. The integration point between the DataView and the business layer is the IDataProvider interface. Below we create an implementation which will bridge the DataView with our business layer and put the DataView in a page so we can see the effects.

1. Implement IDataProvider to retrieve Entries:

    EntriesProvider.java

    ```
    class EntriesProvider implements IDataProvider<Entry> {
        private final EntriesDao entries;
        public EntriesProvider(EntriesDao entries) {
            this.entries = entries;
        }
        public Iterator<Entry> iterator(int first, int count) {
            return entries.list(first, count).iterator();
        }
        public int size() {
    ```

```
            return entries.count();
        }
    public IModel<Entry> model(Entry object) {
        final Long id = object.getId();
        return new LoadableDetachableModel<Entry>(object) {
            protected Entry load() {
                return entries.load(id);
            }
        };
    }
    public void detach() {
    }
}
```

2. Build the guestbook page:

HomePage.java

```
// for markup refer to HomePage.html in the code bundle
public class HomePage extends WebPage {

    @SpringBean
    EntriesDao entries;

    private String text;

    public HomePage(final PageParameters parameters) {
        DataView<Entry> view = new DataView<Entry>("entries",
                new EntriesProvider(entries)) {
            protected void populateItem(Item<Entry> item) {
                item.add(new Label("text", new
                    PropertyModel<String>(item.getModel(), "text")));
                item.add(new Label("created", new
                    PropertyModel<String>(item.getModel(), "created")));
            }
        };
        view.setItemsPerPage(5);
        add(view);
        add(new PagingNavigator("pager", view));

        Form<?> form = new Form<Void>("form") {
            protected void onSubmit() {
                Entry entry = new Entry();
                entry.setText(text);
                entries.save(entry);
                text = null;
            }
        };
```

```
        add(form);
        form.add(new TextArea<String>("text",
            new PropertyModel<String>(this, "text")));
    }
}
```

How it works...

As we are going to use a `DataView` to display the list of guestbook entries the first thing we need to do is create an `IDataProvider` implementation that the `DataView` will use to retrieve the entries from the database. We begin by implementing the interface:

EntriesProvider.java

```
class EntriesProvider implements IDataProvider<Entry> {
    public Iterator<Entry> iterator(int first, int count) {
        return null;
    }
    public int size() {
        return 0;
    }
    public IModel<Entry> model(Entry object) {
        return null;
    }
    public void detach() {
    }
}
```

As the provider needs to retrieve entries we pass in the `EntriesDao` service:

EntriesProvider.java

```
class EntriesProvider implements IDataProvider<Entry> {
    private final EntriesDao entries;
    public EntriesProvider(EntriesDao entries) {
        this.entries = entries;
    }
}
```

 Even though neither `EntriesDao` nor `EntriesDaoImpl` is serializable we can safely keep an instance as a field of `IDataProvider` (which is serializable) because we retrieve it using Wicket-Spring integration which wraps it in a serialization-safe proxy. Please refer to the first recipe for a more complete explanation of this.

Now that we can access our service inside the provider, we can implement the methods used to retrieve data. First the method used to retrieve a page of data from the database:

EntriesProvider.java

```
class EntriesProvider implements IDataProvider<Entry> {
    private final EntriesDao entries;
    public Iterator<Entry> iterator(int first, int count) {
        return entries.list(first, count).iterator();
    }
}
```

And next, the method used to retrieve the total number of entry records in the database:

EntriesProvider.java

```
class EntriesProvider implements IDataProvider<Entry> {
    private final EntriesDao entries;
    public int size() {
        return entries.count();
    }
}
```

 The size() method is necessary because DataView will need to calculate the total number of pages in order to properly display paging information.

The last method we need to implement is the model() method. This method wraps every returned Entry object in a model that is capable of retrieving it from the database if needed. This is useful, for example, when we have a Link that performs some action on the item; the Link can be given the model returned from IDataProvider using which it can retrieve the Entry it needs to operate on. In our recipe we will use a simple LoadableDetachableModel implementation that remembers the id of the Entry and can later load it using that id:

EntriesProvider.java

```
class EntriesProvider implements IDataProvider<Entry> {
    private final EntriesDao entries;

    public IModel<Entry> model(Entry object) {
        final Long id = object.getId();
        return new LoadableDetachableModel<Entry>(object) {
            protected Entry load() {
                return entries.load(id);
            }
        }
```

```
            };
        }
    }
```

 Notice that we pass the Entry object to the model's constructor; this ensures that during the current request the model uses the `Entry` instance already loaded from the database and does not query to retrieve it again – avoiding the n+1 query anti-pattern.

With the `IDataProvider` implemented we can now add the `DataView` to the page:

`HomePage.java`

```java
public class HomePage extends WebPage {
    @SpringBean
    EntriesDao entries;
    public HomePage() {
        DataView<Entry> view = new DataView<Entry>("entries",
            new EntriesProvider(entries)) {
            protected void populateItem(Item<Entry> item) {}
        };
        view.setItemsPerPage(5);
        add(view);
        add(new PagingNavigator("pager", view));
    }
}
```

In the preceding code, in addition to the `DataView`, we also added a `PaingNavigator`; this component will take care of displaying the interface for paging the guestbook entries.

We now have a simple and clean way for displaying a paging list from the database.

There's more...

In the previous example, we have implemented a way to page a database table, but what about sorting? Let's take a look at how to easily create a generic way to support both paging and sorting.

Sorting with IDataProvider

We begin by creating an object that will carry the paging and sorting information from the Wicket layer to the business layer:

QueryParam.java

```
// for a complete listing of this class refer to the codebundle, only
the structure of the class is shown here.
public class QueryParam {
    private final int offset;
    private final int count;
    private final List<SortParam> sort;

    public static enum SortDir {
        ASC, DESC
    }

    public static class SortParam {
        private final String data;
        private final SortDir dir;
    }
}
```

Because we have created a generic way of transferring this information, we can create some utility methods around it which will make building queries that utilize this information easier:

DaoSupport.java

```
public class DaoSupport extends JpaDaoSupport {
    protected String getOrderByString(QueryParam param) {
        // sample code builds the order by clause, refer to the code
            bundle for complete listing.
    }
    protected String applyOrderBy(String jql, QueryParam param)
    {
        if (!param.getSort().isEmpty()) {
            jql += " ORDER BY " + getOrderByString(param);
        }
        return jql;
    }
    protected Query applyPaging(Query query, QueryParam param)
    {
        query.setFirstResult(param.getOffset());
        query.setMaxResults(param.getCount());
        return query;
    }
}
```

We can now use these utility methods to rewrite our business layer to support sorting in addition to paging:

EntriesDaoImpl.java

```
@Repository
@Transactional
public class EntriesDaoImpl extends DaoSupport implements EntriesDao {
    public List<Entry> list(final QueryParam param) {
        return getJpaTemplate().executeFind(
          new JpaCallback<List<Entry>>() {
            public List<Entry> doInJpa(EntityManager em)
                throws PersistenceException {
              Query q = em.createQuery(
                applyOrderBy("SELECT e FROM Entry e", param));
              return applyPaging(q, param).getResultList();
            }
        });
    }
}
```

In Wicket, the sorting information is passed to the IDataProviders using a mixin ISortStateLocator interface. As a convenience, Wicket ships with a SortableDataProvider base class for data providers that support sorting, . Let's create a generic data provider that will bridge SortableDataProvider with our QueryParam transfer object:

EntityProvider.java

```
public abstract class EntityProvider<T>
        extends SortableDataProvider<T> {

  public Iterator<T> iterator(int first, int count) {
    SortParam sp = getSort();
    final List<QueryParam.SortParam> sort;
    if (sp == null) {
      sort = Collections.emptyList();
    } else {
      sort = Collections.singletonList(
       new QueryParam.SortParam(
          sp.getProperty(),
            sp.isAscending() ? SortDir.ASC:ortDir.DESC));;SortDir.
              ASC:ortDir.DESC));;SortDir.ASC:sortDir.DESC));
    }
    return iterator(new QueryParam(first, count, sort));
  }
}
```

```
    protected abstract Iterator<T> iterator(QueryParam param);
}
```

Now we can update our `EntriesProvider` to take advantage of the sorting information:

`EntriesProvider.java`

```
class EntriesProvider extends EntityProvider<Entry> {
    private final EntriesDao entries;

    protected Iterator<Entry> iterator(QueryParam param) {
        return entries.list(param).iterator();
    }
}
```

As `DataView` does not natively support sorting let's replace it with a component that does, the `DataTable`:

`HomePage.java`

```
    // for markup refer to HomePage.html in the code bundle
    public class HomePage {
        @SpringBean
        EntriesDao entries;

        public HomePage() {
            List<IColumn<Entry>> cols = new ArrayList<>();
            cols.add(new PropertyColumn<Entry>(
                Model.of("Created"), "created", "created"));
            cols.add(new PropertyColumn<Entry>(
                Model.of("Message"), "text", "text"));
            add(new DefaultDataTable<Entry>("entries", cols,
                    new EntriesProvider(entries), 5));
        }
    }
```

We now have a table of guestbook entries which can be both paged and sorted.

Creating a model for a JPA entity

Keeping a reference to a JPA entity is a common requirement in web applications, be it as a target for a delete link or as a handle of a row in a table. Traditionally, this has been accomplished by passing the id of the entity in URLs, but in Wicket this is accomplished by passing models to components. In this recipe, we will see how to build a model that can be used to pass around references to any JPA entity. We are going to use the guestbook project demonstrated in the previous recipe as a base:

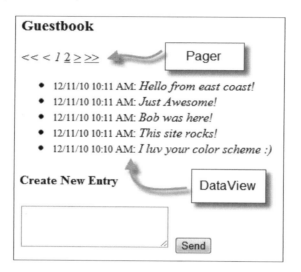

Getting ready

Get started by following the *Getting Ready* section of the previous recipe.

How to do it...

We will begin by building a generic way to identify entities in our application. Then, on top of that, we will build a generic mechanism that can load the entities from the database. Once we have a way to load the entities we can create a model implementation that will do it for us.

1. Create an interface that can be generically used to identify entities:

```
Identifiable.java

public interface Identifiable<ID extends Serializable> {
    ID getId();
}
```

2. Create a service that can be used to generically load entities:

`EntityLoader.java`

```java
@Repository
public class EntityLoader extends JpaDaoSupport {

    @Autowired
    public EntityLoader(EntityManagerFactory emf) {
        setEntityManagerFactory(emf);
    }

    public <T> T load(Class<T> clazz, Serializable id) {
        return getJpaTemplate().find(clazz, id);
    }
}
```

3. Implement the model:

`EntityModel.java`

```java
public class EntityModel<T extends Identifiable<?>> implements
IModel<T> {

    @SpringBean
    private EntityLoader loader;

    private Serializable id;
    private final Class<T> clazz;

    private T instance;
    public EntityModel(Class<T> clazz, Serializable id) {
        this.clazz = clazz;
        this.id = id;
        InjectorHolder.getInjector().inject(this);
    }
    public EntityModel(T entity) {
        this((Class<T>) entity.getClass(), entity.getId());
        instance = entity;
    }
    public T getObject() {
        if (instance == null) {
            if (id != null) {
                instance = (T) loader.load(clazz, id);
            }
        }
        return instance;
    }
    public void setObject(T object) {
        if (object == null) {
```

```
            id = null;
        } else {
            id = object.getId();
        }
        instance = object;
    }
    public void detach() {
        if (instance != null && instance.getId() != null) {
            this.id = instance.getId();
        }
        if (this.id!=null) {
            instance = null;
        }
    }
}
```

4. Modify the data provider from the previous example to use the new model rather than the anonymous `LoadableDetachableModel` subclass it used previously:

`EntriesProvider.java`

```
class EntriesProvider implements IDataProvider<Entry> {
    private final EntriesDao entries;

    public EntriesProvider(EntriesDao entries) {
        this.entries = entries;
    }

    public Iterator<Entry> iterator(int first, int count) {
        return entries.list(first, count).iterator();
    }

    public int size() { return entries.count(); }

    public IModel<Entry> model(Entry object) {
        return new EntityModel(object);
    }

    public void detach() {    }
}
```

How it works...

The model must accomplish the following tasks:

- ▸ It must support detaching - getting rid of all other states other than what is minimally needed to retrieve the entity when needed.

- It must cache the loaded instance - so multiple calls to `getObject()` result in a single load

- It must support being initialized with a loaded entity - so we avoid having to load it again if we need it within the same request

- It must be serializable - so it works properly with Wicket

- It must support swapping entities on the fly - to make linking components easier and allow `IModel`'s `setObject()` method to work properly

- If the entity has not yet been saved we should keep a reference to it across requests until it is saved - this will only work if the entity is serializable and uses a database-generated identifier

Let's get started by implementing the `IModel` interface:

`EntityModel.java`

```
public class EntityModel<T extends Identifiable<?>> implements
IModel<T> {
    public T getObject() {
        return null;
    }
    public void setObject(T object) {
    }
    public void detach() {
    }
}
```

The minimum state we need to identify the entity in the JPA world is its class and id; let's implement a minimal working version of the model:

```
public class EntityModel<T extends Identifiable<?>>
        implements IModel<T> {

    @SpringBean
    private EntityLoader loader;

    private Serializable id;
    private Class<T> clazz;

    public EntityModel(Class<T> clazz, Serializable id) {
        this.clazz = clazz;
        this.id = id;
        InjectorHolder.getInjector().inject(this);
    }

    public T getObject() {
        T instance=null;
        if (id != null) {
```

```
            instance = (T) loader.load(clazz, id);
        }
        return instance;
    }
}
```

 As we are using Spring in this recipe, we inject the `EntityLoader` instance into the model – which allows us to have simpler constructors that do not require the loader to be passed in every time we create a model instance.

So far we have implemented only the first requirement – the model keeps the minimal state necessary to retrieve the entity. Now, let's add the caching to make multiple calls to the model's `getObject()` method efficient:

```
public class EntityModel<T extends Identifiable<?>>
        implements IModel<T> {
    private Serializable id;
    private Class<T> clazz;

    private T instance;

    public T getObject() {
        if (instance == null) {
            if (id != null) {
                instance = (T) loader.load(clazz, id);
            }
        }
        return instance;
    }

    public void detach() {
        instance = null;
    }
}
```

The caching we have now is great, but in a lot of cases we already have a loaded entity – let's add a constructor that will populate our cache with such an instance:

```
public class EntityModel<T extends Identifiable<?>>
        implements IModel<T> {
    private Serializable id;
    private Class<T> clazz;

    private T instance;

    public EntityModel(Class<T> clazz, Serializable id) {
        this.clazz = clazz;
```

```
        this.id = id;
        InjectorHolder.getInjector().inject(this);
    }

    public EntityModel(T entity) {
        this((Class<T>) entity.getClass(), entity.getId());
        instance = entity;
    }
}
```

Our model is now as efficient as possible; we can start adding bells and whistles. First, let's add the support for the `setObject()` method. The method simply swaps the id value for the id of the entity we pass in. It also resets the internal cache to the new instance:

```
public class EntityModel<T extends Identifiable<?>>
        implements IModel<T> {
    private Serializable id;
    private Class<T> clazz;

    private T instance;

    public void setObject(T object) {
        if (object == null) {
            id = null;
        } else {
            id = object.getId();
        }
        instance = object;
    }
}
}
```

The last requirement is to allow our model to keep an entity across requests until it is saved. To accomplish this, we modify our detach logic to only clear the internal entity cache if the entity has been persisted and to update our internal id in case the entity has been saved and is safe to detach:

```
public class EntityModel<T extends Identifiable<?>>
        implements IModel<T> {

    private Serializable id;
    private Class<T> clazz;

    private T instance;

    public void detach() {
        if (instance != null && instance.getId() != null) {
            this.id = instance.getId();
        }
        if (this.id!=null) {
```

```
                instance = null;
            }
        }
    }
```

Our model is now complete; we can start cleaning up our code by replacing this:

EntityProvider.java

```
    public IModel<Entry> model(Entry object) {
        final Long id = object.getId();
        return new LoadableDetachableModel<Entry>(object) {
            protected Entry load() {
                return entries.load(id);
            }
        };
    }
```

With a much simplified version:

```
    public IModel<Entry> model(Entry object) {
        return new EntityModel<Entry>(object) ;
    }
```

There's more...

In the next sections, we will see how to further improve our model implementation and the code that uses it.

Improving entity class resolution

The constructor of the model that takes an instance of an entity directly tries to retrieve its class by using `Object`'s `getClass()` method:

```
    public class EntityModel<T extends Identifiable<?>>
            implements IModel<T> {

        public EntityModel(T entity) {
            this((Class<T>) entity.getClass(), entity.getId());
            instance = entity;
        }
    }
```

Unfortunately this may sometimes run into trouble because under certain circumstances JPA will proxy the entity and `getClass()` will return the class of the proxy and not the entity. To work correctly all the time our model will have to unproxy the entity before retrieving its class. For example, if we were using Hibernate as the JPA provider we could fix our model like this:

```java
public class EntityModel<T extends Identifiable<?>>
        implements IModel<T> {

    public EntityModel(T entity) {
        this(
            (Class<T>) unproxy(entity).getClass(),
            entity.getId());
        instance = entity;
    }
    public static  T unproxy(T entity)
    {
        if (entity instanceof HibernateProxy)
        {
            entity = (T)((HibernateProxy)entity)
                .getHibernateLazyInitializer()
                .getImplementation();
        }
        return entity;
    }
}
```

Unfortunately there is no universal way to unproxy an entity defined in the JPA specification, so there is no way to build a universal model.

A simpler data provider

As we now have a model capable of universally loading entities, we can simplify `IDataProvider` implementations in our application by providing a base class capable of generating entity models across the board:

`EntityProvider.java`

```java
public abstract class EntityProvider<T extends Identifiable<?>>
implements
        IDataProvider<T> {
    public IModel<T> model(T object) {
        return new EntityModel<T>(object);
    }
    public void detach() {
    }
}
```

Once we start using it as a base class, other provider implementations are distilled to just loading and counting records, which leads to cleaner and more maintainable code:

EntriesProvider.java

```
public class EntriesProvider extends EntityProvider<Entry> {
    private final EntriesDao entries;

    public EntriesProvider(EntriesDao entries) {
        this.entries = entries;
    }

    public Iterator<Entry> iterator(int first, int count) {
        return entries.list(first, count).iterator();
    }

    public int size() {
        return entries.count();
    }
}
```

Index

Symbols

@Inject annotation 270
@RequireHttps annotation 261
@SpringBean annotation 266

A

AbstractBehavior class 160
AbstractCheckBoxModel 116
AbstractTab 133
AbstractTabWithCount class 134
addComponentInstantiationListener()
      method 266
AJAX
  used, for swapping panels 213
Ajax feedback
  providing automatically 168-174
AjaxFormComponentUpdatingBehavior 38
Ajax request
  double-submits, preventing 162-166
Ajax validation
  adding, to individual form components
      158-160
  simplifying 161
applicationContext.xml 273
application locale
  forcing manually 94
Application.properties resource 76
authentication process
  implementing, OpenID used 243-246
  working 247, 248
AuthStrategy 239
AuthStrategy.java 238
automatic type conversion
  working 31

B

bean field 210
BeanManagerLocator 271
blockUI 166
borders
  using for decorating components 143-146
built-in error variables
  input 17
  label 17
  name 17
  using 17

C

CAPTCHA
  using, for protection against spam 55-57
CDI 268
CDI integration, Wicket
  about 268, 269
  non-component classes, injecting 271
  Seam-Wicket module, using 268
  working 270
cells, DataTable
  making clickable 106-110
ChallengeModel 59
change notification, over AJAX
  triggering 38, 39
chart data
  feeding to OFC, SharedResource used
      191-197
Chart.data.template 187, 200
Chart.java 179
ChoiceFieldPanel.html 221
clicks, OFC
  responding to 199-203

client-side JavaScript TabbedPanel
    creating 140, 141
    working 142
collapsible border
    about 148
    AJAX used 154
    creating 148-153
component decoration
    automating 64
ComponentFeedbackMessageFilter 66
Component#getResponse() method 70
ComponentInstantiationListener 265
components
    decorating, borders used 143-146
    securing, IAuthorizationStrategy used
        251-255
    swapping, select box used 208-212
ComponentTag object 63
CompoundValidator#validate(IValidatable)
    method 21
ConsumerManager instances 247
Context Dependency and Injection. *See* CDI
ConverterLocator 32
convertInput() method 210
convertToObject() method 28, 29
convertToString() method 28
cookbook.Time object 30
createLabelModel() method 125
CreditCardPayment.java 209
CSRF
    protecting against 258, 259
CSS class, form component
    changing, on validation errors 62, 63
custom error variables
    using 17
custom validator
    built-in error variables, using 17
    creating 12-14
    custom error variables, using 17
    working 15, 16

D

DaoSupport.java 279
data
    exporting, to CSV 120-126
    filtering, DataTable used 100-104
    sorting, DataTable used 96-100
database data
    sorting 105
Database object 37
data export
    moving, to toolbar 127
DataTable
    cells, making clickable 106-110
    data, exporting to CSV 120-126
    making searchable 100
    quick-search type, implementing 100
    rows, making selectable with checkboxes
        110-117
    select/deselect all checkbox, adding
        118-120
decorator work
    making, with AJAX 73, 74
double-submits
    preventing 162-166
dropdown lists
    AJAXifying 38
DynaForm component 214
    select box support, adding 220-222
dynamic forms
    creating 214-219
dynamic portal layout
    creating 222-233
    out-of-bound links, disabling 233, 234
DynamicWebResource 197

E

editor
    changing, to work with mutable model
        object 45
EntityLoader.java 283
EntityModel.java 283
EntityProvider.java 280
EntriesDaoImpl.java 273
EntriesDao.java 273
EntriesProvider.java 277
Entry.java 272
error CSS class
    outputting 62
error(IValidatable,String) method 16
errorKey parameter 16

F

FeedbackPanel
using, to output form component specific messages 65, 66
findPortletBorder() method 231
FormComponent#getConvertedInput() method 11
FormComponentPanel class 42
form component presentation
streamlining, behaviors used 67-73
form component specific messages
outputting, FeedbackPanel used 65, 66
Form#hasError() method 10
form-level custom validation
performing 7-10
Form#onValidate() method 9
form processing
limiting, to validation 175
forms
about 61
decorator work, making with AJAX 73, 74
FormToken object 48

G

getAjaxCallDecorator 166
getColumn() method 231
getCount() method 134
getCssReference() method 147
getData() method 187
getObject() 59, 116, 285
getPortlet() method 230
getResourceStream() method 196
getTitle() method 133
global converters 32
Guava library 247

H

HomePage.java 180
HTTP and HTTPS
switching between 260, 261
HttpsConfig object 261
HttpsRequestCycleProcessor class 260

I

IAjaxCallDecorator 163
IAuthorizationStrategy
using, for securing components 251-255
working 255-257
IAuthorizationStrategy implementation
creating 238
IColumn#getSortProperty() method 98
IConverter interface 28
IDataProvider interface
about 272
sorting with 279-281
Identifiable.java 282
ifAlreadyProcessed() 53
IHeaderContributor interface 180
ILinkListener request interface 201
IndicatingAjaxLink 166
InjectorHolder object 267
InventoryWarningsPanel 223
IRequestTarget 185
IResourceListener interface 182
isInstantiationAuthorized method 239
isSelected() 116
ITab implementation 133
IValidatable#isValid() method 21

J

JPA entity
model, creating 282-288
JPA query 272

L

LazyCountLabel 136
linked selectboxes
creating 34-36
working 36-38
LoadableDetachableModel subclass 284
loading of resources
debugging 92, 93
localized markup
outputting, wicket:message using 86-89
localized resources
overriding, on case by case basis 89-92
localized strings
accessing 80

building 80
feeding, to components using
    StringResourceModel 84, 85
retrieving 80-82
Localizer instance 83
LoginPage.java 237

M

META-INF/persistence.xml 273
modelChanged() method 42
model, for JPA entity
creating 282-288
entity class resolution, improving 288, 289
simpler data provider 289, 290
module resource strings
storing, in package properties 76-79
move() method 231
multiple form components
composing, into single reusable component
    39-44
multiple form submits
preventing 45-53
multiple validators
composing, into single reusable validator
    18-20
MySession.java 237

N

Name domain object
implementing 90
NameEditor component 78
nameFeedback component 66
NameLabel component 77
newCheckBox() method 115
newCheckBoxModel() method 115
newConverterLocator() factory method 31
newLink() method 139
NullPointerException 265

O

OFC
about 177
chart data, feeding using SharedResource
    191-196
charting with 178-185

clicks, responding to 199-203
code, externalizing 186
code, extracting into reusable blocks
    188-191
DynamicWebResource, using for data serving
    197, 198
strings, writing 186, 187
support, adding for multi graphs 204, 205
working 180, 182, 185
OFC Flash component
wrapping, into Wicket 178
onBeforeRespond method 173
onblur event 160
onClick() method 126, 201
onError()method 140, 160
onInitialize() method 221
onLinkClicked() method 202
onResourceRequested method 185
onUpdate method 160
Open Flash Charts. *See* **OFC**
OpenID
authenticating with 243-250
OpenID4Java library 247
OpenIdCallbackPage page 249
OpenIdConsumer.java 248
Order.java 208

P

PackagedTextTemplate class 187
page versioning 54, 55
panels
swapping, AJAX used 213
PasswordPolicyValidator class 15
Payment.java 208
PayPalPayment.java 209
PortalContainer.html 224
PortalContainer.java 230
PortalLayout.java 223
PortletBorder.java 228
Portlet.java 227
PropertyModel 219

Q

QueryParam.java 279
QueryParam transfer object 280

R

RecentOrdersPanel 223
renderHead() method 186, 190
renderIterator() method 231
repeaters
    populating, from JPA query 272-278
RepeatingView 217
RepeatingView#newChildId() method 218
replaceWith() method 213
RequestUtils helper class 183
ResourceModel 132
Resource subclass 197
RestartResponseAtInterceptPageException
    240
rows, DataTable
    making selectable, with checkboxes 110-117

S

SeamApplication class 270
Seam-Wicket module
    about 270
    using 268
SecurePage.java 241
security, Wicket applications
    authenticating, with OpenID 243-250
    base class, using 242
    components, securing with
        IAuthorizationStrategy 251-256
    CSRF, protecting against 258-260
    HTTP and HTTPS, switching between
        260-262
    login page, creating 236-241
    permissions, internalizing in subclasses 257
    subsets of pages, securing 241, 242
    URLs, securing 258-260
    user, forcing for authentication 236-241
select box support
    adding, to DynaForm 220-222
setAttachmentHeader() method 126
setModelObject() method 42
setObject() method 285
SharedResources object 196
SimplePageAuthorizationStrategy 242
SimplifiedAuthStrategy.java 242
size() method 277
slide() method 231

SortableDataProvider base class 280
sort direction indicators
    adding, via CSS 100
spam
    about 55
    protecting, against with CAPTCHA 55-60
SpringComponentInjector 266
Spring integration, Wicket
    about 264, 265
    non-components, injecting 267
    working 266
StockResource.java 193
StockService.java 178
string inputs
    converting, to objects 23-29
StringResourceModel 132
    using 84
StringResourceStream 196
StringValidator 12
stylesheets
    making configurable 147
SubmitOnceForm 51
SWFObject JavaScript library 181

T

tabbed panel
    creating 130-133
    making form friendly 139
    modifying 136, 137, 139
    retrieval of item count, optimizing 134-136
TabbedPanel subclass 137
tabs
    creating, with dynamic titles 130
TextFieldPanel.html 220
TimeServiceImpl bean 265
TimeServiceImpl.java 264
TimeService.java 264, 268
TopSellersPanel 223

U

UI
    blocking, mask used 166-168
updateProcessedForms() function 52
URLs
    securing 258, 259

V

validation constraints encapsulation, avoiding
pitfalls 21
**validation constraints externalization ,
avoiding**
pitfalls 22
validation logic
externalizing 11

W

**wantOnSelectionChangedNotifications()
method 213**
WebComponent class 180
WebMarkupContainer 218
Wicket
Ajax validation, adding to individual form
components 158
built-in validators 12
CDI, integrating with 268-270
integrating, with Spring 264-266
repeaters, populating from JPA query
272-278
StringValidator 12
components, swapping using select box
208-212
dynamic forms, creating 214-219
dynamic portal layout, creating 222-233
OFC library, integrating 177
resource properties, storing 76

WicketApplication.java 237, 239, 274
Wicket applications
securing 235
wicket:body tag 145
wicket:container tag 42
wicket-extensions module 59
Wicket field validator
creating 14
wicket:message
using, to outputting localized markup
86-89
Wicket's resource loading
about 80
extending 80

Thank you for buying
Apache Wicket Cookbook

About Packt Publishing

Packt, pronounced 'packed', published its first book "*Mastering phpMyAdmin for Effective MySQL Management*" in April 2004 and subsequently continued to specialize in publishing highly focused books on specific technologies and solutions.

Our books and publications share the experiences of your fellow IT professionals in adapting and customizing today's systems, applications, and frameworks. Our solution based books give you the knowledge and power to customize the software and technologies you're using to get the job done. Packt books are more specific and less general than the IT books you have seen in the past. Our unique business model allows us to bring you more focused information, giving you more of what you need to know, and less of what you don't.

Packt is a modern, yet unique publishing company, which focuses on producing quality, cutting-edge books for communities of developers, administrators, and newbies alike. For more information, please visit our website: www.packtpub.com.

About Packt Open Source

In 2010, Packt launched two new brands, Packt Open Source and Packt Enterprise, in order to continue its focus on specialization. This book is part of the Packt Open Source brand, home to books published on software built around Open Source licences, and offering information to anybody from advanced developers to budding web designers. The Open Source brand also runs Packt's Open Source Royalty Scheme, by which Packt gives a royalty to each Open Source project about whose software a book is sold.

Writing for Packt

We welcome all inquiries from people who are interested in authoring. Book proposals should be sent to author@packtpub.com. If your book idea is still at an early stage and you would like to discuss it first before writing a formal book proposal, contact us; one of our commissioning editors will get in touch with you.

We're not just looking for published authors; if you have strong technical skills but no writing experience, our experienced editors can help you develop a writing career, or simply get some additional reward for your expertise.

Apache MyFaces 1.2 Web Application Development

ISBN: 978-1-847193-25-4 Paperback: 408 pages

Building next-generation web applications with JSF and Facelets

1. Build powerful and robust web applications with Apache MyFaces

2. Reduce coding by using sub-projects of MyFaces like Trinidad, Tobago, and Tomahawk

3. Update the content of your site daily with ease by using Facelets

4. Step-by-step and practical tutorial with lots of examples

Apache OfBiz Cookbook

ISBN: 978-1-84719-918-8 Paperback: 300 pages

Over 60 simple but incredibly effective recipes for taking control of OFBiz

1. Optimize your OFBiz experience and save hours of frustration with this timesaving collection of practical recipes covering a wide range of OFBiz topics.

2. Get answers to the most commonly asked OFBiz questions in an easy-to-digest reference style of presentation.

3. Discover insights into OFBiz design, implementation, and best practices by exploring real-life solutions.

Please check **www.PacktPub.com** for information on our titles

OSGi and Apache Felix 3.0
Build your very own OSGi applications using the flexible and powerful Felix Framework

Beginner's Guide

Walid Gédéon

OSGi and Apache Felix 3.0 Beginner's Guide

ISBN: 978-1-84951-138-4   Paperback: 336 pages

Build your very own OSGi applications using the flexible and powerful Felix Framework

1. Build a completely operational real-life application composed of multiple bundles and a web front end using Felix

2. Get yourself acquainted with the OSGi concepts, in an easy-to-follow progressive manner

3. Learn everything needed about the Felix Framework and get familiar with Gogo, its command-line shell to start developing your OSGi applications

Apache CXF Web Service Development

Develop and deploy SOAP and RESTful web services

Naveen Balani   Rajeev Hathi

Apache CXF Web Service Development

ISBN: 978-1-847195-40-1   Paperback: 336 pages

Develop and deploy SOAP and RESTful Web Services

1. Design and develop web services using contract-first and code-first approaches

2. Publish web services using various CXF frontends such as JAX-WS and Simple frontend

3. Invoke services by configuring CXF transports

Please check **www.PacktPub.com** for information on our titles

Printed in Great Britain by
Amazon.co.uk, Ltd.,
Marston Gate.